DO NOT REMOVE
CARDS FROM POCKET

T

The Economy of Modern Israel

The Economy of
Modern Israel

Malaise and Promise

Assaf Razin

and

Efraim Sadka

The University of Chicago Press
Chicago and London

ASSAF RAZIN is the Mario Henrique Simonsen Professor of International Economics and Deputy Rector at Tel Aviv University. EFRAIM SADKA is the Henry Kaufman Professor of International Capital Markets at Tel Aviv University.

The University of Chicago Press, Chicago 60637
The University of Chicago Press, Ltd., London
© 1993 by The University of Chicago
All rights reserved. Published 1993
Printed in the United States of America
02 01 00 99 98 97 96 95 94 93   1 2 3 4 5

ISBN: 0-226-70589-7 (cloth)

Library of Congress Cataloging-in-Publication Data

Razin, Assaf.
   The economy of modern Israel : malaise and promise / Assaf Razin and Efraim Sadka.
     p.   cm.
   Includes bibliographical references and index.
   1. Israel—Economic conditions. I. Sadka, Efraim. II. Title.
HC415.25.R38   1993
330.95694—dc20   93-3054
                                                CIP

To our children:
> Ofer, Ronny, and Einat Razin
> Ronnie, Gil, and Shelly Sadka

Contents

Preface

This book is a first account and analysis of economic policy and developments in modern Israel. It covers several unique economic and social phenomena that either coexisted or followed one another, including (1) the massive waves of immigration (*aliya*) which almost overnight changed the economic and social landscape, (2) the exceptionally rapid growth in the early years of the state, which was followed by exceptionally slow growth in more recent years, (3) the coexistence of a flourishing and competitive private sector with a relatively large public sector, (4) the reconciliation of the ruling egalitarian ideology with a policy of economic openness and a probusiness tax structure, (5) the interaction between the economy of Israel and the neighboring economies of the occupied territories (the West Bank and the Gaza Strip) in the face of the Palestinian uprising (Intifada), (6) the slide into a three-digit inflation and the ultimate overnight disinflation, (7) the on-going process of capital market liberalization and privatization and the shrinking role of government, and (8) the unique features that were developed to cope with the effects of inflation in the labor market, the capital market, the tax structure, and the like.

These and other central economic issues constitute the subject matter of this book. Our aim is to draw some lessons that will contribute to economic thinking in general and to the understanding of the economic developments in other countries with similar experiences, in particular.

The book is written for a wide audience of students of economics and professional economists in business, politics, and academia, as well as for all those who are interested in learning about the economy of

Israel and the Middle East. We appeal to a broad body of readers without sacrificing the rigor of economic analysis and argumentation. Thus, technical analysis is relegated to appendices to avoid discouraging readers who may not have a command of technical expertise.

The introduction provides a brief overview of the book. Part I gives historical background and sets the stage for the analysis of the economy of modern Israel. It ends with the study of Israel's unique disinflation experience. Part II is devoted to the stabilization's aftermath. Part III is the first detailed economic analysis of the Intifada in the literature. The recent *aliya* from the Commonwealth of Independent States (the successor of the Soviet Union) and its implications for the Israeli economy in this decade are the subject of part IV. Finally, part V addresses significant policy areas in Israel: the tax system, international trade relations, capital market liberalization, and the privatization process. The epilogue addresses some remaining policy issues that will require further attention in the years to come. We conclude the book with selected data on key economic indicators stretching from the early years of the state until 1991.

Some of the material in the book draws from our previous joint work with Amnon Neubach: *Economic Growth: Embarking on the 1990s* (Maariv Press, 1988; published in Hebrew) and *Challenges to the Economy of Israel* (Maariv Press, 1990, published in Hebrew). We thank Amnon Neubach for permission to use some parts from this joint work. Chapter 12 draws heavily from Efraim Sadka, "An Inflation-Proof Tax System?" *International Monetary Fund Staff Papers,* vol. 38, no. 1 (March 1991): 135–55.

We benefited from comments and suggestions made by the late Eitan Berglas, Bruno Contini, Elhanan Helpman, Zvi Sussman, and two anonymous referees. We thank Nadine Boudot-Trajtenberg for a skillful translation of previous work, originally written in Hebrew, which has been used in some sections of this book. We also thank Stella Padeh for her competent typing of the book. Able research assistance was provided by Edith Yotav. We gratefully acknowledge financial support from the Sapir Center for Development, the Foerder Institute for Economic Research, and Daniel and Grace Ross Chair in International Economics, the Mario Henrique Simonsen Chair in Public Finance, and the Henry Kaufman Chair in International Capital Markets, all at Tel Aviv University.

Introduction

Israel's early economic history is marked by unprecedented growth. The pre-state Jewish population (*yishuv*) accumulated great reserves of capital brought mainly by the immigrants from their countries of origin. Rapid industrialization took place, bringing the share of industrial output in gross domestic product to about one-third just before independence (1948), compared to a share of only about one-fifth in the early 1920s.

The record high rates of economic growth continued in the first two decades after the birth of the state in 1948, with an average annual output growth rate of 10%. This time the growth was fed by a massive wave of penniless refugees from Arab countries and war-torn Europe who immigrated soon after the November 1947 U.N. resolution on the partition of Palestine which led to the birth of the State of Israel on May 15, 1948. This initial wave was later followed by relatively medium-sized waves throughout the 1950s and 1960s. Immigration to Israel is called ascendence (*aliya* in Hebrew) and the immigrants are called ascenders (*olim* in Hebrew). The postindependence growth was generated by high rates of investment (over 30% of GNP), financed through high private saving rates and public borrowing from abroad.

During that period, government involvement in domestic capital formation was immense. The government invested directly in infrastructure (roads, ports, electric power generation and transmission, water supply, etc.), housing for the immigrants, educational facilities, medical care facilities, and so forth. In addition, in both word and deed, the government encouraged pre-state labor-run enterprises (e.g., Hevrat

1

Ha'ovdim) and cooperative organizations (e.g., *kibbutzim, moshavim,* Egged, and Dan bus companies) to invest and create employment opportunities. At the same time, the government aggressively searched for private entrepreneurs and investors and heavily subsidized them. In this respect, the economic system was far from a socialist command economy. Indeed, Israel has always had a flourishing private sector and advanced Western-type market mechanisms with extensive openness to world markets. The public and semipublic sectors operated within the framework of the market economy. Nevertheless, the government was the major intermediary in the capital market, attracting long-term private savings, on the one hand, and offering loans and grants for investments, on the other. Notably, the rate of inflation was low for such a rapidly growing economy, in the single-digit range for most of the period.

Following the Yom Kippur War in October 1973, Israel's unprecedented growth suddenly slowed to rates that were even below those of the industrialized countries of the West. For more than a decade after that war, Israel muddled through high inflation, balance of payments crises, and almost no growth. The inflation rate, which jumped to almost 60% in the first year after the Yom Kippur War, seemed to be under control thereafter when it was brought down to a 30% plateau for several years.

However, following the rise to power of Likud's Menachem Begin in 1977, the inflation rate picked up significantly. The annual inflation rate quickly moved into triple digits and threatened to explode into hyperinflation. At the same time, the deficit in the balance of payments persisted at an intolerable level putting the external debt on a path leading to insolvency. Economic growth slowed even more, and the Israeli economy reached a virtual standstill in the first half of the 1980s.

In mid-1985 the national unity government (headed by Labor's Shimon Peres) launched a comprehensive stabilization program. Inflation was curbed sharply and quickly to 15%–20%. At the same time, the accelerated increase in the external debt was halted and the financial standing of Israel in the international capital markets improved significantly. These accomplishments are still in place today, eight years later. Furthermore, 1992 was the first year since the Yom Kippur War (1973) with a single-digit inflation.

Like Israel, several Latin American countries that faced similar problems launched stabilization programs at about the same time. In some of these countries the stabilization program looked promising at first, but later, failed completely (e.g., Argentina before the recent 1991 stabilization and Brazil). In others (Bolivia, Chile, and Mexico) the stabilization programs proved successful. However, as in Israel, there remained a hard core of inflation of about 10%–20% per annum.

The stabilization program drastically changed the focus of attention of policymakers, economists, members of the business community, and the public at large from the problem of how to cope with high and rising inflation back to the real issues of market structure, international competitiveness, savings and investments, productivity, and growth. This is why we choose to start our detailed analysis of Israel's modern economy in Part I with the stabilization program. This program is discussed from both the economic and political perspectives in chapter 2. However, to introduce the modern economic developments, we provide in chapter 1 a brief account of Israel's economic history, starting with the pre-state *yishuv*. In this chapter we present several hypotheses that were put forth to explain a basic mystery about the economy: What caused the change from exceptionally rapid growth in the early years of the state, and even before, to exceptionally slow growth in more recent years?

The aim of the stabilization program was to bring inflation down to a reasonable and sustainable level. In this respect it was indeed successful. However, it did not, by itself, create the macroeconomic conditions for long-term growth. In the first two years after the launching of the stabilization program, Israel did record exceptional rates of growth of output and productivity and a relatively low rate of unemployment. But this poststabilization boom was short-lived. It was caused by the coincidence of unique events: the sharp decline in the rate of inflation, the pullout of the Israeli forces from Lebanon, and the fall in world energy prices. In the second half of 1987, the economy slid into a recession that continued through 1989. The temporary poststabilization boom had distracted policymakers from the start of a recession, and this late diagnosis led to a longer and deeper recession.

Part II analyzes the economic factors that led to the recession, which were deeply rooted in the frozen exchange rate policy and the high interest rates that prevailed in 1987 and 1988. This policy was taken by the Likud's then–finance minister, Moshe Nissim, and the then–Governor of the Bank of Israel, Michael Bruno. As we shall see, this policy was abandoned after the 1988 general elections. Nevertheless, several major distortions in key relative prices (e.g., the real exchange rate, real short-term interest rates) were only contained by the new policies, but not altogether corrected. These distortions play a significant role even today, preventing a genuine economic recovery.

The Finance Minister of Israel is charged by law with the management of exchange rate policy. Moshe Nissim opted for fixing the exchange rate for reasons of price stability and perceived public credibility. The Governor of the Bank of Israel, through his control of monetary and interest policy, became the de facto architect of exchange rate policy. He persistently used the exchange rate as a monetary anchor for prices and wages, even when the fundamentals were inconsistent with that policy. It was not until mid-1988, 18 months after a complete freeze of the exchange rate, in the face of an almost 30% increase in the price level during that period, that the governor sought to realign the exchange rate. This rather belated attempt to convince the finance minister to adjust the exchange rate failed, because of the approaching national elections (November 1988). After the elections, the new government took a sharp turn in economic policy.

The mid-1987 to 1989 recession was aggravated initially by the uprising in the occupied territories (the West Bank and the Gaza Strip). The Intifada, as this uprising is called in Arabic, exploded on December 9, 1987. It had an immediate and direct effect on the employment in Israel of Arab workers from the West Bank and the Gaza Strip, which fell sharply at its outbreak as a result of both threats issued by the leadership of the Intifada and countermeasures (such as curfews) taken by the Israeli authorities. However, workers from the territories constitute less than 7% of the total number of employees in Israel and are typically among the least skilled members of the work force. Therefore, even though the Intifada had some initial contracting effects on the Israeli economy (and, particularly, on some low-tech sectors, such as construction, where the employment of workers from the occupied territories is concentrated), its impact could not have been long lasting. Overall, the Intifada did not make much difference to the Israeli economy, except possibly in creating a psychological deterrent to foreign investment and credit. It also contributed to political tension between Israel and the United States, thereby, indirectly, leading to a fall in the real value of U.S. aid to Israel.

In contrast, the effect of the Intifada was significant on the economies of the occupied territories. Employment in Israel is the major source of income for the residents of the Gaza Strip and the West Bank, so that the Intifada was economically much more painful to the occupied territories' residents than to those of Israel. Now, more than five years after the outbreak of the Intifada, employment in Israel of Arab workers from the occupied territories is back to its pre-Intifada level. Part III provides an economic perspective on the political conflict between Israel and the Palestinian Arabs.

The national unity government, formed in December 1988, implemented a series of economic measures which deviated sharply from earlier policies. These measures included two realignments of the exchange rate, a new cost-of-living adjustment pact which sterilized the direct effect of devaluations on prices from the cost-of-living adjustment of wages, investment-promoting tax changes such as accelerated depreciation and reduced corporate tax rates, a gradual lifting of some controls on international capital flow, and an intensive exercise of moral suasion to reduce interest rates and financial margins in a concentrated banking industry. However, the growth of output was very slow until a new wave of *aliya* began at the end of 1989 and a residential construction boom pushed output upwards.

Mikhail Gorbachev's *glasnost* policy which allowed Jews to emigrate from the Soviet Union, coupled with stricter immigration quotas imposed by the United States, generated a new large wave of *aliya* from the Soviet Union. By the end of 1991, almost 400,000 new *olim* came from the Soviet Union. Later, the newly established republics of the Commonwealth of Independent States (CIS) continued the policy of allowing unrestricted Jewish emigration. Nevertheless, the pace of *aliya* has slowed significantly, apparently because of the slow, difficult integration of the new *olim* into the Israeli economy.

Past experience in both preindependence Palestine and postindependence Israel suggests that waves of *aliya* typically generate investment booms and accelerate economic growth. The current *aliya*, which joins a relatively viable and modern economy (much different from the war-torn economy of the early 1950s) and is relatively rich in human capital, has even a higher potential to stimulate growth. Part IV is devoted to the new *aliya*. We provide a calibrated model of the Israeli economy in order to simulate the effect of the current wave of *aliya* (whose potential total size is estimated at between 700,000 and one million *olim* toward the end of the century) on capital formation, the balance of payments, and growth.

Part V is devoted to several contemporary topics. Over its brief history, the Israeli economy has attracted international attention and several myths were built around it. One such myth is that the Israeli economy is an Eastern Bloc–type socialist economy, the "last bastion" of

Stalin-type planned economy. We have already pointed out the emphasis that the government has always placed on free enterprise as a means of encouraging capital formation. Despite the obvious presence of government, Israel is a Western-type, modern welfare state with an essentially competitive free market system.

A related myth is the suffocating effect of the heavy tax burden in Israel. While Israel's huge defense outlays, unparalleled by international standards (on average, more than 12% of GNP paid from domestic sources, over the last 25 years), necessitate a higher-than-average tax burden, Israel nevertheless has managed to follow the recent trend in industrialized countries of broadening the tax base and reducing tax rates. Moreover, Israel designed its tax structure in order to shift the burden from savings and investments to consumption and labor income. In addition, Israel has always placed emphasis on reducing the income tax on the business sector. Israel's corporate tax rate is no higher than that in the United States (federal and state) and, as a matter of fact, it is among the *lowest* rates among industrialized countries. Similarly, Israel imposes lower taxes on capital income than on earned income. Chapter 9 describes the unique features of the Israeli tax system. In chapter 10, we develop a calibrated tax-simulation model in order to analyze the efficiency cost of the tax system. Of particular interest are Israel's unique and sophisticated devices for adjusting income tax liabilities for inflation.

Another indication of the Israeli economy's market orientation is its relative openness to international markets. Israel's volume of international trade has always been very high. The volume of exports and imports has been as high as its GNP, in orders of magnitude. The lion's share of Israel's international trade is with the European Community (EC). Israel has an associate membership in the European Community, which amounts to having a free trade agreement with respect to manufactured goods. Israel also has a comprehensive free trade agreement with the United States. In fact, Israel is the only country in the world that has free trade agreements with both the European Community and the United States. Recently, the government launched a unilateral program of (gradual) exposure to imports from other countries (such as Japan and the newly industrialized countries). The method that has been adopted is to first replace administrative trade barriers with tariffs (tariffization) and then gradually to reduce these tariffs. Israel's integration into the world economy is the subject of chapter 11.

The government's attempts to act as a substitute for the "invisible hand'' have been, however, very visible in the capital market, where for many years, the government has been the major intermediary. Individual savings found their way to the government either directly or indirectly. Retirement and long-term savings deposits in pension and provident funds were required to be almost fully invested in nonnegotiable government bonds. Other long- and medium-term savings deposits in commercial banks also ended up with the government (or the Bank of Israel) either through extremely high reserve requirements or through direct investment in government bonds. The government used the savings funds so obtained to finance the deficits in its regular and development budgets and to provide direct or indirect loans for the investments of the business sector. At the same time, the policy of exchange rate management necessitated strict restrictions on capital imports and exports. Over all, the government separated the domestic capital market from the world capital market and segmented the domestic capital market into many sectors with different interest rates, both for lending and for borrowing. However, after the stabilization program of mid-1985 and the fiscal balancing that followed, the government and the Bank of Israel launched major reforms in the capital market that drastically reduced the role of the government as an intermediary. In the first part of chapter 12 we review the special structure of the Israeli capital market and the important liberalization measures taken in the last few years. The government's goal is to reduce the reserve requirements of commercial banks and the mandatory minimum of investment in government assets by savings houses to levels that the Bank of Israel terms "business-like," that is, to levels that would be maintained by prudent businesses even if not required by law or special regulations. The aim is to make private savings finance private investments either through the mediation of private banking or through the security markets, rather than via the government. It is evident, however, that as long as the public sector runs a deficit, part of private savings will be eaten up by this deficit. Similarly, as long as the outstanding public debt is not diminished, a major part of the private stock of financial assets will be trapped there.

A persistent problem of the Israeli economy is the excessive level of government ownership of commercial companies. Despite the declared policy of privatization, very little progress has been made. From an economic point of view, the ultimate aim of privatization is to increase the efficiency of overall resource allocation in the economy and not merely to transfer companies (in many cases with considerable market power) from government to private hands. For this reason, proper privatization requires a restructuring of both the would-be privatized firms and the industries in which they operate in order to increase competition and efficiency. Unfortunately, such an efficient privatization process has not yet started. Moreover, the problem of the government's excessive ownership of business-type companies was recently aggravated by the de facto nationalization of the banking industry. The potential scope and the slow pace of privatization, as well as its guiding efficiency criteria, are the subject of the remainder of chapter 12.

In order to understand more fully the working of economic policies in Israel, it is helpful to pay attention to some important institutional policy features unique to this country. Without attempting to provide an exhaustive list of these features, we nevertheless discuss several of them.

First, most workers are unionized. Unions are organized in several vertical and horizontal overlapping levels: the firm, the professional trade, the industry, and the local level. At the highest level, there is a strong and powerful umbrella organization comprising almost all unions, the General Federation of Labor (Histadrut). The Histadrut runs a health-care program (Kupat Holim) of the health maintenance organization (HMO) type, providing both health insurance and medical care to *all* Histadrut members, even after retirement. This program is by far the largest health-care program in the country, comprising over 70% of the population. In addition, the Histadrut runs large defined-benefit pension funds. Even though not all Histadrut members are covered, most of the unionized employees in the private sector (including Histadrut-owned enterprises) are members of these funds. (Public sector employees are covered by their employers via unfunded pension programs.) Wage bargaining is therefore concerned with not only current wage hikes but also terms of health insurance and pensions.

Wage bargaining is conducted at the plant and firm level, professional trade level, industry level, and national level. Indirectly, the Histadrut is involved in all wage bargaining. Directly, however, it negotiates with the Private Employers' Association (PEA) only at the national level. In recent years, these negotiations centered almost exclusively on the degree of wage indexation, that is, on a cost-of-living allowance (COLA) pact. Typically, the COLA in recent years amounts to a little over 50% of CPI-measured inflation. The government itself is not officially a partner in these negotiations. But unofficially it plays a crucial role as mediator, providing "side payments" to the two official partners (the

Histadrut and the PEA) through economic policy tools, such as payroll tax reliefs, exchange rate adjustments, food and public transportation subsidies, direct transfers to the Histadrut health care system, government support to pension funds, and so forth. Once a pact is reached between the Histadrut and the PEA, it is applied throughout the economy by a government decree (the so-called extension decree).

Second, having a small economy and being poor in natural resources, Israel has always relied heavily on international trade. The exchange rate has always been an important policy instrument. Initially, as the country adopted severe restrictions on international capital flows, the exchange rate served mainly to regulate aggregate real demands and supplies (and, consequently, external imbalances). Gradually, as the economy became more open to international capital flows, the exchange rate policy became interrelated with monetary and inflation policies.

After independence in 1948, the government implemented a policy of a fixed exchange rate, which was in line with the Bretton Woods currency system in the industrialized world economy, albeit with discrete realignments. After some rapid realignments intended to unify the many exchange rates governing international transactions in the late 1940s and early 1950s, later realignments took the form of discrete, infrequent devaluations necessitated by the differential inflation (relatively minor in annual terms) between Israel and its trading partners. In 1975, when inflation accelerated considerably, a new policy of crawling peg was adopted. In the late 1970s, in view of the increased relaxation of foreign exchange controls, the exchange rate policy was changed to a managed float. The sharp acceleration of inflation in the late 1970s, fueled by the monetary expansion which was generated by growing public deficits, and the consequent rise in domestic interest rates attracted massive flows of financial capital into the country. The Israeli currency (then the Israeli lira) appreciated substantially in real terms. Following the second oil price shock in 1979–80, the economy suffered a severe deterioration in the balance of payments. A new exchange rate policy, of the purchasing power parity (PPP) type, was implemented. That is, the Israeli currency was depreciated in accordance with the differential inflation between Israel and its trading partners, so as to keep constant the relative prices of Israeli goods in the world markets. The PPP exchange rate policy was de facto abandoned in 1982 when unsuccessful attempts were made to conquer inflation by slowing down devaluations. These attempts abruptly ended with a bank shares crash at the end of 1983.

After the stabilization program of July 1985, the fixed exchange rate regime returned. The ensuing real appreciation of the Israeli currency finally led to a recession. Consequently, following a sharp devaluation of the Israeli sheqel, in 1989 a new policy of target zones was put in place. A band of ±5% was set around a fixed central exchange rate. Within this band, the rate was supposed to float according to supply and demand. However, unlike the European Monetary System (EMS) of target zones, the Bank of Israel practically determines the daily variations of the exchange rate within the target zones, very often disregarding private demands and supplies. Nowadays, the fixed central exchange rate has been replaced by an upward crawling central exchange rate with a preannounced path. Accordingly, the band is upward crawling too.

Since the time that exchange rate policy became an anti-inflation tool and monetary policy became largely accommodating, finance ministers have often opted to delay devaluations (even ones deemed necessary by economic fundamentals) until a prior ad hoc agreement has been reached with the Histadrut about keeping the effect of the devaluation on the CPI from influencing wages through the COLA. This habit often causes long delays in realigning the exchange rate and stimulates occasional speculative attacks on the foreign currency reserves.

Overall, in one way or another, the government has always intervened on a daily basis in the determination of the exchange rate. The official or unofficial (declared or undeclared) pegging of the exchange rate in the presence of massive international capital movement has undermined the effectiveness of monetary policy. For instance, an attempt to contract the money supply tends to raise domestic interest rates and thus attracts capital inflows. Within the "rules of the game" of a pegged exchange rate, such inflows expand the money supply and undermine the initial contractory attempt. Similarly, an attempt to execute an expansionist monetary policy is undermined by capital outflows. As the tendency in Israel nowadays (as well as elsewhere in the world) is for greater liberalization of international capital flow regulation, the traditional policy of pegging the exchange rate has to be rethought.[1]

1. Following the similar currency crunch in Europe in September 1992, Dornbusch (1992) put it succinctly: "In the aftermath of the European currency turmoil, exchange rate regimes that target inflation convergence have become suspect. To varying degrees, Mexico, Argentina and Israel are suspect. Real exchange rates have appreciated significantly over the past years, prospective gains in competitiveness are not in sight and plausible explanations about the justification for substantial real appreciation are running thin. Faced with an increasingly overvalued exchange

We believe that understanding these institutional policy features of the Israeli economy will prove useful to the reader in following our analysis of the economic developments and contemporary issues in Israel.

---

rate, governments are still reluctant to make corrections because the exchange rate is the only or chief anchor of a program, the economies are thought to be substantially indexed and the financing with hot money might be put in question if the government blinks. Credibility was built, typically, by a firm exchange rate policy, if the exchange rate is allowed to go, will everything go with it? Yet, if competitiveness is not recovered, how can increasing imbalances be financed except at interest rates that ultimately make debts and the economy itself unviable?''

I
Historical Overview, 1920–85

1

From Rapid Growth to Standstill, Accelerating Inflation, and Debt Crisis

The economic history of Israel can be meaningfully traced back to the early 1920s and to the so-called *yishuv* which consisted of the Jewish population (about 80,000 strong) under the British Mandate in what was then Palestine. Many of these pioneers wanted to create a democratic, socialist homeland for the Jewish people in Palestine and consequently established various agricultural (*kibbutzim* and *moshavim*), construction, and service cooperatives and organized a strong labor movement. Alongside these collectivist undertakings, privately owned small businesses and farms flourished as well.

Following the insightful observations of Michael Bruno (1989*a*) based on the studies by Jacob Metzer (1985) and Jacob Metzer and Oded Kaplan (1990), one can provide an anatomy of the economic growth that started in the 1920s and reached rates remarkable by international comparison, slowed down sharply after the Yom Kippur War and the energy crisis of 1973, and came almost to a standstill in the early 1980s.

Between 1920 and 1948, the population grew by a factor of 7.5 and the gross domestic product (GDP) by a factor of 25. Thus, per capita GDP more than tripled during this period, implying an annual growth rate of 4.9%.

Four features of the growth of the pre-state economy are noteworthy. First, following social and political turmoil in Europe, the *yishuv* population grew rapidly through waves of migration before and immediately after World War II and reached 600,000 by 1948, when the State of Israel was established. The distinct characteristics of a modern industrialized economy could be detected even in the early 1920s. For instance, the product of the manufacturing sector was already relatively high (over 20% of GDP), compared to the product of the agricultural sector (less than 15% of GDP). The Second World War gave a further push to the manufacturing sector which increased its share of GDP to about one-third in 1945. Second, the rate of capital accumulation was quite impressive, with the net stock of capital growing by about 15% annually between 1922 and 1935. The lion's share of this capital formation was financed by capital import, of which about 85% was in the form of unilateral transfers by immigrants (*olim*). In addition, the stock of cultivated land increased by about 4% per annum during that period. Third, employment grew at a rate of 12.3% per annum. Fourth, total factor productivity grew by about 7%–8% annually. Consequently, the net domestic product grew about 20% annually between 1922 and 1935.

Jacob Metzer (1985) suggests that "a convenient starting point for observing Israel's economic growth performance is 1952. This year marked the end of the country's period of infancy—the War of Independence, the redrawing of borders, the formation of institutions, and a massive influx of immigrants." In the next two decades the annual growth rates of population, GNP, and GNP per capita were about 3.6%, 9.1%, and 5.3%, respectively. The sharp decline in the economy's growth rate following these two decades is graphically depicted in figure 1.1.

The period which started with the Yom Kippur War and lasted until the recent wave of immigration which began in 1990 is known as the "lost years." Between the years 1973 and 1985 the product of the business sector grew at a relatively meager rate of about 3% per annum. After a short-lived episode of increased growth, following the 1985 stabilization program, the growth rate fell even lower to about 2% in 1989.

Following Jacob Metzer and Michael Bruno, we can provide several explanations for the abrupt slowdown of the Israeli economy in the period after the Yom Kippur War. Figure 1.2 exhibits these factors graphically. First, the annual increase of labor inputs to the business sector fell considerably. This was caused primarily by (1) the decline in the growth rate of the 14+ age group because of low (occasionally even negative) immigration, (2) the decline in labor force participation (e.g., from 51.6% in 1961–72 to 49% in 1973–81) due possibly to the increase in the relative share of the military sector, (3) the relative shift of civilian employment from the business sector to the public sector

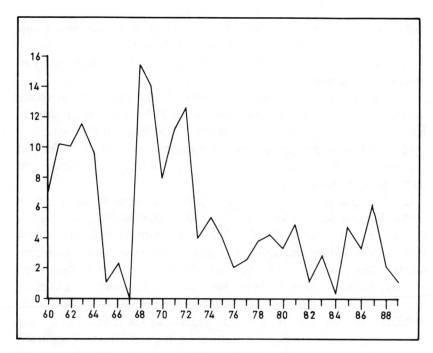

Figure 1.1: Annual rate of growth of GNP, 1960–89.

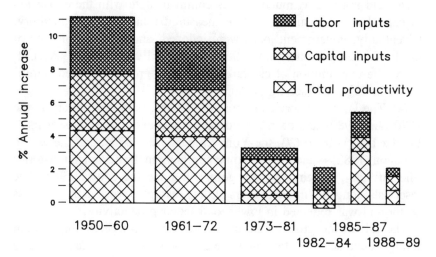

Figure 1.2: Growth factors in the business sector, 1950–89. The contribution of labor and capital inputs to growth are based on labor share of 0.68 and capital share of 0.32.

Sources: Bruno (1989a) and Bank of Israel (1991a).

(for instance, the relative share of employment in the business sector fell from 77.2% in 1961–72 to 73.6% in 1973–81).

Second, total factor productivity fell dramatically. This decline had several explanations:

(1) The two major supply shocks (energy and raw materials price increases) that occurred in 1973–74 and in 1979–80 were apparently felt much more in Israel than in the other industrialized economies.

(2) Inflation picked up and caused a wasteful shift of resources and managerial attention from production lines to financial maneuvers and rent-seeking activities.

(3) The government was a major source of loans to the business sector. For politico-economic reasons, long after inflation accelerated, the government continued to extend these loans at a relatively low interest rate, without indexation (thereby waiving the due inflation premium). This amounted to heavily subsidizing, at greatly differentiated effective rates, investments in the business sector, resulting on average in a low (and perhaps even negative) marginal productivity of capital. Similarly, the tax system provided tremendous tax reliefs to business investments in fixed assets in a time of high inflation. This again amounted to an implicit subsidy that gave rise to excessive capital formation in the business sector. Therefore, the product of the business sector did not rise as much as was commensurate with the expansion in capital input, resulting in low measured total factor productivity. (Eventually, government loans were indexed, and by the beginning of the 1980s inflation-based tax relief was gradually diminished. Accordingly, the contribution of capital formation to growth declined significantly in 1982–84 (see fig. 1.2)).

(4) The length of service required of reservists in the military in the 1970s and 1980s had been considerably extended due to three wars— the Six Day War (1967), the Yom Kippur War (1973), and the war in Lebanon (1982)—and the Palestinian uprising in the occupied territories (the Intifada), which has been going on since the end of 1987. The reservists' long and frequent tours of duty disrupted work in the business sector and was reflected in lower total factor productivity.

The fall in the growth rate coincided with an acceleration in both foreign debt accumulation and the inflation rate. Yet, despite these internal and external economic problems, the standard of living (measured by per capita private consumption) continued to rise. An ever-widening gap began to appear between the insignificant growth in the economy's productive capacity and the growth in the overall level of

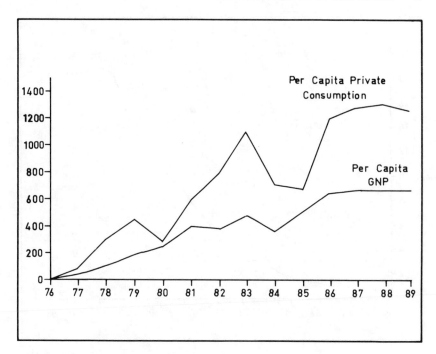

Figure 1.3: Developments in real GNP and private consumption relative to 1976 levels ([GNP/1976 GNP] − 1).

consumption spending (see fig. 1.3). The principal source of finance for this gap was foreign loans, with the result that the net external debt rose unremittingly to reach $19.7 billion by the end of 1984 (see fig. 1.4). At that time, Israel had the world's largest per capita external debt (approximately $4,500).

At the same time, the government's inability to keep spending in check and to maintain a consistent, balanced, and restrained economic policy, led to spiraling inflation which reached frightening, three-digit levels—375% in 1984 (see fig. 1.5). This inability to deal systematically with the country's basic economic and social problems stemmed from, inter alia, the desire to rapidly increase the standard of living in the short term. A striking example was the policy of fixing the nominal prices of subsidized goods and public services. While this policy had the effect of protecting living standards for a few months, in the longer term it was set to collapse, to the detriment of broad sectors of society and particularly low-income groups. A survey conducted by the National Insurance Institute (the Israeli analogue of the Social Security

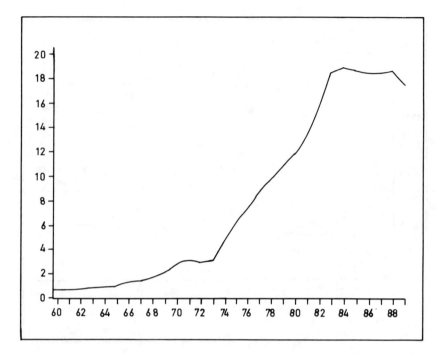

Figure 1.4: Net external debt, 1960–89 (billion current $).

Administration) shows that between 1978–84, transfer and subsidy payments became significantly less effective in their ability to combat poverty. Out of the total number of families, the proportion of poor families, that is, families whose disposable income brought them below the poverty line, rose by approximately one third, from 6% to 8%.

Moreover, during the years when inflation was at its peak, tax receipts, mainly those from the business sector, fell drastically (by an amount equivalent to some 8.5% of 1984 GNP). This decline led to an increase in the budget deficit, which reached some 12% of GNP between 1980 and 1984 (see fig. 1.6). The budget deficit was what fed inflation. High inflation and the large public sector debt led to fears that the government would either fail to honor its liabilities or impose heavy taxes; this led to the flight of capital abroad. The ultimate consequence of this process was the bursting of the bubble in the stock market (January 1983) and, more striking, the bank shares crisis (October 1983). High inflation undermined nominal accounting statements, clouding the real picture prevailing in all sectors of the economy and hindering decision making (particularly in agriculture and industry).

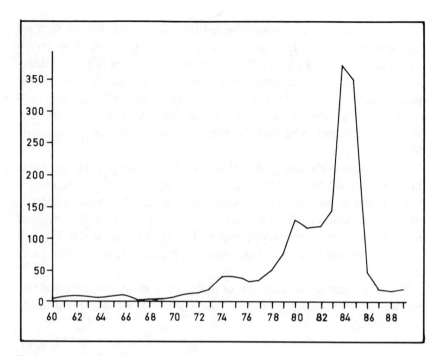

Figure 1.5: Annual inflation rate, 1960–89.

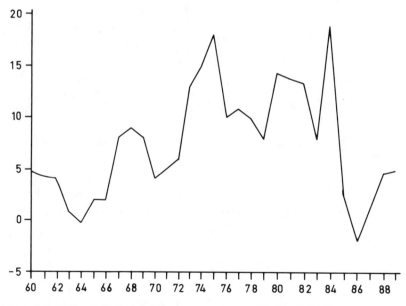

Figure 1.6: Domestic budget deficit as a percentage of GNP, 1960–89.

As government policy was designed far more for short-term than for long-term success, there was a constant need for frequent sharp policy changes. The overall picture painted by government policy was, therefore, one of alarming inconsistency, inconsistency which reflected the underlying weakness of those at the helm. Ultimately, by the mid-1980s, Israel's inflation rate and national debt reached intolerable levels, and threatened to rupture the country's entire economic and social fabric.

It was against this background that in mid-1985 the government made the bold decision to implement a new economic policy which, even if it was harsh in its short-term effects, was designed to solve the basic problem of inflation. Emphasis was placed on stabilizing the economy through fiscal and monetary restraint. The relative price stability that this policy achieved has, in fact, endured up to today, some eight years later.

The main economic features of the stabilization program and the political decision-making process which led to it are described in the next chapter.

2

Stabilization

Inflation has become almost universal among countries that have undergone social and political transitions and suffered from political instability. Inflation itself weakens the power of government and simultaneously feeds on the ensuing political turmoil. Israel is not the only country which has had such an experience. Many Latin American countries struggled with high rates of inflation. More recently, many economies in the former Communist Bloc are experiencing high inflation in their transformation to market systems. Some economies ran into inflation suddenly, and then found it difficult to extricate themselves. Stabilizing an economy is an extremely demanding political task. Even in the economic literature, the process of stabilization is not fully understood. No country has managed to stabilize its economy on its first such attempt; they all went first through a sequence of unsuccessful experiments. Israel was no exception.

This chapter provides an overview of the stabilization program in Israel. We begin by reviewing several unsuccessful stabilization experiments, both in Israel and elsewhere. These experiments typically relied on devaluation slowdowns and price synchronizations that were inconsistent with the economic fundamentals. We then highlight the successful stabilization program which Israel implemented in July 1985. We also provide a short account of the political decision-making process surrounding the stabilization program. Attention is paid to the roles played in the design and implementation of the program by the pillars of the political economic system: the government, the Histadrut, and the Private Employers Association (PEA). We conclude this chapter with an account of the recent Latin American experience that reveals some successes along with a few failures.

2.1. Unsuccessful Stabilization Experiments: Devaluation Slowdowns and Price Synchronizations

In the past, several attempts were made at slowing the rate of inflation. These were based on holding back devaluations and/or using administrative measures aimed at restraining price increases or actually freezing prices, even though it was evident that the economic fundamentals were not in line with these "anti-inflation" measures. Examples are the "Five-Five" policy of Yoram Aridor, Likud finance minister during 1982–83, and the Peres-Moda'i package deals which were implemented at the end of 1984 and in the first half of 1985.

Aridor's Five-Five policy was an attempt to synchronize key prices such as the exchange rate and the prices of subsidized commodities (mostly basic food items and public transportation). This policy was called Five-Five because it was based on limiting devaluations to no more than 5% per month and holding back increases in the controlled prices of subsidized commodities to 5% per month. This was at a time when monthly rises in the CPI were averaging 7%. Shimon Peres was the Labor prime minister during the years 1984–86 in the national unity government whose Likud finance minister was Yitzhak Moda'i. They struck several package deals with the Histadrut and the PEA aimed at stabilizing the economy with very little pain. In a typical such package the government promised to abstain from raising the prices of subsidized commodities or taxes, while the Histadrut agreed to abstain from demanding "unwarranted" wage hikes; and the PEA agreed to refrain from "unwarranted" price increases. None of these deals lasted long.

Similar experiments were made in other countries, and all of them failed for lack of suitable fiscal and monetary backing. The main side effects of these measures, both at home and abroad, were a drop in the foreign exchange reserves, increased consumption, and rapid growth in the external debt. In order to stop the accumulation of a large debt, which would lead to a debt crisis, a sharp change in economic policy was soon required. And with this change, consumption fell, growth slowed or stopped, and inflation rose again to high levels. Thus in Israel, inflation continued to rise despite attempts to reduce it.

Argentina and Chile provide striking examples of similar attempts to restrain inflation by limiting the rate of devaluation without appropriate

Table 2.1 Slowed-down Devaluations: Argentina, Chile, and Israel, 1978–81

Year	Real Exchange Rate (index)	Private Consumption (index)	Trade Balance (million $)	Change in Central Bank Reserve (million $)
		Argentina		
1978	100	100	2913	−2297
1979	73	101	1783	−4381
1980	72	109	−1373	2749
1981	85	107	−3347	3347
		Chile		
1978	100	100	−426	−724
1979	88	119	−355	−1128
1980	75	122	−676	1402
1981	—	132	2677	−77
		Israel[a]		
1981	100[b]	100	−1371[c]	−2280[d]
1982	96[b]	106	−1837[c]	−1940[d]
1983	91[b]	115	−2741[c]	−2307[d]
1984	98[b]	110	−2130[c]	−803[d]

Source: Helpman and Razin (1987)
[a] The years 1981–84 have been moved backward by one quarter to adjust for the period of delayed devaluations (1982.4–1983.3).
[b] Calculated from the import price index and the GDP deflator.
[c] Current account minus defense imports and interest payments.
[d] Growth in reserves minus unilateral transfers to the government of Israel.

fiscal and monetary backing. In Argentina, the slowed-down devaluation program known as Tablita was applied from December 1978 until February 1982. In February 1978, Chile implemented a restricted devaluation policy, which turned into a complete freezing of the dollar exchange rate from June 1979 until June 1982, again without fiscal and monetary backing. Israel adopted a delayed devaluation policy from September 1982 to October 1983 (the Five-Five program). Table 2.1 shows the great similarity between the main economic developments in each of the countries in question: a considerable appreciation of the real exchange rate, a large growth in private consumption, a worsening of the trade deficit, and a rapid drop in the foreign exchange reserves. In each country, the growth of external debt and the drop in reserves forced the government to implement sharp changes in policy. This shattered the illusion that "deluxe" stabilization could be achieved without any accompanying fiscal and monetary restraints which, though painful in the short term, provide the long-term basis for growth and price stability.

2.2. The Stabilization Program: July 1985

2.2.1. The Political Arena

From 1974 to 1985, the Israeli economy was embroiled in a mass of increasingly complex problems that posed a continual threat to its stability. Hindsight, as well as contemporary analyses, show that this situation was caused by a weak government, which lacked resolve and had at best a poor understanding and awareness of the real seriousness of these problems. Years of high inflation and the government's mishandling of the economy give rise to a belief that democratic government is incapable of dealing with economic problems of the type experienced in Israel. Such a state of affairs makes it all the easier to appreciate the significance of the government's decision to initiate a stabilization program in July 1985 and the achievements made following its implementation. This decision marked the end of a long, hard process of consultation and compromise which had to be endured before the economy recovery program could be drawn up.

In the early 1980s, the realization had already developed that only drastic measures could help the Israeli economy to recovery. The scene was set for a series of studies that offered potential solutions. Members of the academic community, the administration, and the business community were all hard at work looking for a magic formula to solve the country's economic woes. The formula was to solve simultaneously the inflation problem and the persistent balance of payments deficit. But the weakness of all solutions offered was the implementation phase and the mustering of political clout necessary for carrying out a comprehensive economic stabilization program.

An analysis of past economic decision making shows that the various problems that threatened the economy were always overshadowed by the demands of pressure groups. Sometimes it was the need to finance the country's defense requirements, a need regarded as of paramount importance. At other times, it was the "social lobby" that led the field in the fight against cuts in transfer payments and subsidies; and if not this lobby, then it was the industrialists or the agricultural sector.

The realities facing the national unity government headed by Labor's Shimon Peres, when it took up office in September 1984, were such that it preferred to avoid resolute action and to seek interim solutions, which were ineffective in providing any basic remedy to the country's economic ills. Between September 1984 and the beginning of April 1985, two package deals were implemented (see section 2.1). These packages were limited in their application and of doubtful effectiveness. Their significance, however, lies in the fact that they resulted from tripartite talks between the government, the Histadrut, and the PEA. These meetings, which started out informally for the purpose of consultation and exchanging opinions, eventually solidified into a socioeconomic advisory body. In turn, this conclave grew into a forum for negotiations and discussions between the three central factors in the economy. During the discussions preceding the formulation of the economic stabilization program, it became increasingly apparent that a solution could only be found via a truly comprehensive array of measures. Also clear at the time was the fact that any delay in deciding on a resolute course of action would mean a worsening of the situation in every branch of the economy. Indeed, some involved in the tripartite discussions presented an apocalyptic scenario for the country's economic and social future. Accordingly, it was no longer impossible to accept the need for drastic and significant policy measures. Michael Bruno (1991) correctly points out that "the Prime Minister of Israel by tradition seldom takes an interest or intervenes in economic issues. His or her preoccupation centers on matters of defense and foreign policy, while economic leadership and the substance of economic policy are usually delegated to the Minister of Finance who may or may not be vested with the full power." Shimon Peres as prime minister, however, was a much needed exception. Once he was convinced that only a comprehensive program would work, he effectively led the entire process in close cooperation with the finance minister, Yitzhak Moda'i. The prime minister's extensive involvement in the package deals and his inclusion of other parties in the decision-making processes gave the impression that he would be announcing some truly significant measures. At the time, there was a public consensus that drastic measures were required. The U.S. administration, through Secretary of State

George Shultz, both urged the Israeli government to launch a comprehensive program and pledged financial aid conditional upon its implementation.

A special team of experts was appointed by the prime minister to plan the components of the economic program. The team included Professors Eitan Berglas of Tel Aviv University and Michael Bruno of the Hebrew University in Jerusalem, Mordechai Frankel from the Bank of Israel, Amnon Neubach, special economic advisor to the prime minister, and Dr. Emmanuel Sharon, Director-General of the Ministry of Finance. The team worked in remarkable confidentiality and communicated frequently with the prime minister and the finance minister. The team came up with a comprehensive program that included up-front devaluation and wage cuts (through COLA suspension) and tight fiscal and monetary measures (see sec. 2.2.2).

At this stage, the policymakers realized that the decision-making process had to plan for battles on at least four fronts:

(1) The fight from within the government would have to include the various ministries and the Likud-Labor factions.

(2) Some accommodation with the Histadrut would have to be reached concerning the issues of cost-of-living allowance (COLA) and wage erosion, worker redundancies (hidden unemployment), the use of emergency decrees in order to implement the economic stabilization program, and the threat of unemployment posed by the draconian measures envisaged in the program (the "cold turkey" approach to economic remedies).

(3) Public opinion would have to be confronted and public confidence in the government rebuilt. The government would have to prepare to cope with the public reaction to such a comprehensive and drastic range of measures. Other factors which had to be taken into account were the response by the capital market, developments in the foreign exchange reserves, and a potential draw on saving deposits should the public's confidence in the government be undermined.

(4) The government would have to work "behind the scenes" to strengthen Israel–U.S. relations. The Americans were becoming increasingly concerned at the Israeli government's irresolute economic stance, and wanted to ensure that the government would not flinch from making vital decisions in real time. They were willing to help, provided they could be convinced that the Israeli government really meant business this time. For this purpose, they established a Joint Economic Development Group (JEDG) with Israel to consult on the economic

program and follow through on its implementation. Notable American economists (Stanley Fischer from MIT, Herbert Stein from the American Enterprise Institute) along with high-ranking State and Treasury Department officials were members of the group.

Although only a very small group of people had been informed of all the program's components, the attitude adopted by the prime minister in his meetings with all the involved parties led to the belief that a wide-ranging program was definitely in the offing. Each party involved immediately tried to promote its own interests at the expense of everyone else's. At the sessions chaired by the prime minister, an effort was made to formulate the program in a manner acceptable to the public without watering down any of the measures planned for solving the country's basic economic problems.

Ultimately, the decision on the content of the economic stabilization program hinged on developments on four fronts:

The cabinet. During the last week of June 1985, various news reports suggested that the government was on the verge of adopting a new economic policy. Because of the complex nature of the new policy, an increasing number of people had to be informed of its components before preparations for its final implementation could be completed. The members of the cabinet were invited to attend what they were told was to be a long meeting on the afternoon of Sunday, June 30, 1985. At the meeting, the minister of finance and part of the team appointed by him presented the main features of the program. Except for Deputy Prime Minister Yitzhak Shamir, Transport Minister Haim Corfu and, of course, Finance Minister Yitzhak Moda'i (who had actually presented the program to the government), all the Likud ministers present vehemently objected to the program, warning of its inherent dangers in terms of great pathos. Foremost among the program's opponents was the minister of housing, David Levy, who, in the course of the cabinet meeting, decided to inform the media of his vigorous objection to the program. The cabinet meeting continued throughout the night, and it was early morning before there was any sign that a decision was going to be adopted. As expected, most of the ministers present, even those who in principle supported the program, objected to the cuts proposed in their own ministries' budgets. Only the realization that a decision had to be reached made it possible for the prime minister to push through an agreement to cut the budget, reduce subsidies, and implement changes in other policy areas. In the early morning of July 1,

1985, after a grueling night's work, the prime minister was able to tell the public that the government had adopted a new economic policy.[1]

The wage front. Before the announcement of the economic stabilization program, the government and the Histadrut made several attempts to reach an agreement on wage controls, but the Histadrut remained opposed to any erosion in wages and/or violation of COLA agreements. On the Saturday evening before the June 30th cabinet meeting at which the economic program was presented to government, the prime minister, the finance minister, and the secretary-general of the Histadrut met to discuss the program. The Histadrut secretary-general vehemently opposed any attempt to use emergency decrees to override binding labor contracts. When the program was being presented to the government, it was said that emergency decrees were necessary in order to implement all the components of the program simultaneously. The use of emergency decrees was aimed at controlling prices, suspending the COLA for a limited period, avoiding wage increases, and allowing public sector employees to be dismissed at short notice.

The Histadrut secretary-general regarded the use of emergency decrees as a gross violation of the network of employer-employee relations. However, when it was announced that the use of emergency powers to curb wages and dismiss workers was conditional on the agreement of the Histadrut, he grudgingly agreed to discuss the subject with the government. The Histadrut and the workers eventually agreed to shoulder the burden of promoting economic recovery, on the condition that the burden would be shared with other sectors of the economy.

Within a few days of the announcement of the program, Histadrut officials sat down with the government to discuss changes in the COLA agreement (which would lead to temporary wage erosion) and worker dismissals. After two weeks of intense negotiations, all disagreements were resolved. In the short term, most of the program's objectives on the wage front were achieved. However, in the long term, the trade unions managed to recoup much of the erosion in their real wages.

Public support for the measures. The public's favorable response to the program, as soon as it was implemented, clearly played a role in its success. This program satisified the expectations caused by the wait

---

1. The active and authoritative role played by Shimon Peres was a remarkable contrast to the passive, unenthusiastic role played by Prime Minister Menachem Begin in 1983 when another stabilization program, the "dollarization" program, was poorly designed, interminably debated, leaked to the press, and then abruptly aborted.

for a significant change in economic policy. This positive response from the very outset proved that the prime minister's fears of an unfavorable public reaction were groundless, and the government managed to consolidate public opinion behind it. One reason for this success was the great effort made at ensuring that the burden which had to be borne for economic recovery was shared fairly among all sectors of the economy. It was clear from the start that the exchange rate needed to be adjusted and subsidies cut, while avoiding excessive impact on prices and wages. Obviously these measures would reduce the purchasing power of salaried workers' earnings. Lower-income groups were also hit by subsidy cuts. Therefore, concurrent with the erosion of the real wage, a surtax was imposed on the self-employed. Also the tax burden on firms was sharply increased by closing large loopholes that they enjoyed in the presence of high inflation.

Israel–United States relations. The Americans were expecting a comprehensive range of policy measures and were delaying legislation related to an emergency aid package amounting to $1.5 billion spread over two years. U.S. embassy staff in Israel and the Israeli government were exchanging information on the implementation, extent, and timing of the program and were holding discussions on its objectives. Secretary of State George Shultz and Prime Minister Shimon Peres were also exchanging correspondence on the subject. This can be described as a mutual consultation process aimed at strengthening Israel through both political and material support.

2.2.2. The Economic Perspective

The stabilization program consisted of a major realignment of key prices and fiscal and monetary restraint. The launching point was a remedial adjustment in the exchange rate. The sheqel was devalued by 19% against the dollar on June 30th, which followed another devaluation of 20% spreading over the earlier part of the month, leading to a cumulative devaluation of some 42% during the month of June. (In fact, the exchange rate at that point reached a *real* level that was never experienced again until the present.) Government subsidies of basic food items and public transportation were severely slashed.

The direct effects of the devaluation and the cut in subsidies on the consumer price index (CPI) were planned to be sterilized by the COLA with the threat to enforce this by emergency decrees if necessary. Later, however, the government reached a negotiated settlement with the Histadrut under which real wages, especially in the public sector, would be allowed to recoup much of this decline through a predetermined schedule lasting about one year.

The cut in subsidies was just one of the ingredients of the fiscal restraint exercised by the government. In addition, there was a cut in domestic defense spending following the pullout of the Israeli army from most of Lebanon. Tax revenues increased substantially. A significant part of the increase in tax receipts was a direct consequence of the lower inflation rate. Indeed, when inflation rates are high, the time lapse between the accrual of the tax liability and the actual payment of that liability erodes the total amount of tax revenue collected in real terms (the so-called Tanzi effect). Thus, when inflation rates drop, real tax collections automatically rise. Another cause for the growth in tax revenues was the adoption of the Steinberg Commission's recommendations on the taxation of the business sector under conditions of inflation (1985) and the imposition of a temporary surtax on the income of the self-employed.

One member of the team of experts who designed the program, Professor Michael Bruno, also suggested that a 10% tax be imposed on the existing stock of the public's financial assets. The proposal, which amounted to a confiscation of part of the public's assets, could have had disastrous effects on government credibility and was flatly rejected by the other members of the team and eventually by the government.

Figure 2.1 shows the effects of the ensuing fiscal restraint. The public sector domestic deficit fell to 0%–2% of GNP, from about 12% prior to the stabilization. Together with $1.5 billion of emergency aid provided by the United States government, this helped to generate an overall budget surplus amounting to some 2% of GNP. The effects of monetary restraint are shown in figure 2.2. A curbing of the M_3 monetary aggregate (which includes means of payments, interest-bearing unindexed assets, and resident deposits linked to foreign currencies) became immediately apparent after the implementation of the stabilization program. This sharp decline in the money supply came at a time when the demand for money grew drastically because of the lower expected rate of inflation. As a result, monetary restraint also expressed itself through a sharp rise in real interest rates immediately after the program was implemented (see fig. 2.3). These measures naturally contributed to a fall in aggregate demand by the private sector (both consumption and investment) and, consequently, to an almost immediate economic stabilization.

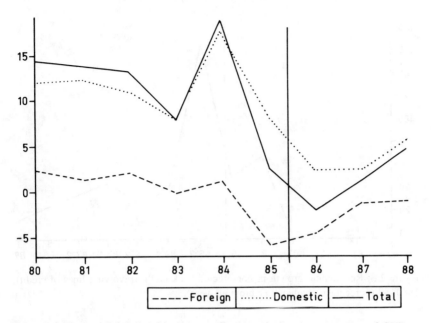

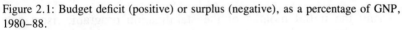

Figure 2.1: Budget deficit (positive) or surplus (negative), as a percentage of GNP, 1980–88.

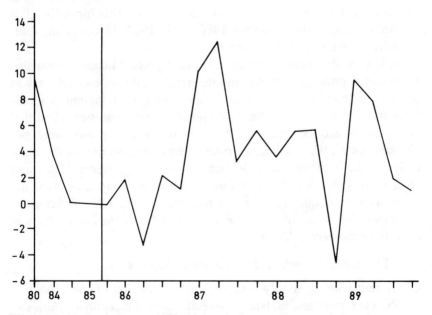

Figure 2.2: M_3 developments, 1980–89 (nominal, quarterly rates of change).

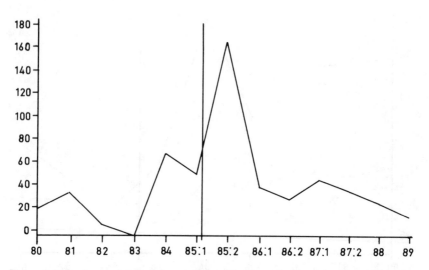

Figure 2.3: Real annual growth in nondirected bank credit (revolving lines of credit), 1980–89 (percentage change over previous year).

During the initial months of the stabilization program, fiscal and monetary restraint led to a moderate rise in unemployment of between 0.5 and 2 percentage points, over and above the average monthly rate of some 6% for January–June 1985 (see fig. 2.4). This higher level of unemployment continued during 1986 but in 1987 fell below the level recorded on the eve of the program.

During the deliberations of the team of experts, Michael Bruno also suggested a prolonged exchange-rate freeze. Others objected. It was finally concluded that the exchange rate would be continuously monitored in conjunction with the development of nominal wages and that no freeze would be executed if nominal wage increases were not checked. Later, when Michael Bruno became the governor of the Bank of Israel, he implemented a de facto exchange-rate freeze. This, and other factors that will be fully discussed in later chapters caused the economy to subsequently fall into a recession, which was characterized by record high levels of unemployment in 1989, on the eve of the new *aliya* from the Soviet Union.

2.3. The Latin American Experience in Recent Years

Concurrent with or shortly after the implementation of the economic stabilization program in Israel, several Latin American countries— Bolivia, Mexico, Chile, Argentina, and Brazil—initiated their own sta-

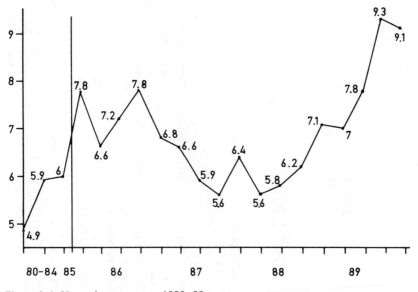

Figure 2.4: Unemployment rate, 1980–89.

bilization programs. Bolivia, Chile, and Mexico adopted orthodox programs that tackled such fundamental causes of inflation as budget deficits and monetary accommodation. By contrast, Argentina and Brazil chose heterodox programs that, aside from a few orthodox components, consisted mainly of measures that dealt directly with only the symptoms of the inflationary crisis. These measures included a wage, price, and exchange rate freeze as well as a regulation mechanism supervising their evolution. The first three countries' stabilization attempts have been successful; the latter two countries', after some temporary success, have failed abysmally. In fact, these countries' inflation rates were higher after their stabilization programs had been in effect than they were before. For instance, in Argentina, the monthly rate of inflation in June 1989 reached 100%. In Brazil, monthly inflation rates during 1989 amounted to between 25% and 30%. Table 2.2 provides a summary of the politico-economic cyclical developments inherent in heterodox attempts to stabilize the economies of Argentina and Brazil.

The entries in table 2.2 reflect the striking fact that economic programs designed to combat only the symptoms of inflation (e.g., by freezing prices or the exchange rate), instead of to uproot its basic causes (e.g., by cutting the budget deficit and maintaining a balanced budget in the long term) do not succeed in achieving economic stability

Table 2.2 Heterodox Attempts at Stabilization in Argentina and Brazil, 1985–89

Program (Date of Implementation)	Fall in the Inflation Rate	Duration of Program's "Success" (monthly inflation of less than 50%)	Type of Heterodox Measures	Monetary Policy	Fiscal Policy
Argentina					
Austral (June 1985)	From 30.5% in June to 3.1% in August	11 months	Freeze in wages, prices, and the exchange rate	Accommodation	Partial cut in the budget deficit
Primavera I (August 1986)	From 8.8% in August to 6.1% in October	2 months	Ceiling on wage and price rises and delayed devaluations	Partial restraint	None
Februar (February 1987)	From 6.5% in February to 3.4% in April	1 month	Freeze in wages, prices, and the exchange rate	Partial restraint	None
Austral II (October 1987)	From 19.5% in October to 3.4% in December	1 month	Freeze in wages, prices, and the exchange rate	Partial restraint, then accommodation	Decision to cut the budget deficit which was not put in practice

Primavera II (August 1988)	From 27.6% in August to 9.0% in October	0	Guidelines got delaying wage and price rises, and delayed devaluations	Partial restraint	Marginal and temporary cut in the budget deficit
Brazil					
Cruzado (February 1986)	From 22% in February to −0.5% in April	9 months	Freeze in wages, prices, and the exchange rate	Monetary expansion	Growth in the budget deficit
Brasser (June 1987)	From 25.8% in June to 4.5% in August	1 month	Freeze in wages, prices, and the exchange rate	Accommodation	None
"Stage by Stage" (April 1988)	None	0	Ceiling on wage and price rises and delayed devaluations	Accommodation	None
Summer (January 1989)	From 36.5% in January to 4.3% in March	1 month	Freeze in wages, prices, and the exchange rate	Accommodation	None

Source: Kiguel and Liviatan (1991).

for more than a few months. In this respect, the Austral, Primavera, and Cruzado programs in Argentina and Brazil were essentially no different from Yoram Aridor's Five-Five policy and the Peres-Moda'i package deals.

The aforementioned stabilization programs of Argentina and Brazil during the second half of the 1980s are fundamentally different from Israel's 1985 stabilization program. The latter can be described as orthodox in principle, as it was based on a substantial reduction in the public sector's budget deficit, by an amount equal to approximately 10% of GNP. The Israeli program therefore resembled its counterparts in Bolivia, Chile, and Mexico. These countries too, it should be noted, were left with a hard core of inflation of about 20% per year.

In 1991, Argentina abandoned its old heterodox policies and adopted tough orthodox measures. The tax burden was significantly increased; the heavy losses of government enterprises were sharply reduced through an extensive privatization process; monetary restraint was exercised. In doing so, Argentina has been able thus far to experience the kind of relative stabilization enjoyed by Bolivia, Chile, Israel, and Mexico.

II

Poststabilization Recession

3

A Recovery That Faded Away

As described in Part I, inflation in Israel was brought down, almost overnight, from the triple digits to 10%–20% annually. At the same time, the accelerated increase in Israel's external debt was brought to an end, and Israel's financial standing in international capital markets improved. However, the 10%–20% annual inflation that remained appeared to be hardcore. It is noteworthy that this has also been the experience in other high-inflation countries that managed successful stabilization programs.

Most inflation-ridden countries experience very slow economic growth as well. Israel was no exception. Stabilization therefore cannot be an end by itself, but rather a stopover on the road to renewed growth. It remains to be investigated whether stabilization was indeed followed by economic growth. This is relevant not only as an episode in Israel's modern economic history, but also in terms of the lessons that can be applied to other inflation-ridden economies.

This and the next chapter are devoted to the study of poststabilization economic developments in Israel. At first, it seemed that after it was stabilized, the Israeli economy began a recovery. Its growth rate and factor productivity picked up significantly shortly after the stabilization. However, as we explain in this chapter, this boom proved to be short-lived since it stemmed from one-shot favorable factors. Sustainable growth was elusive. In fact, shortly after this boom, the economy slid into a severe and long recession. Chapter 4 addresses the question of whether this recession was a necessary by-product of stabilization, an

avoidable outcome of adverse external shocks, or the result of a mis-
guided macroeconomic policy that accompanied the stabilization.

3.1. Short-Lived Recovery

First signs of economic recovery became apparent soon after the launching of the July 1985 stabilization program and its accompanying policy
measures. After an initial GDP decline of about 4% per annum in the
second half of 1985, compared to the first half of the year, GDP rose
in 1986 by 3.6%, and the business sector product increased even more
—by some 5.7%. The economic upswing continued at an even more
rapid rate in the first half of 1987, when GDP grew at an annual rate
of about 6.5% and the business sector product by some 8% annually
over the second half of 1986. These were the highest growth rates
experienced by the Israeli economy since the Yom Kippur War until
the recent wave of immigration.

Since 1985, after many years of stagnation and even decline, business
sector productivity recorded a substantial rise of about 4% per annum—
exceptional growth by comparison with Israel's early record as well as
by international standards. In the second half of 1986 and the first half
of 1987 this was accompanied by a substantial increase in investment
(15% and 6.7% in annual terms, respectively), coming after sharp declines of 11.3% in 1984 and 7.8% in 1985. Immediately after the
implementation of the stabilization program, the unemployment rate
rose moderately but began to fall by mid-1986, with the decline continuing into 1987.

The short-lived boom did not result in a deterioration of the balance of
payments, certainly not at the time. In 1985 and 1986, current account
surpluses of 1.1 and 1.6 billion current dollars, respectively, supported
by a special U.S. emergency grant of $1.5 billion and a decline in the
world price of oil, were recorded for the first time in Israel's economic
history.

Among the principal causes of GDP growth was an exceptional productivity increase, which resulted from a coincidence of favorable factors: First, the drastic reduction of inflation (and particularly the narrowing of the random fluctuations in its monthly rate) shifted work
effort away from financial activities (chiefly designed to afford protection against the inflationary erosion of monetary assets or to generate
inflationary profits which contributed nothing to real GDP) to real productive activities. Second, the drop in world energy prices raised the
value added of domestic production, expressing itself in a rise of pro-

ductivity. Third, the withdrawal of the Israeli Defence Forces from most of Lebanon eased the burden of military reserve duty and its disruptive effect on work. However, these factors had a one-time effect on productivity, which would run its course in the year or two following the stabilization program. The inflation rate became more or less stable and its random fluctuations became much more moderate. Even a further decline in the inflation rate to a level comparable to that prevailing in Organization for Economic Cooperation and Development (OECD) countries would not significantly lighten the business sector's burden of inflation-induced financial activities and would therefore also have no significant effect on productivity growth. In the period under discussion, oil prices were relatively low in real terms compared to their level after the oil crises of 1974 and 1979–80. Subsequently, they did not decline further (in fact, there was a temporary increase in prices during the Gulf crisis).

Despite the remarkable performance, several problems remained unresolved and became increasingly prominent in subsequent years:

(1) The rise in productivity was due to nonrecurrent factors, such as the one-shot drop in inflation. The problem of low productivity remained unsolved.

(2) The inflation rate remained high compared to those of Israel's trading partners. The stabilization program and the curbing of inflation were associated with a fixed nominal exchange rate (except for a slight correction in January 1987). Thus, a continuing erosion of the real exchange rate (i.e., a real appreciation of the sheqel) developed, causing a steady fall of profitability in the business sectors producing for export or import substitution (manufacturing, tourism, etc.).

(3) High real interest rates (serving as an important means of curbing domestic demand within the framework of the stabilization program) did not decline in the period under discussion to levels that would permit a renewal of economic growth. On the contrary, the high interest rates aggravated the financial crises of various enterprises (such as Koor Industries, Polgat Textiles, Carmel Carpets) and economic sectors (such as *kibbutzim* and *moshavim*).

(4) Although the savings of the public sector increased as the persistent public deficit turned into a surplus, a sharp decline in the private saving rate caused the national saving rate to fall. This drop in the national saving rate, from 21.7% of total resources (GNP plus unilateral transfers from abroad) in 1985 to 16.5% in 1987, slowed down wealth accumulation which otherwise could have generated further growth.

Table 3.1 Wages, Returns to Capital, and Productivity in the
Business Sector, 1986–87 (percentage rate of growth)

Year	Total Productivity P_T	Labor Productivity P_L	Wages g_W	Returns to Capital g_S
1986	3.8	3.5	9.1	−12.0
1987	4.1	3.0	8.1	−7.9

Source: Bank of Israel (1989, p. 78). Based on the assumption that the respective shares of capital and labor in GDP are 25% and 75%.

(5) For 1985 as a whole, real wages contracted by 6.4% over 1984, despite the rise in real wages in the first half of 1985. Real wages rose again in 1986 and 1987—by 9.1% and 8.1%, respectively. These wage increases exceeded the rise in the marginal product of labor as measured by the change in labor productivity. As such, it slashed returns to capital in the business sector. This was partly offset by the rise in total productivity, over and above the growth in labor productivity, which contributed to an increase in the returns to capital. However, overall, returns to capital in the business sector were eroded substantially, just when the cost of capital rose. This reduced the profitability of investment in the business sector (see app. 3.1). Table 3.1 presents figures for the returns to capital in 1986 and 1987. We observe that returns to capital declined by 12% and 7.9% in 1986 and 1987, respectively.

3.2. Slide into Recession

The remarkable expansion of GDP and economic activity that characterized the period following the July 1985 stabilization program (the year 1986 and the first half of 1987) came to an abrupt end in the second half of 1987 (see table 3.2). In 1986, GDP grew by 3.6% and the business sector product by 5.7%. In the first and second quarter of 1987, the business sector product rose at annual rates of 2.4% and 22.5%, respectively. However, in the second half of 1987, before the outbreak of the Intifada, business sector product as well as total GDP began to decline. The unemployment rate, which in the year following the stabilization program had risen temporarily (from about 6% in the first half of 1985 to 6.4% in the first half of 1986), later fell back to the low level of the prestabilization period. Unemployment also remained low in the second half of 1987 and the first half of 1988, and began to rise only in the second half of 1988, reaching 9.3% in the second quarter of 1989.

In medicine, early diagnosis of an illness is crucial for proper treatment. The same holds in economic policy. A real-time identification of reversals in economic trends is vital for updating and revising economic policies. However, several factors can impede the timely observation of trends. First, most data on economic variables (such as GDP, unemployment rate, level of investment, etc.) appear naturally only with the significant delay of a quarter or even a whole year. Second, a change of trend in the level of economic activity is not immediately reflected in all economic indicators. A fall in the demand for a product does not immediately lead to a decline of output, because initially firms tend to accumulate inventories with the wishful thought that the contraction of demand is temporary and also because, in part, some production costs are in the short run sunk costs. In Israel, a decline in output also does not express itself in an immediate contraction of employment, since firms do not rush to shed workers because of the high costs (financial

Table 3.2 Economic Activity, 1985–89
(annual percentage changes, seasonally adjusted)

Year and Quarter	GDP	Business Sector Product	Unemployment[a]
1985 1	− 0.8	7.4	
2	26.2	14.8	
3	− 16.8	− 20.3	
4	− 0.8	22.5	
Annual Average	3.9	5.3	6.5
1986 1	7.0	2.0	
2	− 0.4	2.0	
3	4.5	8.2	
4	13.4	12.6	
Annual Average	3.6	5.7	7.1
1987 1	0.8	2.4	
2	13.0	22.5	
3	− 0.8	− 2.0	
4	− 2.4	− 8.9	
Annual Average	5.2	7.0	6.1
1988 1	19.3	19.3	
2	− 16.1	− 16.1	
3	0.8	2.0	
4	5.7	7.8	
Annual Average	2.1	1.1	6.4

[a] Percentage of unemployed out of (civilian) labor force.

and other) that layoffs require firms to bear. For example, though economic activity had already slackened in the second half of 1987, no significant rise in the unemployment rate appeared until the second half of 1988.[1]

In hindsight, it seems that policymakers were late in perceiving that economic trends were headed toward recession. The Bank of Israel's periodic report on economic developments, published in September 1987 said: "The turnaround in domestic economic activity began in the second half of 1986, as the economy emerged from the standstill during the first year after the adoption of the emergency stabilization program."[2] At the time, there was a guarded assessment that the economy was about to resume its growth.

The aforementioned Bank of Israel report stated: "Another important feature of recent developments is the growing indication of the beginning of structural change in the economy—a change which, if continued, will bring forth accelerated stable growth." The authors of the national budget for 1988 judged that there would be no return to the impressive growth rates in GDP and business sector product of 1987 but still believed that the "GDP will grow by 3.7 percent and the business sector product by 4.6 percent," growth rates that in no way indicate the beginning of recession. As the data in table 3.2 illustrate, the growth rates of GDP and the business sector product in 1988 were in fact miniscule: 2.1% and 1.1%, respectively.

Even by March 1988, the Bank of Israel still hesitated to say that the economy was clearly turning toward recession: "The slowdown in business activity that made itself felt in the last quarter of 1987 followed a steady and rapid expansion during the three preceding quarters. The question that therefore poses itself is what caused activity to slow in the last quarter, and whether this is a temporary phenomenon or indicates a reversal of the expansionary trend that marked business activity during 1986 and, even more so, the first three quarters of 1987."[3] The Bank of Israel's annual report for 1987, published at the end of May 1988 after the Central Bureau of Statistics had published data on the economic growth of 1987, was clearly on an optimistic note: "Following the initial shocks caused by the stabilization program, a process set in of progressive adaptation to the changed economic environment. This

---

1. It should be noted that higher public sector employment also moderated the rise in unemployment.
2. See Bank of Israel (1987).
3. See Bank of Israel (1988a).

process has apparently not yet run its course. So far, three stages are discernible in it: (1) a sharp drop in the inflation rate and a large cut in the budget deficit, with a slowdown in economic activity, (2) the consolidation of stability and a surge in domestic demand, and (3) a rise in business sector activity and employment, associated with changes in the structure of demand and product."[4] In mid-1988, when the annual report was published, the Bank of Israel had not yet perceived that the third of these stages had in fact ended by the third quarter of 1987.

This significant delay (of nearly a year) in diagnosing the turnaround in the economy delayed any decision to adopt corrective policy measures and caused the recession in economic activity to accelerate, as witnessed in 1989.[5]

APPENDIX 3.1 Wages and Productivity

This appendix analyzes the relationship between changes in the marginal product of labor, total factor productivity, labor productivity, and the returns to capital.

Let output (Y) be produced by two factors of production, labor (L) and capital (K), according to the production function,

$$Y = F(K, L, T), \tag{A3.1}$$

where T is the total productivity index. Denote the growth rates of Y, L, and K by g_Y, g_L, and g_K, respectively. Differentiating (A3.1) with respect to time, we obtain

$$g_Y = a_K g_K + a_L g_L + P_T, \tag{A3.2}$$

where P_T is the growth rate of total factor productivity.

In equation (A3.2), a_K and a_L measure the shares of capital and labor in output, respectively, as determined by their marginal product, namely,

$$a_K = \frac{MP_K K}{Y} = \frac{MP_K}{AP_K}, \tag{A3.3}$$

---

4. See Bank of Israel (1988b).

5. This prolonged lag in recognizing the change of trend in economic activity by policymakers was not shared by others in the business and academic communities. Thus, for example, the evaluations and forecasts of Economic Models Ltd., published in July 1987, stated: "The leading indicators for the first half of 1987 indeed point to a substantial rise in industrial production, exports, investment and private consumption. However, in our view, this is a temporary phenomenon, and a slowdown is expected in the second half of 1987, compared with the first half of the year." In September 1987, even before the outbreak of the Intifada, the same company made the assessment that the previous twelve months' acceleration of economic activity had in fact ended, and "since the conditions for structural change had not yet materialized, especially in the industrial sector, economic activity returns to a path of moderate growth, of 2–3 percent per annum." (See Economic Models Ltd. 1987a, 1987b.)

$$a_L = \frac{MP_L L}{Y} = \frac{MP_L}{AP_L}, \tag{A3.4}$$

where MP_i and AP_i are the marginal product and the average product, respectively, of factor $i (i = K, L)$. Assuming constant returns to scale, we have

$$a_K + a_L = 1. \tag{A3.5}$$

Labor productivity growth (P_L) is defined as the growth rate of the average product of labor and is equal to the growth rate of output minus the growth rate of labor, i.e.,

$$P_L = g_Y - g_L. \tag{A3.6}$$

Equations (A3.2), (A3.5) and (A3.6) yield the relationship between the growth rates of total factor productivity and labor productivity:

$$P_T - P_L = g_Y - a_K g_K - a_L g_L - (g_Y - g_L) = a_K(g_L - g_K). \tag{A3.7}$$

In other words, the growth rate of total factor productivity exceeds the growth rate of labor productivity if and only if the growth rate of labor exceeds the growth rate of capital.

In the various measurements of productivity growth rates it is usually assumed that the production function is of the Cobb-Douglas type, i.e.,

$$F(K, L, T) = TK^{a_K}L^{a_L}. \tag{A3.8}$$

In this case, the shares of capital and labor in output (a_K and a_L) are constant, and a constant ratio is also maintained between the marginal and the average product of the two factors. It follows that the growth rate of labor productivity is equal to the growth rate of the value of the marginal product of labor.

With returns to capital (equity) being a residual, namely output net of wages, the return per unit of capital is equal to

$$s = \frac{(Y - WL)}{K} \tag{A3.9}$$

where W is the real wage. Hence, differentiating (A3.9) with respect to time and employing equations (A3.2), (A3.5) and (A3.7), yields

$$g_s = \frac{[P_T - a_L P_L - a_L(g_W - P_L)]}{a_K}. \tag{A3.10}$$

Thus, wage growth in excess of labor productivity growth reduces real returns to capital. There is, of course, another factor which may act in the opposite direction, namely growth of total factor productivity in excess of labor productivity growth (multiplied by labor's relative share in total product) which contributes to an increase in the real return to capital.

4

Anatomy of Recession

In its modern history Israel had not experienced serious recession, except for a short period in 1966–67. The recession that started in the second half of 1987 therefore took policymakers by surprise. In contrast to the 1966–67 recession, which was policy-initiated (intended to check an adverse balance of payments trend that had developed), the recent recession was unplanned. The authorities did not perceive it as the inevitable outcome of the economic policy of 1986–1988. On the contrary, as illustrated in the preceding chapter, their assessment was even that the prevailing policy would gradually bring economic growth.

A persistent core of inflation of about 15%–20% per annum accompanied the recession. In fact, it may be said that the recession cum inflation was caused primarily by the distortion of several key relative prices, namely, the real exchange rate and real short- and long-term interest rates, coupled with on-going monetary expansion.

The first signs of slowdown had already surfaced in the third quarter of 1987, before the outbreak of the Intifada. The uprising was therefore not a factor that pushed the Israeli economy into recession; it merely deepened it.[1] In any event, because the Intifada has not been growing in intensity, its economic impact may be regarded as a one-time adverse shock to the level of GDP; it cannot explain a continuing fall in GDP growth rates.

---

1. For the effects of the Intifada on the economy, see Part III below.

4.1. Monetary Expansion

The money supply measure relevant for issues of monetary policy is customarily taken to be the M_3 aggregate, which comprises cash held by the public, demand deposits with the banks, unindexed short-term sheqel deposits (such as Pakam), government bills (Makam), and short-term foreign currency–indexed deposits (Patam). Regarded from the asset side of the banking system's balance sheets, M_3 equals the sheqel value of the Bank of Israel's net foreign currency reserves[2] plus net domestic credit extended by the banking system to the private sector and the government (see app. 4.1). In the analysis that follows we employ this decomposition of M_3. Note that in order to describe the interrelationships between the money supply and price levels, wages, and interest rates, it is necessary to look at the nominal rather than the real changes in the money supply.

Intervention in the foreign currency market by the central bank in order to peg the exchange rate impairs the bank's control over the money supply. Under a fixed–exchange rate regime, capital inflows (when not fully controlled, as was the case in Israel) must increase the supply of money. When the Bank of Israel announces a fixed–exchange rate policy and the public becomes convinced that the bank will adhere to that policy, if domestic nominal interest rates are higher than abroad, there will, of course, be capital inflows: loans will be taken up abroad at low interest and invested in Israel at high returns. As a result, the money supply increases. Such a process actually developed during 1986–87. Bank of Israel data show that the M_3 aggregate increased between 1985 and 1986 by a nominal 45% and by another 32% between 1986 and 1987. These expansions were made up of increases in the central bank's foreign reserves, by 61% from 1985 to 1986 and 56% from 1986 to 1987, and increases in net domestic credit of 34% and 16% for the same periods.

The one-shot drop in inflation that followed the July 1985 stabilization seems to have caused a substantial change in the public's attitude toward the holding of unindexed financial assets. It is plausible that the demand for money expanded significantly in this period. The increased money supply of 1986 therefore served at least in part to satisfy this larger demand for money.

Since 1987, however, there has been no substantive change in the inflation rate, nor are there other reasons to assume that there were

2. Net of the Bank of Israel's liabilities to the rest of the world.

further significant changes in the demand for money. The continued rise in the money supply therefore exerted pressure on the price level. On the other hand, if freezing the exchange rate for a long period is inconsistent with the fundamentals of the economy, expectations of an exchange rate realignment typically start to build up. These expectations generate capital outflows. Such capital outflows express themselves in a fall in the Bank of Israel's foreign reserves, shrink the money base and, with it, all the monetary aggregates. This, in fact, occurred in the second half of 1988.

As expectations of a devaluation strengthened in 1988, the rate of growth of nominal M_3 declined to an average of 18%. Because the GDP growth rate in 1988 was only 2.1%, the 18% growth rate of M_3 could still sustain the two-digit core inflation.

As stated earlier, the M_3 aggregate is equal to the sum of the sheqel value of the Bank of Israel's net foreign reserves and the net domestic credit extended by the banking system to the public and the government. It is noteworthy that despite the 1988 decline in the growth rate of M_3, its net domestic credit component, which is supposed to be the Bank of Israel's principal policy instrument, expanded at an accelerated rate. From an expansion of no more than 16% in 1987, net domestic credit grew by some 30% in 1988. The expansion rate of net domestic credit spiraled in the second half of 1988 to an annual rate of 60%. This expansion actually financed the public's stepped-up foreign currency purchases, caused by expectations of an imminent devaluation. The expansion of net domestic credit was a result of the Bank of Israel's reaction to the rise in the interest rates in the short-term unindexed segment of the credit market. The complementary image of the accelerated growth of net domestic credit, which contrasted with the relatively moderate expansion of M_3, was the sharp decline in the foreign currency reserves.

4.2. Exchange Rates and Wages

Excessive money supply growth expresses itself in price increases. However, a frozen exchange rate limits increases in the prices of traded goods, such as manufactured goods and tourism services, which are exposed to competitive imports. Indeed, prices of such goods rose only at a rate approaching the average world rate of inflation. However, prices of nontraded goods (mainly services), which are not exposed to competitive imports, continued to rise. Naturally, these price increases were accompanied by wage increases in these sectors. Competition

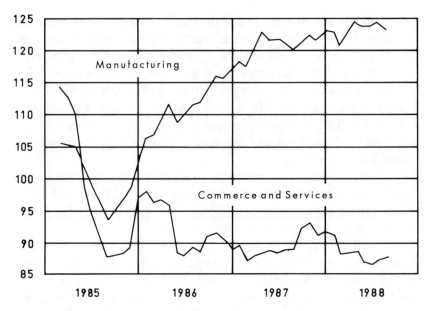

Figure 4.1: Index of real wages, 1985–88 (1984 = 100; nominal wages deflated by industry price indexes).
Source: Neubach, Razin, and Sadka (1990).

for workers caused wage increases to spread even to industries facing competition from imports or producing for export, despite the slower rate of increase in their prices. As a result, profit margins in these industries were slashed, and firms were compelled to shrink.

Figure 4.1 charts the changes in real wages for two sectors: manufacturing, which represents mainly internationally traded goods, and the commerce and service sector, which produces mainly nontraded goods.[3] The real wage in each sector was calculated by deflating the nominal wage by the price index of the product of that sector. Figure 4.1 shows that real wages in manufacturing rose between 1984 and 1988 by a cumulative 20%, while real wages in the service and commerce sector declined in the same period by 5%. The preceding discussion clearly indicates the adverse effect of prevailing economic policy on manufacturing, a leading sector of the economy (the product of the manufacturing sector accounts for almost 30% of the business sector product). Such a great rise in real wages—nearly twice the increase in labor productivity—severely cut into the profitability of manufacturing.

3. Services are evidently mainly nontraded. The product of the commerce sector is the domestic value added by marketing. Thus, it represents mainly nontraded goods.

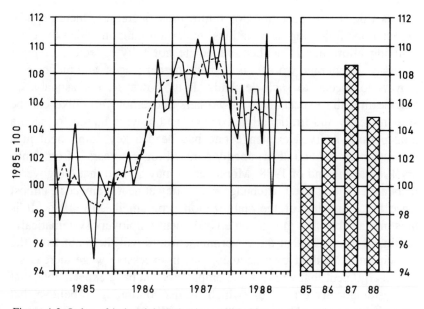

Figure 4.2: Index of industrial production, 1985–88 (monthly and annual averages).

It is therefore no surprise that the product of the industrial sector was among the first to be hurt by the prevailing economic policy. Figure 4.2 shows that the growth of industrial production came to a halt in the third quarter of 1987; industrial production then began to decline. Due to the input-output interrelations between the industrial sector and the other sectors in the economy, the decline in industrial output necessarily sparked a chain reaction in all economic sectors.

The index of industrial production is published with a relatively short lag (about three months), and so should serve as a leading indicator of economic trends. As such, its downturn ought to have lighted, in nearly real time, a red light for policymakers. This is particularly so because a theoretical economic analysis of the effects of the economic policy would have clearly indicated the erosion in the profitability of the industrial sector.

It has variously been argued in the Finance Ministry and the Bank of Israel, that one of the principal causes of the recession was an exogenous wage rise. The explanation offered was that "employers were prepared to accede to wage demands in the (erroneous) hope that they would eventually be bailed out by an accommodative government policy. Such a policy could be a devaluation."[4]

4. See Bruno (1989*b*).

It is true that expectations of future price increases, including the expectations following devaluations, under a regime in which the cost-of-living allowance is neither immediate nor fully reflective of price increases, encourage workers to demand higher wages, and induce employers to accede to such demands. It is, however, unreasonable to assume that the expectations of workers and employers alike can be systematically and irrationally erroneous and upward-biased for such a long period. A fixed exchange rate had been a key component in a policy announced and determinedly pursued for two years—from January 1987 to the end of 1988. Moreover, it may be said that the government adhered to a fixed–exchange rate policy at nearly any cost, almost since the launching of the stabilization program in July 1985. It is thus implausible that in such an environment employers systematically continued to expect that the government would bail them out from the consequences of their own acquiescence in excessive wage increases.

The argument that workers and employers can have expectations that are systematically erroneous (which means continuing to believe that the government would come to their aid with a devaluation) is also not supported by the data on nominal wage increases in the various industries. If this argument were true, nominal wage increases would have been higher in traded goods sectors, where devaluation has a greater impact on prices as perceived by firms, and lower in sectors producing nontraded goods. Thus, for example, nominal wage increases in manufacturing should have been greater than those in the personal services sector and others like it. The data, however, indicate the opposite: between the second half of 1985 and the second half of 1987, nominal wages in manufacturing rose by 89%, whereas in the sectors of personal services and other nontraded goods, nominal wages rose by 97%.

A popular argument against a devaluation goes as follows. After all, the sole role of a devaluation is to erode real wages. Therefore, it is preferable to endeavor to achieve a direct cut in nominal wages rather than to devalue the currency. The problem with this line of argument is that it ignores the fact that devaluation also changes relative prices between different sectors, especially between traded and nontraded goods. It thus affects real wages (in terms of producer prices) differentially in the various sectors. A devaluation reduces real wages in the traded goods industries at a higher rate than in the sectors producing nontraded goods. However, nominal wages are determined by the competition of all sectors for workers—and therefore vary according to occupation, seniority, and so forth—and not in accordance with an industry breakdown. Mechanical engineers with similar qualifications, for example, earn more or less the same wage in all industries. Therefore, even if a restrictive monetary policy and other macroeconomic measures, particularly tripartite wage negotiations between government, employers, and the trade unions, could produce downward pressure on nominal, and consequently real, wages without devaluation, it must be assumed that such wage cuts would spread more or less evenly over the various sectors. The distortion of relative real wage levels in the various sectors would remain unaffected by a uniform wage cut.

One factor which clouded the economic landscape and, in particular, made it difficult to "read the map" of the effects of economic policy was the development of exports, especially industrial exports. On industrial exports, the Bank of Israel's 1988 annual report says: "The 1988 exchange rate freeze against the dollar did not prevent significant expansion in industrial exports to the United States and an increase in their share in total exports" (Bank of Israel 1989, p. 198). In the first half of 1987 total industrial exports rose in real terms, seasonally adjusted, by 5% over the second half of 1986, then by an additional 8.4% and 6.5% in the second half of 1987 and the first half of 1988, respectively. When economic activity slows down, exports obviously tend to rise, diverting supply from the slack domestic market to international markets which are unaffected by the level of domestic activity. But a hysteresis effect was apparently also at work, preventing the decline in profitability caused by the freezing of the exchange rate from promptly affecting the level of exports.[5]

4.3. Interest Rates

The short-term interest rate is directly affected by the supply of the monetary aggregates. These aggregates, however, have only a marginal effect on real long-term interest rates in the long run.

The main instrument of monetary policy in Israel is short-term monetary loans. These loans are extended by the Bank of Israel to commercial banks through two channels. The first is the discount window which amounts to a stepped-up supply curve of loans, designed individually

5. Hysteresis exists because there are sunk costs in the entry into and exit from foreign markets. Therefore, as long as exporters believe that there is a reasonable chance that the erosion of profitability will cease in the future, they will postpone a decision to get out of their foreign markets. A similar phenomenon occurred in Japanese exports to the United States. Despite the strengthening of the yen, Japanese exporters did not quickly raise the dollar prices of their products and continued to export at lower yen prices. For an explanation of this phenomenon, see Dixit (1988).

for each bank. The second is a monetary auction of a given size of loans, on which commercial banks compete with quantity–price (interest) sealed bids. Thus, through both channels different commercial banks receive loans at different interest rates.

It is noteworthy that, because of regulations and tax barriers, international capital mobility in Israel is far from free. In the absence of sufficient exposure to the world markets, interest rates in the Israeli capital market also change in response to variations in the market power of the domestic banking industry which determines the gap (or financial margins) between lending and borrowing rates.[6]

4.3.1. Short-Term Interest Rates (The Unindexed Sheqel Segment of the Credit Market)

The drastic fall of the inflation rate in 1985 was accompanied, within a short time, by a downward adjustment of expectations to a new low inflation rate. This led to an increase in the demand for *real* money balances to a higher steady-state level. Such an increase in money demand could have been satisfied in principle by a one-shot fall in prices, thereby raising the *real* value of money balances. But this does not usually happen in Israel as prices are downward sticky. Alternatively, if capital imports are not restricted, they can finance the increase in money demand. (However, the consequent increase in money supply would have renewed inflationary expectations; see below.) In fact, capital imports were severely restricted. With sticky prices and restriction on capital imports, the increase in money demand typically exerts upward pressure on the short-term real interest rate. This pressure became even stronger as a result of the monetary restraint that was a necessary component of the stabilization program.

Such a rise in interest rates seems to be inevitable in practice and was typical of similar stabilization programs elsewhere. Theoretically, it would be possible to think of a finely tuned and effective combination of two monetary measures which would bring about price stabilization without entailing a sharp rise in real short-term interest rates: (1) a one-time increase in the money supply, which would satisfy the higher demand for *real* money balances (as a result of the fall in the expected inflation rate), and (2) immediately afterwards, a drastic reduction of the growth rate of the money supply, which would cut the inflation rate

---

6. The two largest commercial banks, Bank Hapoalim and Bank Leumi, account for 70% of total bank assets, indicating a highly concentrated industry.

and inflationary expectations. In practice, however, it is difficult to make such a policy credible because, on the one hand, it would increase the money supply, and on the other, promise to reduce its rate of expansion immediately afterwards. In practice, therefore, it would seem to be unavoidable to start a stabilization program with immediate monetary restraint and pay the price for that by a rise in real short-term interest rates, at least temporarily.

Several other factors contributed to the rise in real interest rates and, in particular, to their persistence at a high level. In consequence of the sharp initial rise of interest rates that followed the stabilization program, as well as the erosion of the real exchange rate, enterprises and various economic sectors were in financial distress. Thus banks were exposed to higher risk in lending to the public, and the risk premium further raised lending rates, especially for short-term credit.[7]

An additional cause of the rise in real short-term interest rates (in the unindexed sheqel segment of the credit market) seems to be related to the high concentration of the banking industry. The Israeli financial market is far from regulation-free and competitive. The excessive regulations (e.g., restrictions on the minimum period for which indexed credit may be granted) establish, in effect, two segmented financial sectors: an indexed sector and an unindexed sector. They differ both in their borrowing and lending rates and in the financial margins prevailing in each. (For a more detailed description of the Israeli capital market, see chapter 12.)

The unindexed sheqel segment is generally under looser regulatory control, and in this segment the commercial banks have more discretion in adjusting interest rates to the demand for credit. When long-term credits fall due and firms in financial distress are unable to roll them over by taking fresh long-term loans, their demand for short-term credit increases and becomes less elastic. Figure 4.3 in fact indicates a continuing decline in net medium- and long-term credit flows, relative to business sector product. When the supply of credit is concentrated in a relatively small number of large commercial banks, higher and less elastic demand for credit will express itself in high lending rates and a larger spread between lending and borrowing rates. (For a detailed explanation of this phenomenon, see Figure A4.1 and appendix 4.2.)

7. This phenomenon is particularly noticeable in the case of short-term credit (overdraft facilities), because the rolling over of long-term credits for firms in financial distress (and therefore late in servicing their debt) is shifted to short-term accounts.

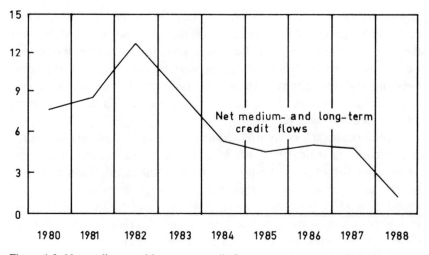

Figure 4.3: Net medium- and long-term credit flows as a percentage of business sector product, 1980–88.

Source: Bank of Israel (1989, diagram H-2).

Figure 4.4 indicates the substantial rise in importance of unindexed short-term credit following the stabilization.

Table 4.1 presents a time series of interest rates in the unindexed sheqel segment of the credit market. The sharp rise in average real lending rates in 1984–85 is prominent. Since then, real interest rates have fallen, but their level remains high in comparison to the 1970s and the early 1980s. The table also indicates a very sharp increase in 1984–85 in the gap between lending and borrowing rates and in financial margins which, as the reader will recall, are caused by (1) the high degree of concentration in the banking sector, (2) the decline in the elasticity of demand for credit, and (3) the rise in the risk premium.[8] Also noteworthy are the temporary fluctuations in sheqel interest rates which result from expectations of price rises in general and devaluation in particular. The sheqel interest rate thus includes, in addition to the

8. Financial margins are lower than spreads between lending and borrowing rates because the former take account of the central bank's reserve requirements, which oblige the banks to redeposit with the central bank, at a relatively low interest rate, part of the public's deposits. Thus, e.g., although the difference between borrowing and lending rates was 39.8% in 1987, this does not represent the banks' profit from lending. The reason is that the banks are not able to use all the funds they borrow from the public at the (negative) lending rate of −1.2% in order to grant credit at 38.6%. Rather they have to deposit part of these funds with the Bank of Israel at the relatively low interest determined by the central bank.

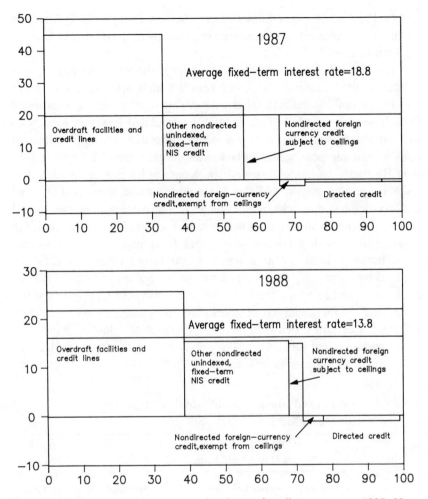

Figure 4.4: Real short-term interest rates by shares of credit components, 1987–88 (percent per annum). The average fixed-term interest rate is based on weighted monthly averages. It therefore differs from the average rate of interest obtained from the weighted quarterly averages shown in the diagram.

Source: Bank of Israel (1989, diagram H-4).

risk premium (which also exists for indexed credit), a premium for expectations of price changes, including devaluations. Thus, when expectations of devaluation rise, demand increases for sheqel credit destined to finance speculative purchases of foreign currency made to profit from the expected devaluation. Of course, such an increase in demand for credit raises nominal interest rates, as in fact happened toward the end of 1988 when expectations of devaluation strengthened. After the devaluations, interest rates resumed the downward trend that characterized the year 1988.

The rise in the interest rate on short-term sheqel credit has various effects on the economy. First, companies which suffered severe profit erosion in real operations (also as a result of the factors mentioned earlier) were compelled to cover their accumulated losses by turning to the short-term credit market. For such enterprises, the higher interest rates in that segment were the last straw (e.g., Carmel Carpets, Horowitz Brothers, *kibbutzim, moshavim,* Koor, Solel Boneh, et al.). The financial burden aggravated the crisis which these firms had reached and accelerated cutbacks in output and employment. Second, in all sectors the rise in short-term interest rates increased the cost of holding inventories, and thus caused inventories to contract. In other words, firms found it more difficult (or less profitable) to absorb a fall in demand by increasing their inventories (e.g., Soltam, Ordan, Tadiran, et al.), and had to adjust their current activities more rapidly to the fall in demand. In fact, analysis of investment in inventories in recent years indicates a certain downward trend in inventories relative to business sector product (see table 4.2). We must, however, remember that investment in inventories is influenced by other factors, such as expecta-

Table 4.1 Unindexed Sheqel Credit: Real Interest Rates and Financial Margins, 1970–88

| Period | Real Short-term Interest on Unindexed Sheqel Credit | | | | Average Real Short-term Interest on Total Bank Credit |
	Lending Rate[a]	Deposit Rate[b]	Spread[c]	Financial Margins	
1970–75	0.4	−8.7	9.1	4.5	
1976–77	−0.1	−14.1	14.2	5.7	
1978–83	7.0	−23.4	30.4	17.5	3.7
1984–85	77.8	−9.5	87.3	33.8	22.5
1986	33.4	−2.1	36.8	15.1	8.2
1987	38.6	−1.2	39.8	18.4	18.8
1988	25.4	−4.1	29.5	16.0	13.8

Source: Bank of Israel (1989, p. 243).
[a] From 1978, on overdraft facilities.
[b] On certificates of deposit or overnight deposits.
[c] Lending rate minus deposit rate.

Table 4.2 Investment in Inventories as a
Percentage of Business Sector
Product, 1980–88

Year	
1980	1.0
1981	−1.7
1982	0.9
1983	0.2
1984	1.6
1985	0.6
1986	3.4
1987	0.2
1988	0.0

Source: Central Bureau of Statistics (1989a).

tions of higher prices and devaluation, the tax code, and actual inflation.[9]

4.3.2. Capital Imports and the Long-Term Cost of Funds

In the presence of restrictions on international capital mobility, domestic interest rates differ from those prevailing in international capital markets. In practice, long-term credit from domestic sources was substantially more expensive (as a result of effective restrictions on capital imports) than the cost of raising funds abroad (adjusted for exchange rate changes). At the same time, returns on certain financial investments abroad are higher or appear safer than the return obtained by Israeli savers (as a result of effective restrictions on capital exports).

Freezing the exchange rate (perceived as a credible policy by the public) in the presence of inflation requires a fairly rigid enforcement of restrictions on capital imports in order to maintain some control over the money supply. When the sheqel interest rate far exceeds the foreign currency–denominated interest rate abroad and when this is accompanied by official declarations of intent to adhere to a fixed–exchange rate regime, it is evidently profitable to import capital. That is, it pays to borrow at low interest rates abroad and invest the funds in Israel for a

9. The tax code does not regard business inventories as fixed assets, so that, ceteris paribus, the higher the actual inflation rate, the more profitable is the holding of inventories (see chapter 9).

high nominal yield. This capital inflow remains profitable as long as the public does not expect a devaluation in the near future and does not, therefore, fear exchange rate losses that would offset the profits arising from the difference between domestic and foreign interest rates. The well-founded fear of a "monetary flood" that would occur if unlimited capital imports were permitted required strict enforcement of the restrictions on capital imports particularly on short-term, but also on long-term, capital imports.

The restrictions on capital imports were tightened by, among other things, the imposition of a 3% surcharge on credits taken up abroad. The surcharge increased the business sector's cost of raising funds abroad and allowed domestic long-term interest rates to remain relatively high. A ceiling was also imposed on the borrowing rate on credits taken up abroad. Thus, only firms that could obtain credits abroad at a rate below the ceiling were allowed to borrow abroad. This eliminated whole segments of Israeli firms (i.e., those considered high risk) from the international capital market. In addition, other factors augmented domestic demand for long-term credit. One of these was the rise in demand for consumer goods (especially durables such as automobiles, VCRs, etc.), caused by a too low real exchange rate.[10]

As a result of the high dispersion of long-term credit among different borrowers, the many different purposes for which such credit is taken up and granted, and so forth, it is difficult to arrive at a precise estimate of the marginal cost of long-term credit. Nevertheless, in this credit segment the differences between borrowing and lending rates are relatively small. This permits us to take the changes in real yields on long-term financial assets as an approximation of the business sector's real cost of raising capital. Figure 4.5 indicates a substantial rise in the yields on long-term (risk-free) financial assets soon after the adoption of the stabilization program. Although there was subsequently a clear downward trend in these yields (and the 3% surcharge on capital imports was abolished), it was only toward the end of 1988 that these yields began to approach their level of the 1970s. Eventually, albeit with a lag, the high cost of raising capital depressed investment and contributed to the onset of recession.

10. The resulting increase in demand for credit was, it might be noted, partly moderated by restraint in public consumption.

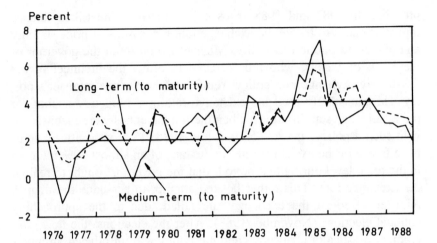

Figure 4.5: Real rates of return on government bonds, 1976–88.
Source: Bruno (1989*b*).

4.4. Poststabilization Lessons

In the first two years after the launch of the stabilization program Israel recorded exceptional rates of growth of output and productivity and a relatively low rate of unemployment. However, the poststabilization boom was short-lived. It was caused by the coincidence of once-and-for-all factors. First, the sharp decline in the rate of inflation enabled nonfinancial enterprises in the business sector to shift resources from financial activities to genuinely productive activities. Second, the pull-out of the Israeli forces from most of Lebanon relieved the burden of military reserve duties and reduced its adverse impact on the continuity of the work process. Third, the fall in world energy prices enhanced productivity in a country which is entirely dependent on a foreign supply of energy.

A slide into a recession could have been detected as early as the second half of 1987. The recession continued well into 1989. Then some early indications of recovery were seen toward the end of 1989, by the time the new wave of *aliya* started. It seems that the temporary poststabilization boom distracted policymakers, and their late diagnosis led to a longer and deeper recession.

The 1988–89 recession had several causes: It had, for instance, deep roots in the pegged exchange rate policy and high interest rates that prevailed in 1987 and 1988. Moshe Nissim (then the Likud finance minister) chose to freeze the exchange rate for reasons of price stability and perceived public credibility. Michael Bruno (then the governor of the Bank of Israel), who thus became in effect the architect of the day-to-day exchange rate policy, reinforced the finance minister's policy. He persistently used the exchange rate as a monetary anchor for price and wage stability, even when the fundamentals were inconsistent with such a policy. It was not until mid-1988, 18 months after a complete freeze of the exchange rate, in the face of an almost 30% increase in the price level during that period, that the governor sought to realign the exchange rate. This rather belated attempt to persuade the finance minister to adjust the exchange rate failed, due to the approaching national elections (November 1988). After the elections, the new government drastically changed economic policy and introduced an ambitious recovery program.

The stabilization program dictated a sharp cut in the rate of expansion of the nominal monetary aggregates, and this was in fact done. (In theory, a one-shot expansion of the supply of money, followed by a fall in the money growth rate, would have been the ideal policy. However, in practice, the initial monetary expansion would have generated inflationary expectations which could undermine the stabilization). Monetary restraint, together with a rise in the demand for money as inflationary expectations abated, caused a sharp rise in real interest rates (particularly on unindexed sheqel credit). This rise deterred the Bank of Israel from continuing its sharp monetary restraint, a policy consistent with the single-digit inflation rates in Israel's trading partner countries. At the same time, the central bank and the Ministry of Finance adhered to a declared and determined policy of freezing the exchange rate, which in turn further reduced the Bank of Israel's ability to check the rate of growth of the monetary aggregates. The real appreciation of the sheqel against the currency basket, which followed from this policy, cut further into the business sector's profitability (especially in the industries producing tradeables for export and import substitution, such as manufacturing, agriculture, et al.) This sector had already been hurt by the higher interest rates.

To these recessionary factors, one should add the rise in the cost of raising capital following the tighter restrictions on capital imports. These restrictions were intended to prevent a massive monetary expansion swelled by capital inflows. Such inflows became profitable in the face of the frozen exchange rate and the high nominal interest rates generated by a 15%–20% inflation. Profitability in the nonfinancial business sector was further eroded by the increase in the effective tax burden on the business sector stemming from the decline in inflation. This low profitability made it difficult to roll over long-term credits by raising fresh long-term loans. Thus the business sector was increasingly forced to resort to "distress borrowing," especially in the short-term unindexed sheqel credit segment, in order to roll over loans as well as to cover current losses. Consequently, the demand for unindexed sheqel credit rose and became less elastic. Under market conditions far from perfectly competitive, as in Israel's concentrated banking sector, these developments facilitated a rise in lending rates together with the widening of financial margins.

The initial rise in interest rates was apparently an unavoidable by-product of stabilizing the economy which had experienced rampant inflation. But the monetary policy pursued subsequently should be viewed as the fundamental force driving the economy into recession, a recession further deepened by the Intifada and the rise in the effective tax burden. Part III provides a detailed account of the Intifada and discusses its effect on the Israeli economy, on the one hand, and on the economies of occupied territories, on the other.

Appendix 4.1 Composition of Monetary Aggregates

The monetary aggregate M_3 is conventionally defined, by using the liability side of a consolidated balance sheet of the banking system, as the sum of currency in circulation (C_a), sheqel-denominated demand and time deposits (D_1), and foreign currency denominated deposits (D_2). That is,

$$M_3 = C_a + D_1 + D_2. \tag{A4.1}$$

Ignoring the Bank of Israel's equity (which is typically negligible relative to total assets or liabilities), a schematic version of its balance sheet looks as follows:

Bank of Israel

Assets	Liabilities
R	C_a
B_g	C_b
B_{p1}	
B_{p2}	
H	H

where,

C_b = commercial banks' reserves
R = international reserves (net of external indebtedness)
B_g = Bank of Israel's credit to the public sector
B_{p1} = Bank of Israel's credit to the private sector
B_{p2} = Bank of Israel's credit to commercial banks
H = money base

From this balance sheet we get

$$H = C_a + C_b = R + B_g + B_{p1} + B_{p2}. \tag{A4.2}$$

A schematic consolidated balance sheet of the commercial banks looks as follows:

Commercial Banking System
(consolidated balance sheet)

Assets	Liabilities
	E
C_b	B_{p2}
B_{p3}	D_1
	D_2

where B_{p3} denotes commercial banks' credit to both the nonbanking private sector and the public sector and E denotes equity.

Hence, from the balance sheet we get

$$E + D_1 + D_2 + B_{p2} = C_b + B_{p3}. \tag{A4.3}$$

Equations (A4.1)–(A4.3) yield

$$M_3 = C_a + D_1 + D_2 = R + B - E, \tag{A4.4}$$

where $B = B_g + B_{p1} + B_{p3}$ is the net domestic credit of the banking system (central and commercial) to the nonbanking private and public sectors. That is, since typically E is negligibly small (relative to $R + B$), it follows that the money supply is approximately equal to the sheqel value of the international reserves plus net domestic credit.

APPENDIX 4.2 The Determination of Interest Rates in a Noncompetitive Market

In order to highlight key factors that influence the spread between borrowing and lending rates, we present an extreme case of noncompetitiveness on the

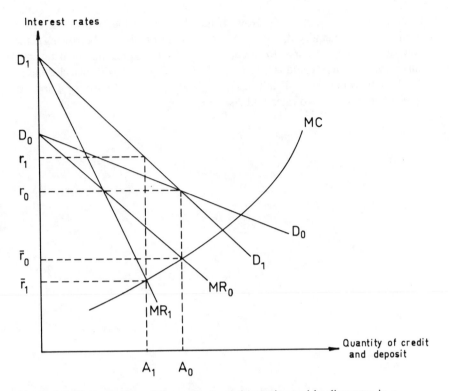

Figure 4.6: Determination of the gap between borrowing and lending rates in a monopolistic market. Borrowing rates—$\bar{r}_1$, $\bar{r}_0$; lending rates—r_1, r_0; demand curves of the public for credit confronting the bank—D_0D_0, D_1D_1; marginal revenue curves (from interest on credit) of the bank—MR_0, MR_1; bank's marginal cost of mobilizing deposits—MC.

supply side in which the industry consists of a single bank. For simplicity, we further assume that there are no reserve requirements and no discount-window lending by the Bank of Israel, so that the borrowing rate paid to depositors represents the bank's marginal cost of raising funds. We assume that the initial demand curve for credit faced by the bank is D_0D_0 in figure 4.6, and the marginal revenue curve (in terms of interest on credit) is MR_0. The bank's marginal cost curve (namely, borrowing rate) is MC. In this situation, the bank will set its borrowing rate at $\bar{r}_0$ and its lending rate at r_0.[11] The quantity of credit (and deposits) will then be A_0 and the spread between borrowing and

11. To avoid complicated diagrams, we ignore the possibility that the bank can also act as a monopsonist toward its depositors. This possibility in fact increases the interest rate spread even more.

lending rates will be $r_0 - \bar{r}_0$. Now, if the elasticity of the demand for credit declines at the quantity A_0 (as, e.g., in the case of distress borrowing), the new steeper demand curve for credit will be D_1D_1 and the marginal revenue curve will be MR_1. The quantity of credit (and deposits) will then decline to A_1; the borrowing rate will fall to $\bar{r}_1$, the lending rate will rise to r_1, and the spread between the two rates will rise to $r_1 - \bar{r}_1$.

III

The Uprising in the West Bank and Gaza: Intifada

5

The Economies of the West Bank and the Gaza Strip

The uprising in the West Bank and the Gaza Strip (which have been occupied by Israel since the Six Day War in 1967) broke out in December of 1987. The Intifada, as the uprising is called in Arabic, came almost out of the blue following a fatal collision between an Israeli truck and a bus carrying Palestinians from Gaza working in Israel. Immediately after the accident, the groundless rumor spread in the Gaza Strip that it was a deliberate Israeli act to kill Palestinians. Riots broke out and immediately spread to the West Bank as well. These riots crystallized a new local leadership that transformed them into a continuous political struggle against the Israeli administration.

The Intifada started at a time when the Israeli economy was already sliding into recession. The Intifada, by itself, could not have pulled the Israeli economy into a severe slump because the economies of the West Bank and Gaza are very small relative to the Israeli economy. However, the Intifada did cause a decline in the national income of the West Bank and the Gaza Strip. Initially, the Intifada incorporated elements of economic warfare, but the strong dependence of the Palestinian economies on the Israeli economy prevailed and the use of economic weapons faded away.

An analysis of recent economic developments in Israel cannot be complete without investigating the economic effects of the Intifada. This chapter provides an overview of the structure of the economies of the West Bank and the Gaza Strip, their interactions with the Israeli economy, and their development since 1967. Chapter 6 first investigates the economic effects of the Intifada, concluding that they were minor in Israel but quite sizeable in the West Bank and Gaza. The second part of chapter 6 describes a fascinating element of the Intifada—the use of economic weapons and counterweapons in the conflict between the residents of the territories and the Israeli administration. We find that eventually the leadership of the Intifada realized that the use of economic weapons was self-defeating.

5.1. Facts and Figures

The economies of Israel, the Gaza Strip, and the West Bank are interconnected by a wide-ranging network of mutual ties, but differ greatly in their size and stages of development (see table 5.1). The population of the occupied territories is about one-third of Israel's population, but their combined GNP is only 8% of Israel's GNP. Accordingly, per capita GNP in the territories is less than one-quarter of that in Israel. While Israel's domestic product is slightly larger than its national product (mainly because of interest payments on the external debt), in the territories the opposite is true, and the GDP there is far lower than the GNP, which contains a contribution from the earnings of local Arabs who work in Israel and other countries. Domestic product per employed person in the territories is less than half of the corresponding figure for

Table 5.1 Israel, the West Bank, and the Gaza Strip—Comparative Indicators, 1986[a]

	Israel	West Bank	Gaza Strip
Population (thousands)	4,298	826	536
Gross national product (million 1986 $)	28,435	1,397	572
Gross national product per capita (1986 $)	6,615	1,691	1,067
Gross domestic product (million 1986 $)	29,141	1,111	352
Gross domestic product per employed person (1986 $)	19,747	10,100	7,040
Capital per employed person (1986 $)	51,497	6,769	8,556

Sources: Central Bureau of Statistics (1988b) and Zaka'i (1989).
[a] Because of the biennial cyclical nature of the agricultural branch (particularly in olive production, which is the main agricultural sector in the West Bank), we report average annual data on the West Bank and the Gaza strip for the two years 1985–86.

Table 5.2 Labor Force and Employment in the West Bank and the Gaza Strip, 1968–86

Year	Population	Labor Force	Employed Persons	Persons Employed in Israel
		Total (thousands)		
1968	938	156	135	5
1978	1,195	217	214	69
1986	1,362	269	261	95
		Average annual percentage rate of growth		
1968–86	2.1	3.1	3.7	
1968–78	2.1	3.4	4.7	
1978–86	2.0	2.7	2.5	

Source: Central Bureau of Statistics (1988*b*).

Israel. One of the reasons for this is the relative scarcity of capital: the amount of capital per employed person in the territories is only one-sixth that in Israel.

After 1967, the economies of the West Bank and the Gaza Strip enjoyed accelerated growth produced primarily by their increasing openness to the Israeli economy. In addition, for at least part of the period in question, Jordan experienced similar growth. It is difficult to assess whether the economic growth in Jordan contributed to the growth in the territories, or whether it was the other way around.

Between 1968 and 1986, the population of the occupied territories grew by about 50%, while the local labor force increased by around 75% (see table 5.2). The number of employed persons doubled, and the number of those obtaining employment in Israel reached 95,000. Although residents of the territories employed in Israel make up only 7% of the Israeli work force, they account for close to 40% of all employed persons living within the territories. There is no doubt that this phenomenon has had important consequences for the economic structure of the territories and for their considerable economic dependence on Israel.

The territories' GNP grew by an annual average of 6.5% after 1968, a rate which was considerably higher than the annual 2% increase in their population (see table 5.3). However, most of this growth occurred during the first decade after the Six Day War, when it averaged 10%

Table 5.3 GNP and Balance of Payments in the West Bank and the Gaza Strip, 1968–86

Year	GNP	Exports	Imports	Deficit in the Trade Account
	Total (million 1986 $)			
1968	440	110	270	160
1978	1,130	360	950	590
1986	1,550	420	1,190	770
	Average annual percentage rate of growth			
1968–86	6.5	6.9	7.7	8.2
1968–78	9.8	12.7	13.4	13.2
1978–86	4.0	1.8	2.8	4.7

Source: Central Bureau of Statistics (1988*b*).

per year. During the subsequent decade, the growth rate was only 4%. The overall average GNP of the territories in 1985–86 was approximately 2 billion 1986 dollars, compared to 440 million 1986 dollars in 1968. The territories' exports (not including labor services) to Israel and other countries grew four-fold in real terms between 1968 and 1986, when they reached $400 million. Imports of goods grew at a slightly higher rate (by a factor of 4.5) and amounted to $1.2 billion in 1986. The trade deficit totaled $770 million in 1986, compared to 160 million 1986 dollars in 1968. The overall deficit in the current account (including labor services) was much lower, and came to $200 million in 1986.

5.2. Interdependence with Israel

The economic relationship between Israel and the territories is a classic example of the integration of a "large" and a "small" economy. Economic theory suggests that in such a case, the small economy becomes very dependent on the large economy, while the large economy's dependence on the other is insignificant. Moreover, the benefits that always derive from such integration are also unevenly divided, with the small economy usually benefiting more than the large one (see appendix 5.1). This happens because the terms of trade in the small economy (the relative prices of goods and factors of production) improve and approach those existing in the large economy.[1] In our case, in which the

1. See the classic article by Paul A. Samuelson (1939).

territories' exports to Israel consist mainly of labor services, the terms of trade of this factor of production (i.e., wages) improved to the benefit of the residents of the territories. This improvement was reflected in the high growth rates of GNP and standard of living in the territories, as can be seen from tables 5.2 and 5.3. By contrast, in Israel's large economy, imported labor was not a significant component of the work force employed in Israel, and the relative benefit to Israel was therefore limited.

The dependence of the territories' economies on that of Israel is apparent from the indicators shown in tables 5.4 and 5.5. Since labor is a key component in the overall trade (including that in goods) between Israel and the territories, the extent of the territories' economic dependence on Israel can be measured by the number of the territories' residents employed in Israel as a percentage of the total number of employed residents of the territories. This ratio is 36.4%—and is even higher for the Gaza Strip alone, 45.7%. However, residents of the territories employed in Israel account for less than 7% of all persons employed in Israel, indicating the Israeli economy's much lower dependence on workers from the territories. Furthermore, since the workers from the territories are on average less skilled than Israeli workers, their share in the effective labor employed in Israel is much lower than 7%, about 4%–5%.

A good indicator of a country's economic dependence on others is the ratio between domestic product and national product. As national accounting shows, a country's national product comprises the product originating in that country (the domestic product), plus the product generated abroad by factors of production (capital and labor) that are

Table 5.4 Indicators of Economic Interdependence between Israel and the Occupied Territories: Employment, 1986

Residents of the Territories Employed in Israel	Total	As a Percentage of Total Employment of Territories' Residents	As a Percentage of Total Work Force Employed in Israel
Total	95,000	36.4	6.5
Gaza Strip	43,000	45.7	2.9
West Bank	51,000	30.0	3.5

Source: Central Bureau of Statistics (1991c).

Table 5.5 Indicators of Economic Interdependence between Israel and the Occupied Territories: Output and Foreign Trade, 1986

| | Israel | Occupied Territories | | |
		Total	West Bank	Gaza Strip
Percentage of national product not from domestic sources		25.7	20.5	38.5
Percentage of domestic product in foreign hands	2.4			
Exports of goods and services as a percentage of GNP	40.8	19.0	17.0	25.9
Imports of goods and services as a percentage of GNP	56.3	57.9	43.0	108.7

Source: Central Bureau of Statistics (1991c).

owned by that country's residents, minus that part of the domestic product that is created by foreign factors of production. In other words, a country's national product is equal to the domestic product plus the net earnings of the country's residents that have been generated abroad. In line with this indicator, the proportion of the territories' national product that is not from domestic sources is over 25%. In the Gaza Strip, this proportion approaches 40%. In Israel, by contrast, the proportion of the domestic product which is generated by foreign-owned factors of production is less than 2.5%. In light of this great dependence on foreign-generated product, yet another indicator of the territories' economic dependence on Israel is the fact that their exports of goods and services (mainly labor services) to Israel account for 45% of their national product—in the Gaza Strip alone, 56%. However, imports of goods and services from the territories account for only 3.2% of Israel's domestic product.

Since the Six Day War (1967), the State of Israel has maintained an administrative system which operates in accordance with international conventions relating to occupied territories. In legal terms, the territories have not been annexed by the State of Israel (except for East Jerusalem and the Golan Heights), and they are therefore subject to Jordanian law (the West Bank) and Egyptian law (the Gaza Strip), as they were before 1967. However, the economies of the territories have been integrated with the Israeli economy. They are covered by the Israeli umbrella of customs, tariffs, and other import taxes and are also subject in part to Israeli laws relating to foreign exchange and the control of capital movement. The Jordanian dinar and the Egyptian lira coexist with the Israeli sheqel as legal tender in the territories. The gathering of Israel and the territories under this umbrella has created a kind of common market for the movement of capital, goods, and services, subject to certain significant restrictions.[2] In the absence of sea or airports, the territories' imports of durable goods and investment goods come via Israel.

From a budgetary point of view, expenditure on the supply of local civilian services in the territories is more or less covered by revenues collected from residents of the territories, and thus they do not represent an additional burden on the Israeli budget. Initially, expenditures exceeded revenues and the deficit was covered by oil revenues from the Sinai Desert (this was returned to Egypt following the Camp David Peace Treaty). In recent years, revenues from tax collection in the territories and taxes levied on workers from the territories employed in Israel have increased, and they effectively cover most of the expenditures on civilian services. In 1987, for example, spending on civilian services totalled $370 million (in 1986 prices), while local revenue amounted to $280 million. The difference, of approximately $90 million, was largely covered by payroll taxes on workers from the territories employed in Israel.[3]

APPENDIX 5.1 The Benefits Incurred by Merging of the Labor Markets of a Small and a Large Country

We will assume there are two countries, one "large" and the other "small." The movement of workers from the small to the large country will cause a marginal change in the large country's labor market and, thus, will not have any significant effect on wages in the large country. For the sake of this

2. These restrictions almost totally prohibit agricultural exports from the territories to Israel. They also prohibit residents of the territories from investing in real or financial assets in Israel. The transfer of goods to Jordan is also subject to Jordanian imposed restrictions. For example, industrial exports to Jordan are only permitted if their raw materials have been purchased in Jordan; and agricultural exports to Jordan are subject to quotas.

3. It should be noted that revenue figures for the territories do not include government receipts from taxes and duties levied at Israeli ports on imports destined for the territories.

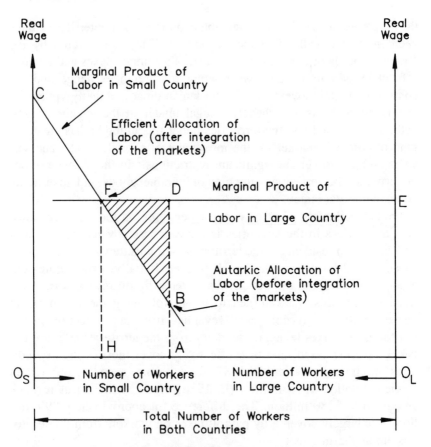

Figure 5.1: Integration of the labor markets of a large and a small country.

discussion, we will assume that the differences in size between the two countries are so great that the movement of workers from the small to the large
country has absolutely no effect on wage levels in the large country. In other
words, we will assume that the marginal product of labor in the large country
which is faced by the small economy is constant.

Figure 5.1 shows the marginal product curves of employed persons in both
countries. The number of workers in the small economy is measured from left
to right at point O_s. The number of workers in the large economy is measured
from right to left, from point O_L. The segment O_sO_L is equal to the total
number of workers in both markets, where O_sA is the number of workers in
the small economy and AO_L is the number of workers in the large economy.
Before the integration of the two economies, real wages in the small economy
will be at level AB and its national product (which is equal to the domestic
product in this autarkic case) will be the area under the marginal product curve,

which is equal to O_sCBA. Real wages in the large economy will be at level AD, and its national (and domestic) product will be $ADEO_L$. When workers are allowed to cross the border, they will move from the small economy, where wages are relatively low, to the large economy, where wages are relatively high. The movement of workers will push wages up in the small economy until they are equal to those in the large economy. This will be achieved at point F, by the crossing over of AH residents from the small economy to work in the large economy. What benefits are incurred from the integration of the two economies? While the small country's domestic product will decline to O_sCFH, its residents' income will be incremented by $HFDA$ derived from labor in the large economy. Its national product will therefore be O_sCFDA. That is, the growth in its national product as a result of the integration is equal to the area of the shaded triangle FDB. But in the large economy, there will not be any growth in national product. Although its domestic product will grow by the area of the rectangle $HFDA$, this entire growth will consist of payments to foreign factors of production, so that its national product will remain equal to the area of the rectangle $ADEO_L$.

6

The Economic Effects of the Intifada

6.1. Employment, Income, and Trade

When the Intifada erupted in December of 1987, it had an immediate effect on the employment in Israel of workers from the territories. There was a sharp drop in the export of labor services from the territories to Israel, due to pressure both from the local leadership of the uprising and from the Israeli army (which enforced curfews and cordoned-off entire areas). This decline in employment was evident not so much from a reduced number of those counted as working in Israel, as from their frequent absenteeism and their reduced working hours.

Table 6.1 shows that there was a decline of almost 45% in the number of hours worked in Israel by residents of the territories during the first quarter of 1988, the first quarter following the outbreak of the Intifada. However, this decline was strongly reversed as early as the second quarter of that year, although the employment in Israel of workers from the territories did not return to its pre-Intifada level until 1990. Employment in Israel of the territories' workers suffered a temporary setback when it came to a virtual stop during January and February of 1991 (the Gulf War period), but it is estimated that by the second half of 1991, employment again regained its pre-Intifada level. Certainly, the recession in Israel had a negative effect on the employment in Israel of workers from the territories. But undoubtedly, the sharp decline in employment was caused primarily by the Intifada.

It is not easy to identify any change in the level of employment *within* the territories following the Intifada. Data are available only on the number of those employed annually, and not on the total number of

Table 6.1 Employment in Israel of Residents of the Occupied
Territories, 1987–90

Year and Quarter	Hours per Week		Work Days per Month	
	Thousands	Index (100 = 1987)	Thousands	Index (100 = 1987)
1987 4	4,733	101.7		
Annual average	4,654	100	1,211	100
1988 1	2,661	57.2		
2	3,666	78.8		
3	4,044	86.9		
4	3,749	80.1		
Annual average	3,529	75.8	915	75.6
1989	3,616	77.7	1,002	82.7
1990	3,835	82.4	1,121	92.6

Source: Central Bureau of Statistics (1991c).

hours worked in the territories during each quarter.[1] Table 6.2 does, however, indicate that the number of those employed in the territories, particularly in the West Bank, increased slightly during 1988–89, compared with 1987, and employment rose significantly in 1990, by 8% over the preceding year.

It is interesting to note that there was especially large growth in agricultural employment in the territories. A possible explanation is that most disturbances were in urban, rather than agricultural, areas. It is also likely that some of those who intermittently absented themselves from work in Israel found additional, part-time agricultural employment in the villages.

We can also make rough estimates of the effect of the Intifada on the overall employment of residents of the territories both in Israel and in the territories. The total number of workers from the territories employed in Israel fell from 104.7 thousand in 1987 to 104.3 thousand in 1988. This fairly gentle reduction, however, conceals a dramatic drop in the average work week of workers from the territories. If the number of workers in 1988 is adjusted for this decrease (a decline from 44.5 hours per week during 1987 to 33.8 hours per week in 1988),[2] the

1. In general, some caution should be exercised in interpreting the data collected after the outbreak of the Intifada, since it interrupted the sampling of economic data in the territories.

2. See Central Bureau of Statistics (1991c, table 27.27). It is interesting to note that the decline in the average number of working hours was steeper in the Gaza Strip than in the West Bank,

Table 6.2 Employment in the Territories, Selected Years
(thousands of workers per year)

Year	Total	West Bank	Gaza Strip
1970	152.7	99.8	52.9
	(38.7)	(42.5)	(31.6)
1975	138.6	91.9	46.7
	(31.8)	(34.6)	(26.3)
1980	140.6	94.3	46.3
	(28.4)	(33.2)	(18.8)
1985	152.7	103.8	48.9
	(24.4)	(27.3)	(18.0)
1986	164.9	114.6	50.3
	(24.9)	(28.4)	(16.6)
1987	168.8	114.7	54.1
	(22.8)	(26.0)	(16.0)
1988	172.5	119.0	53.5
	(27.3)	(32.1)	(18.6)
1989	174.6	115.4	59.2
	(23.7)	(26.4)	(18.4)
1990	188.8	128.0	60.8
	(26.6)	(29.5)	(20.4)

Source: Central Bureau of Statistics (1991c).
Note: Figures in parentheses are agricultural employment as a percentage of total employment.

appropriate figure for the number of persons employed in Israel fell from 104.7 thousand in 1987 to 79.2 thousand (in 1987 equivalent terms) in 1988. This represents a decline of 24.4% in employment in Israel. On the reasonable assumption (in the absence of other indicators) that there was no significant change in the number of hours per week worked by those employed within the territories, the total number of persons from the territories employed in Israel or the territories (adjusted to the decline in the average number of working hours per week in Israel) fell from 273.5 thousand workers in 1987 to 251.7 thousand (in 1987 equivalent terms) in 1988. This represents an 8% decrease in employment during the first year after the start of the Intifada.

Despite and perhaps partly because of the 8% decline in employment, the real wages of workers from the territories who were employed in

apparently due to the more intense pressure exerted by the local leadership behind the uprising. In the West Bank, the average number of hours fell from 46.0 per week in 1987 to 35.9 hours per week in 1988. In the Gaza Strip, the corresponding decline was from 42.4 hours per week in 1987 to 30.9 hours per week in 1988.

Table 6.3 Real Wage[a] of Workers from the Occupied Territories, 1984–88 (annual percentage change)

Year	Employed in Israel			All Workers[c]		
	West Bank	Gaza Strip	Total[b]	West Bank	Gaza Strip	Total
1984	−8.9	−17.0	−12.5	−1.2	−8.9	−3.9
1985	−5.3	−8.9	−7.0	−5.3	−12.7	−7.9
1986	19.5	31.9	25.1	12.4	20.6	15.3
1987	16.5	33.7	23.5	14.1	28.7	19.2
1988	21.0	13.2	19.8	15.4	10.6	13.7
1989	−0.3	2.6	0.6	−5.6	−2.2	−4.4
1990	−5.8	−3.1	−4.8	−3.4	−3.2	−3.3

Source: Constructed from data published by the Central Bureau of Statistics (1987, 1988a, 1989b).
[a] Wage in current prices, adjusted by CPI in relevant area.
[b] Weighted by working hours of territories' residents in Israel.
[c] Weighted by employment of territories' workers in Israel and in the territories.

Israel and the territories rose by 13.7% in 1988 compared with 1987 (see table 6.3). As a result, the wage income of the residents of the territories did not fall sharply during the first year of the Intifada. While employment in Israel of territories' residents dropped by 24%, their wage income declined by only 9% due to the 19.8% rise in their real wages.[3] Note that in comparison to pre-Intifada years, the rise in the overall real wage of workers from the territories, working both in Israel and in the territories, was moderate in 1988. This moderation may be the result of the slowdown in economic activity in Israel. It should be recalled that wage rises in Israel were also more restrained during 1988, and in 1989 and 1990 real wages actually fell.[4] Eventually, the decline in real wages in Israel pulled down the real wage of territories' workers (both in Israel and in the territories) by 4.4% and 3.3% in 1989 and 1990, respectively. All in all, total wage income of West Bank's residents working in Israel rose by about 4% per year during the first three years of the Intifada (1988–90). For workers from Gaza in Israel, there was a decline of 8% per year during that period.

3. The real wages of workers from the territories are defined as wages at current prices, adjusted for the rise in the CPI in the territories. The inflation rate in the territories during 1987–88, it should be noted, was substantially lower than that in Israel (see table 6.4).
4. The annual rate of growth in real wages in Israel fell from approximately 8% in 1986 and 1987 to some 6% in 1988. During 1989 and 1990, real wages actually fell by about 1.3% and 0.9%, respectively.

Table 6.4 CPI in Israel, the West Bank, and the Gaza Strip,
1982–90 (annual percentage change)

Year	Israel	West Bank	Gaza Strip
1982	120.3	107.4	114.6
1983	145.7	139.8	151.2
1984	373.8	360.7	373.0
1985	304.6	320.6	337.6
1986	48.1	50.0	49.6
1987	19.9	13.1	11.0
1988	16.3	8.7	11.1
1989	20.2	14.5	15.7
1990	17.2	13.0	16.9

Source: Central Bureau of Statistics (1989*b*, 1991*c*).

During the Intifada, economic developments in the West Bank and
Gaza differed considerably. A distinct two-year cycle is evident in the
West Bank's olive crop, causing a biennial cyclical movement in its
product (see table 6.5). The years 1986 and 1988 saw record olive
harvests there, resulting in a 74.1% higher agricultural product in 1986
and a 100% increase in 1988! Thus although the domestic product
(excluding olives) of the West Bank (i.e., from industry, construction,
trade and services, etc.) fell by 15% in 1988, its overall domestic
product increased by 2%–5%. Rough estimates from Central Bureau of
Statistics put the annual rate of growth of GDP during the first three
years of the Intifada (1988–90) at about 2%–4%. During the same
period, the annual rate of growth of GDP excluding olives was about
0.5%–1.5%, showing the relatively good olive crops during the Intifada. The growth rate of GDP fell short of the rate of growth of the
population, resulting in a decline in GDP per capita during the first
three years of the Intifada. National disposable income, which includes
wage income earned in Israel, rose by about 5%–6% per year during
1988–90. Investment data are skimpy from 1988 on. We can only guess
that investment in fixed assets fell considerably. The available data
clearly indicate such a trend for public investment, with declines of
about 53% and 43% in 1988 and 1989, respectively.

A two-year cycle is also evident to some extent in the Gaza Strip,
reflecting mostly the pattern of the citrus crop, which accounts for 20%
of its agricultural product.[5] Accordingly, the effect of the Intifada on

5. Peaks and troughs in the Gaza Strip's citrus crop and in the West Bank's olive crop are not
synchronized.

Table 6.5 Macroeconomic Indicators for the Occupied Territories, 1986–89 (annual percentage change)

Year	GDP	Per Capita GDP	Business Product	Agriculture	Industry	Construction	Other Sectors	GDP Excluding Olive Crops	National Disposable Income	Per Capita National Disposable Income	Gross Investment in Fixed Assets			Population
											Total	Private	Public	
							West Bank							
1986	23.4	20.2	30.7	74.1	29.4	3.2	20.6	12.0ᵃ	21.8	18.6	20.7	20.8	20.4	2.7
1987	−7.7	−10.1	−11.0	−34.0	−1.9	1.4	−6.5	1.5	2.0	−1.1	9.4	5.6	32.4	3.6
1988	2/5	−1.1	7/12	100	−8	−25/−23	−30/−20	−15	−2.0/0.0	−5.0/−3.0			−53	3.1
1989	−4.0	−6.2							−1.0	−4.0			−43	2.3
							Gaza Strip							
1986	6.3	2.8	8.4	−5.4	35.3	10.3	7.2	10.3ᵇ	14.2	10.4	11.8	7.8	41.6	3.4
1987	12.3	8.2	19.8	20.4	35.9	2.2	29.9	13.4ᵇ	15.6	11.6	9.5	6.3	30.5	3.8
1988	−13/−12	−16.3/−15.4	−18/−16	−1	−22	−21	−28/−21	−18.9/−16.3	−15/−14	−18			−28	4.0
1989	11.0	7.0							1.0	−3.0			−12	3.7

Source: Central Bureau of Statistics (1991*c*).
Note: Read "x/y" as "x to y."
ᵃ GDP excluding agriculture for the West Bank in 1986.
ᵇ GDP excluding agriculture for all years in the Gaza Strip.

domestic product in the West Bank and in the Gaza Strip is best examined by comparing 1986 with 1988 and 1987 with 1989. The Gaza Strip's GDP fell by 12%–13% in 1988, compared with the 6.3% increase achieved in 1986. GDP rose by about 11% in 1989 compared to the 12.3% rise in 1987. All nonagricultural sectors in Gaza were badly affected in the first year of the Intifada (1988), particularly industrial output, where a decline of 23% was recorded in 1988, compared with 35.5% growth in 1986. In general, GDP was less affected by the Intifada than was national disposable income, because the Intifada disturbed mostly the work of Gaza's residents in Israel. Indeed, national disposable income fell by about 18% and then by 3% in 1988 and 1989, respectively. As work in Israel almost regained pre-Intifada levels in 1990, national disposable income rose in 1990 and reached its pre-Intifada level at the end of that year. Over the first three years of the Intifada, gross investment in fixed assets declined by about 4.5% per year, despite an increase of 1% per year in residential structures.

6.2. Economic Weapons and Counterweapons

6.2.1. Background

From the mid-1960s until the beginning of the 1980s, the economies of the West Bank and the Gaza Strip underwent rapid development. The GNP of the West Bank rose at an annual rate of 7.6%, and that of the Gaza Strip at 8.1%. Although this development was neither steady nor uniform, it made possible a constant increase in the standard of living of the population of both areas. However, the pace of economic development was not balanced throughout the period. From the mid-1960s to the mid-1970s, the annual growth rate of output was 14%. In the mid-1970s, this growth slowed to 7%, and since 1980, it has been insignificant. Only in 1986–87 did these economies again experience any significant growth.

The integration of the economies of Israel and of the West Bank and the Gaza Strip, together with their geographic proximity, opened up the Israeli labor market to a population that was eager to seek work. This integration of two structurally different economies certainly led to increased economic activity and accelerated growth.

In 1970, there were 20,000 residents of the territories working in Israel. This number grew continually until 1987, when it reached 110,000. This corresponds to an annual growth rate of around 10%. From the point of view of the Israeli economy, in 1970 the 20,000 employees from the territories constituted less than 3% of the total number of persons employed in Israel; while in 1987, 110,000 employees from the territories raised that share to 8%. The Israeli economy's opportunity to employ workers from the territories led to some delay in implementing technological improvements in several branches of industry and in construction. For the most part, however, this influx of labor brought clear economic benefits.

An examination of the economies of the occupied territories shows that employment in Israel has been an important source of income. In 1970, the 20,000 employees accounted for 12% of all employed persons resident in the territories, and the figure of 110,000 from 1987 represented 40% of the total. Such a large number of workers employed in Israel, but continuing to reside in their original homes, contributed not only to a growth in national product, but also to a transfer of skills and expertise to the economies of the occupied territories. Another aspect of the economic relations which developed between Israel and the territories has been the opening-up of the Israeli economy to the export of goods to and from the territories.

Economic growth in the occupied territories was not the result of industrialization. Rather, it was led by increased activity in the trade and services sector. Thus, the main visible results of this growth were an improvement in the standard of living and in the standard of dwellings. Most investment was in residential construction and contributed little to the industrialization of the economy.

In the late seventies, two simultaneous but counterbalancing developments occurred in the territories and in the Middle Eastern oil-producing countries. The West Bank and the Gaza Strip experienced slowed economic growth, although, at 7% of GNP per year, their growth rate was still high compared to concurrent growth rates in the Middle East and worldwide. However, the reduced rate of growth in the territories, following the slowdown in Israel's economic growth rate and the availability of large pools of manpower in the territories, was partly offset by rapid growth in Jordan and the Middle Eastern oil-producing countries and the consequent demand for labor. Economic growth in these countries—annual GNP growth rates of 8% in Jordan and 12% in the oil-producing states—resulted from the large growth in revenues which followed the sharp rise in oil prices.

Residents of the West Bank were among those who responded to the demand for labor in Jordan and the oil-producing countries. Their search for work produced a net emigration of 17,000 people between 1976 and

1980, which in turn led to increased transfer payments to the territories in the form of remittances. In the wake of falling oil prices and the resulting economic slowdown in Jordan and the oil-producing states, this emigration dropped to 9,000 persons in 1982 and to about 3,000 in 1983. This slowdown in economic activity was concurrent with the growth in the supply of workers between the ages of 25 and 34 and with low economic growth in Israel. The growth in this manpower population group was the result of high birth rates and a considerably reduced demand for labor in the oil-producing countries and Jordan.

That such regional economic and political changes have a significant effect on the economies of the occupied territories emphasizes their great dependence on Israel and neighboring countries. This dependence derives from the lack of indigenous growth factors in the territories themselves, a fact made obvious once the period of rapid development following the economic integration with the Israeli economy petered out. The traditional social structure of the economies of the territories affected the scale and nature of economic activity. Despite the high level of savings, perhaps a consequence of the great political and economic uncertainty, there has been almost no significant investment, except for housing. The territories lack major business enterprises for initiating investment and raising capital funds on a large scale, because of the perceived investment risk caused by political uncertainty. Likewise, direct foreign investment has been sparse.

The significant reduction in economic growth in the occupied territories in the late 1980s, together with the widespread belief that there can be no political solution for the territories while they remain under military rule, provided a somber background for political and social developments at the beginning of 1988.

6.2.2. Economic Weapons

Since the start of the uprising it has been obvious that the aim of its leadership in the occupied territories has been to portray the Israeli administration as unable to fulfill its duties in the territories. A comprehensive, integrated approach was necessary in order to achieve this objective. This approach has included the boycotting of civilian services supplied by the military government, on the one hand, and the creation of an alternative network of services on the other. However, the economic dependence on Israel of the territories' residents was so great that this strategy had only limited success. The longer the struggle continued, the more burdensome it became to the local population. The price paid is expressed by the fall in the standard of living and the inability to produce alternative, independent administrative networks. The objectives of the Israeli administration were to keep the scale of violence and civil disturbances to a tolerable minimum, and to continue providing civilian services when possible.

The territories' economic dependence on Israel forces them to coexist with both Israel and the military government, in violation of the guiding principles of the Intifada. Since its very beginning, the Intifada has needed grass roots support. The leadership of the uprising has been capable of distinguishing between the various instruments at its disposal, and in consideration of public opinion in Israel and abroad, the leadership has preferred to use civil disobedience and low-scale violence which do not lead to large-scale bloodshed. Accordingly, a rich menu of cold civil measures (as opposed to live fire) has been used in the West Bank and the Gaza Strip as part of the Intifada. Only recently, the increasingly powerful Hamas Muslim fundamentalist movement turned the uprising into a conflict dominated by terrorists.

The forms that the struggle has taken have differed between the West Bank and the Gaza Strip because of significant differences in the population and geography of these regions. The Gaza Strip is a small, separate area, which the military can control without any great effort. This should not be taken to mean that the population is especially docile, but that the nature of the territory and its entry and exit points make it relatively easy to control. This is not the case with the West Bank. There, the territory is much larger; there are a larger number of crossing points; maintaining control is more difficult; and the population is larger and more amorphous. Accordingly, the manifestations of the struggle and the countermeasures adopted by Israel have differed in the two regions.

The principal economic instruments employed by the leadership of the Intifada have been: general strikes, full and partial commercial strikes, tax revolts, measures to prevent territories' residents from working in Israel, boycotts of Israeli goods, and attacks on Israeli factories and businesses. We briefly examine these methods and their effectiveness.

General strikes. General strikes have been used by the Palestinians since the early 1920s. They were frequently employed during the Great Arab Revolt of 1936–39, which accelerated the process of economic segregation between Jews and Arabs. At the peak of the Intifada, there was, on average, one full day of strike per week which encompassed all sectors of life and activity in the territories. Since advance warning was given before each such day, the population learned to live with the strikes, for instance, by buying food before the strike took effect. In addition, many workers violated the strikes by staying overnight in Israel for the duration of the strike and going to work. The leadership of the uprising also showed some pragmatism by permitting maintenance workers in various factories in the territories to work during strikes, in order to ensure that production and maintenance schemes were kept in good order.

Commercial strikes. Frequently, commercial strikes were called by the leadership of the uprising. Attempts by the Israeli administration to force stores to open for the entire day failed, and this failure was regarded as a victory for the leadership. Notwithstanding the damage done to commerce and tourism in East Jerusalem, the residents of the territories appeared to have learned to live with this form of frequently interrupted commerce, as well. All shops were open until midday. Since most store owners live close to their shops, they were actually able to sell goods directly from their homes when their shops were closed. In addition, the selling of goods in courtyards and by the roadside became common practice. The reduced commercial activity was more the result of lower income levels than of the restricted hours of commerce. At the start of the Intifada, the leadership allowed industrial plants, as opposed to shops, to work until 4 P.M. Subsequently, the leadership removed even this restriction and workers are now permitted to remain in the plants for an unlimited time. The leadership of the uprising effectively controls the streets and has ways of enforcing its decisions.

Tax revolts. The tax revolt was initiated selectively and consisted mainly of attempts to avoid or delay tax payments. There were a few cases, such as that in Beit Sahur in the West Bank, in which there was a real revolt, whereby the various organizations behind the uprising violently attacked those who were paying taxes. The case of Beit Sahur is exceptional, however, in both the residents' determination not to pay taxes and the military government's determination to levy tax payments by force.

Clearly, the decline in economic activity in the territories has contributed to the fall in tax receipts in the occupied territories. In 1988, tax receipts fell by 40% in the West Bank and by 20% in the Gaza Strip. But it is not clear to what extent the decline in tax revenues can be attributed to the tax revolt rather than to the general recession in economic activity.

Measures to prevent territories' residents from working in Israel.
The departure every morning of 110,000 workers from the territories to places of employment in Israel has a substantive effect on the economic ties between the territories and Israel. Thus, the labor of the territories' residents became a constant target for attack by the leadership of the uprising and their strike forces.

At the start of the Intifada, the leadership called on the residents of the territories not to go to work in Israel. However, financial necessity forced workers to defy this call. Moreover, the value of this tactic was undermined by an unexpected development. The large number of curfews and strikes in the Gaza Strip, compared to the West Bank, led Israeli employers to prefer to employ workers from the West Bank. Thus, one group (workers from the West Bank) actually obtained work and income at the expense of the other (workers from the Gaza Strip).

In the West Bank, there were local strike forces which attempted to damage buses carrying workers to Israel, without harming the workers themselves. But in any case, apart from this limited activity, both the leadership of the uprising and local bodies realized that economic necessities are overriding, and that action must not be taken against efforts to comply with these needs.

The biggest battle over the controlled departure of workers to Israel took place in the Gaza Strip during July and August of 1989. As part of the Israeli attempt to control the exit of workers to Israel, the authorities decided to issue permits for this purpose. The local leadership decided to combat the granting of these licenses with all the means at its disposal. Working with prepared lists, its men visited people's houses in order to confiscate their work permits. As a countermeasure, the Israeli administration announced that as of July 1989, no one would be allowed into Israel without a permit. As a result, the number of vehicles leaving daily for Israel fell to 1,500, compared with the pre-Intifada peak number of 3,000 private cars per day leaving the Gaza Strip for Israel. In July and August 1989, the number of vehicles leaving the Strip was very low. In effect, a war of nerves was being fought between the leadership of the uprising and the Israeli military government. At the same time, the leadership of the uprising was subject to mounting pressure from workers and heads of families who were left without employment and thus with no source of income. This pressure finally forced

the local committees to retreat from their positions and not only allow
workers to leave for Israel with permits, but also return the work permits
which they had confiscated.

By October 1989, some 4,000 vehicles were leaving the Gaza Strip
daily for Israel, reflecting the increased number of workers going out
of the Strip, following the two-month period when there was a very
significant decline in departures. During the last two months of 1989,
the number of vehicles leaving daily for Israel leveled off at around
3,000. According to estimates by administration staff, toward the end
of 1989 a record number of 45,000 workers were leaving the Gaza Strip
for Israel every day.

The leadership's attempts to fight the Israeli military government at
the workers' expense proved unsuccessful. At the same time, workers
from the territories managed to find an increasing number of alternative
solutions. Many of them stayed in Israel overnight without permits,
close to their places of work. This method, which is illegal under Israeli
law, is yet another way of bypassing the directives of the local leadership and the military government.

Boycotts of Israeli goods. Since the start of the Intifada, its leadership
has called for a boycott of Israeli goods. In this, the leadership was
relatively successful, and very few goods with Israeli labels were seen
in shops in the territories. A total boycott of Israeli soft drinks and
cigarettes was very successful. There have, however, been a few set-
backs. In the summer of 1989, the war against the sale of Israeli-grown
melons and watermelons was abandoned. In some cases, identifying
labels have been replaced, and Israeli products were marketed in the
territories thus.

The leadership's policy regarding the boycott of Israeli goods was
clear. In all those cases where local substitutes were available, the sale
of Israeli-produced items was banned. In all cases where there were no
alternatives, the sale of Israeli goods was allowed in practice.

In practice, the commercial ties between Israel and the territories and
the freedom of movement which exists served to provide the residents
of the territories with an ample chance to purchase Israeli products. The
extent to which purchases of Israeli goods declined because of
the boycott is difficult to assess. According to Israeli manufacturers,
the boycott appeared effective only with respect to cigarettes and soft
drinks.

Attacks on Israeli factories and businesses. The objectives of the uprising and the desire to attack anything that represents Israeli sovereignty included Israeli factories, banks, and territorial transportation networks that were identified with Israel. As a first stage, a boycott was imposed on the use of Israeli banking services in the territories. This development forced the banks to close their branches in the territories, which had not been profitable even before the Intifada. In the West Bank, the closure of branches of Israeli banks was accompanied by increased activity on the part of the Cairo-Amman Bank, whose first branch in the territories was opened in Nablus in 1987. Although the opening of the bank reflected a clear understanding between the governments of Israel and Jordan, the local leadership had its reasons for not attacking it. In fact, they allowed the bank to open branches in other towns in the West Bank. In the Gaza Strip, where no effective alternative banking facilities exist, branches of Israeli banks moved to the industrial area in the north of the Strip. (The local Palestine Bank operates to a very limited extent in Gaza.)

During the first two years of the Intifada, there were isolated attempts to sabotage and attack factories and business property. It is difficult to assess precisely the extent of the damage which resulted, but it seems almost negligible. The main damage was caused to buses carrying workers and other passengers within the West Bank. Estimates by Egged, the Israeli bus cooperative, indicate that since the start of the Intifada, about 1,000 buses have been damaged, 10% of them beyond repair.

In its objective to disrupt life in the occupied territories, the uprising's leadership succeeded to some extent. The Israeli economy, however, appeared to have adjusted to the situation without sustaining any appreciable damage. The real price for the disruption of economic activity was paid by the civilian population of the West Bank and the Gaza Strip.

6.2.3. Counterweapons

The goal of the Israeli Administration in the territories during the Intifada was to prove that law and order can be maintained under Israeli rule and that the civil uprising was being suppressed effectively. In this respect, the Israeli administration was faced with a dilemma: how to curtail acts of violence and disruptions of everyday life, while concurrently enforcing curfews and making preventative arrests in order to keep riots and mass demonstrations in check. The Israeli administration, which considers itself responsible for maintaining services to the public, was concerned with the question of how the population can cope with the new situation and to what extent they are capable of adapting to the continual disruptions in everyday life. For example, in the Sha'ati refugee camp in Gaza, which houses some 30,000 people, there were approximately 200 days of curfew during 1988. In the Jabalia refugee camp, where some 20,000 people live, there were 150 days of curfew. In addition to those detained by curfews, there were approximately 5,000 persons imprisoned in detention facilities in the Gaza Strip, corresponding to about 5% of the work force.

Curfews, arrests, strikes, and riots came on top of the fall in the value of the Jordanian dinar (which until the Intifada, had been the principle means of saving) and the rise in the prices of basic commodities. The administration believed that part of the population of the territories, particularly those in Gaza, were likely to reach the breadline or even starve. Hindsight shows that the endurance and adaptability of the residents of the territories exceeded expectations, for several reasons that had not been anticipated.

In the refugee camps, the U.N. welfare and relief agency (UNWRA) increased the supply of food and provided greater financial assistance. Other charitable and international relief organizations also provided extensive material support. At the same time, the strength of the family cell and the rural (or semirural) structure of Palestinian society made it possible for residents of the territories to cope with the new situation and the accompanying economic distress. Also, as was already mentioned, workers from the territories managed to some extent to continue work in Israel, albeit intermittently.

Since the Intifada started, there has been, in effect, a war between the residents of the territories and the Israeli administration. In this, as in any other war, both sides have used a wide variety of methods to prevent the other side from achieving its objectives. The Israeli administration has adopted numerous measures to prevent the leadership of the uprising and the territories' residents from achieving any real gains. Some of these measures are discussed below.

Curfews and cordoning. As both a punitive and palliative measure, the Israeli administration ordered a large number of curfews in the occupied territories. Some areas were placed under curfew and cordoned-off for up to an entire month. During May and June of 1989, there were eight full days of curfew throughout the Gaza Strip, and about 360 local curfews in the refugee camps and other areas. The curfews had an immediate effect on local economic activity, on the opportunity to go out to work and trade, and on the pattern of everyday life.

The replacement of identity cards and vehicle registration numbers. In both the Gaza Strip and the West Bank, the Israeli administration replaced all identity cards and vehicle registration numbers as a way of identifying tax dodgers and persons wanted by the authorities. These measures were implemented in several stages, each one of which involved the loss of many working days and disruption of daily life. To date, the administration has carried out four major operations to replace identity cards. The replacement of identity cards between April and June of 1988 considerably reduced the intensity of the uprising by enabling better monitoring of insurgents. In the Gaza Strip, between June and November of 1989, over 90,000 exit permits to Israel were issued and 150,000 identity cards were replaced. The battle over exit permits was one of the most difficult confrontations of the Intifada, and the leadership in the territories were forced to bow to economic pressure.

Regulations of savings. Until December 1987, residents of the territories were allowed to make regular bank deposits of about 5,000 Jordanian dinars, on the condition that such deposits be reported. In order to make it more difficult for terrorist organizations to transfer funds, the Israeli administration restricted the sum that could be deposited to 200 dinars. But despite the restrictions imposed, the residents of the territories continued to receive some 16 million dinars per month from abroad (these being the sums that were actually reported). Attempts to limit the funds entering the territories were also aimed at preventing the leadership from assisting families suffering from the economic effects of the Intifada.

Withholding export licenses. The fight over agricultural exports was a political struggle, in which farmers in the territories endeavored to cut themselves off from Israel's institutional marketing networks (Agrexco and the Citrus Marketing Board) and to market independently to Europe. Here, the Israeli administration was forced to bow to external pressure (mainly from Europe) and permit direct agricultural exports to Europe. These exports failed badly in 1988 because of low quality and poor marketing, but recovered in 1989.

Tax enforcement. The significant decline in tax receipts, which was partly due to the tax revolt, forced the administration to enact a series of enforcement measures. This process began with the requirement to present proof of payment of taxes when applying for an exit permit to Jordan, when renewing a driving license, or during any other administrative procedure. The war over tax collection reached the stage at which the village of Beit Sahur was subjected to an extended curfew and large amounts of assets were confiscated in order to cover the debts of those who had refused to pay their taxes.

To summarize, even though the Intifada is still intense, the economic warfare waged during its first two to three years seems to be over. Recall that the rapid economic growth in the occupied territories after the Six Day War was achieved through strong economic integration with Israel. This integration, which suffered temporarily from the early, economic components of the uprising, is so vital to the residents of the territories that it eventually escaped the Intifada.

IV

Ascending to Israel: *Aliya*

7

The Current *Aliya* and Its Setting

7.1. Pre-*Aliya* Turnaround in Economic Policy

Following the November 1988 general elections, the new finance minister, Shimon Peres, shifted policy in an attempt to pull the economy out of the recession. Toward the end of 1989, some signs of economic recovery could have been detected, in particular, with respect to business output. Unemployment, however, was still high, affecting 9% of the labor force. At that time, the rapid disintegration of the Soviet Union brought a new wave of mass immigration (*aliya*), which simultaneously raised the growth rate of output and the level of unemployment.

We start the chapter with a brief description of Peres's pre-*aliya* policy turnaround and its consequences, but the main issue of this chapter is the peculiarly Israeli phenomenon of *aliya*. Section 7.2 first provides the historical background and then presents the main characteristics of the new immigrants (*olim*). The heart and soul of this part is chapter 8, which calibrates an elaborated model of the Israeli economy and studies the macroeconomic consequences of the *aliya*.

In the spring of 1988, well before the general elections held in November, it became evident that the stubborn policy of freezing the exchange rate, in effect since January of 1987, inflicted a heavy toll on the economy (see Part II). Academic economists, leading members of the business community, and even some senior government officials wrote articles, books, and memos pointing out the detrimental effects of the policy.[1] Even so, its full impact, especially on employment, had not yet materialized.

---

1. See, e.g., Neubach, Razin, and Sadka (1988).

Table 7.1 Macroeconomic Indicators, 1988–89
(quarterly percentage changes)

Year and Quarter	GDP	Unem-ployment Rate	Gross Domestic Investment[a]	Consumption		Exports	Imports[c]
				Private	Public[b]		
1988 1	4.5	5.9	−7.4	5.3	1.6	3.7	0.7
2	−4.3	5.9	2.5	−5.3	−0.5	−7.7	−4.6
3	0.2	6.8	−1.1	1.2	0.6	−3.2	−1.9
4	1.4	7.0	1.2	1.9	1.4	5.2	6.0
Annual percentage change	2.1	6.4	−1.9	3.8	3.5	−2.1	0.0[b]
1989 1	0.5	8.3	−6.6	−3.1	−0.7	2.5	−6.0
2	1.3	9.2	9.2	2.2	−1.5	2.3	4.9
3	−1.8	9.0	−12.9	−0.8	1.6	−0.5	−2.0
4	2.4	9.1	14.0	1.1	0.9	1.9	3.9
Annual percentage change	1.3	8.9	−2.7	−1.0	0.4	4.6	−1.1[b]

Source: Central Bureau of Statistics (1990).
[a] Includes inventories.
[b] Excludes direct military imports.
[c] Excludes direct military imports, ships, and aircraft.

It was obvious to all that an exchange rate realignment was inevitable. The only question was its timing: was it to be before or immediately after the general elections? Eventually, domestic politics prevailed and the exchange rate freeze was extended until after the elections. Speculative attacks on foreign currency reserves accelerated immediately after the elections and forced the government to change its policy of exchange rate freeze. Two adjacent devaluations totalling about 13.5% took place in the last week of 1988. Since then the government has conducted a much more flexible exchange rate policy, following more or less an implicit purchasing-power-parity (PPP) rule.

The policy change did not yield immediate results. The poststabilization recession continued well into 1989 (see table 7.1). In fact, the GDP growth rate for the entire year of 1989 was only 1.3%, even lower than the GDP growth rate in 1988. This represents a decline in GDP per capita, that is, a negative rate of growth.

The extended recession was noticeable in almost all sectors. The product of the business sector grew by only 1.3% in 1989, compared to the remarkable 6%–8% annual growth rate in 1986–87. Gross domestic investment (including inventories and residential housing) fell by about 2.7%. In fact, gross capital formation in the business sector and infra-structures fell by an even higher rate, 9.1%, which was partly offset by a 6.7% rise in investment in residential structures. Private consumption fell by 1%, its first decline since the major economic crisis of 1984.

Nevertheless, the new economic measures taken by the new government, especially the more flexible exchange rate policy which enabled a reduction in interest rates, produced (with a lag) some clear signs of recovery toward the end of the year. The recovery, coupled with measures that improved the country's international competitiveness, was apparent in the growth of exports by about 4.6% and the decline in civilian imports of about 1.1%. The export growth was even more remarkable in leading high value-added sectors, such as manufacturing (exports of low value-added sectors, such as polished diamonds, declined). The export-led recovery appeared in other sectors of the economy later that year. In the last quarter of 1989, GDP grew at a quarterly rate of 2.4%, which on an annual basis is about 10%; gross domestic investment grew at a quarterly rate of 14% and private consumption at a rate of 1.1%.

The recovery can be credited to several measures adopted by the government. Flexing the exchange rate was one. In addition, a new pact on the cost-of-living adjustment (COLA) for wages was signed between the General Federation of Labor (the Histadrut) and the umbrella organization of private employers (PEA), with the blessing and the active encouragement of Finance Minister Shimon Peres (this is why the pact is called "a triangular pact"). As is common in Israel, this pact was then extended by the government to the public sector. Specifically, the pact slashed the first six percentage points of inflation per annum from the COLA. Eighty-five percent of any inflation over 6% per annum is then compensated for by the COLA.

Accelerated depreciation was allowed in the manufacturing sector.[2] The corporate tax rate was uniformly reduced from 45% to 43% in 1989, with an additional one percentage point reduction per annum scheduled for the next three years.[3] Long-term capital imports were partially liberalized, narrowing the long-term interest rate differential between Israel and the world capital market. Moral suasion by the Bank of Israel and the Finance Ministry helped reduce financial margins in

2. In 1991, depreciation was further accelerated to 100%. The accelerated rate was terminated on June 30, 1992.

3. In 1992, the corporate tax rate was 40%. It is scheduled to go down gradually to 36% in 1996.

the short-term unindexed credit market. The recovery by itself reduced the magnitude of distress borrowing and further contributed to the decline in the short-term interest rates.

The policy turnaround and the continued recession in early 1989 brought about significant changes in the major relative prices in the economy. Figure 7.1 indicates that the policy brought an end to the erosion of the *real* exchange rate. Similarly, figure 7.2 shows that the escalation in real wages in both the private and public sectors stopped completely. Finally, figure 7.3 shows the steady decline in the short-term unindexed rate of interest which sharply reduced the gap between the interest rate and the rate of inflation, thereby lowering the short-term *real* rate of interest.

The upward trend in unemployment came to a halt in mid-1989 (fig. 7.4), but not even a hint of a downward trend could be detected. It is noteworthy that the lack of such a downward trend does not necessarily mean that a continued recessionary force is at play, for there was concurrently a labor supply increase reflecting the baby boom that followed the Six Day War (1967).

In due course, the economic recovery would have been reflected by a decrease in the rate of unemployment. But then the massive influx of

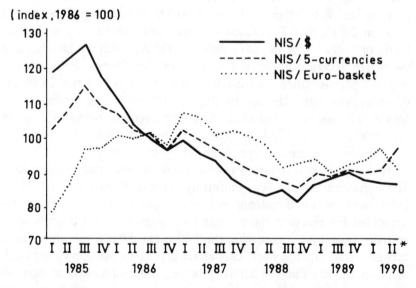

Figure 7.1: Relative price of industrial output: selected trading partners/Israel. *April and May only.

Source: Bank of Israel (1990).

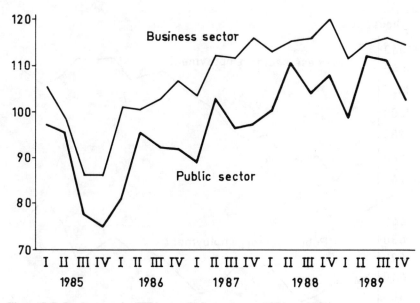

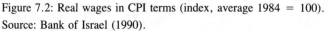

Figure 7.2: Real wages in CPI terms (index, average 1984 = 100).
Source: Bank of Israel (1990).

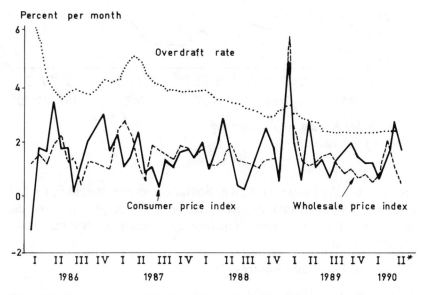

Figure 7.3: Interest rate and inflation. *Overdraft rate—April only; inflation—April and May only.
Source: Bank of Israel (1990).

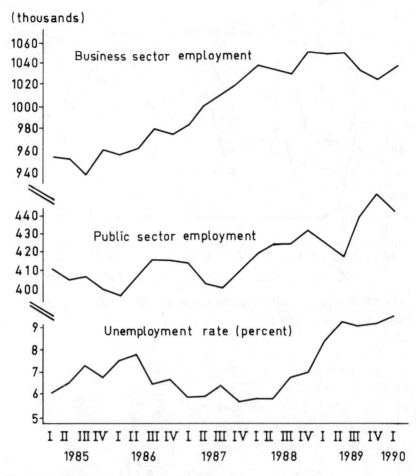

(thousands)

Figure 7.4: Employment and unemployment.
Source: Bank of Israel (1990).

immigrants (*olim*) from the former Soviet Union that started in the last quarter of 1989 and rapidly accelerated in 1990 sharply increased the labor force. This labor supply expansion, inevitably, pushed the rate of unemployment upward.

7.2. *Aliya:* **Facts and Figures**

7.2.1. Historical Background

Past experience in Israel and pre-state Palestine suggests that migration to Israel, called *aliya* ("ascending") in Hebrew, comes in waves. The first wave came in 1881–82 when Palestine was part of the Ottoman (pre-Turkey) Empire.[4] These waves continued through the era of the British Mandate in Palestine and with increasing frequency and intensity after the establishment of the State of Israel on May 15, 1948. The waves of *aliya* were closely associated with sharp rises in capital formation and productivity which manifested themselves in remarkable economic growth.[5]

The two major waves of *aliya* during the British Mandate in Palestine took place in 1919–26 and 1933–36. In 1926, at the height of the first wave, the number of *olim* (immigrants) that came to Palestine reached almost 30% of the total number of Jews then living in Palestine. During each one of the years 1933–35, after the Nazis rose to power in Germany, the number of *olim* that arrived to Palestine amounted to about 20% of the established Jewish population. The birth of the State of Israel in 1948 brought a massive, unprecedented wave of *aliya*. In less than three years the Jewish population more than doubled. Altogether over the first forty years of Israel as an independent state (1948–88), the Jewish population rose from about 0.65 million people to about 3.659 million people, with *aliya* contributing about 1.857 million to the increase. Figure 7.5 provides an overview of the waves of *aliya* since the creation of Israel.

One of the most distinctive features associated with *aliya* is the high rate of economic growth. Table 7.2 indicates that *aliya* produced massive investments, both in residential structures and in nonresidential capital. These investments were so substantial that they increased the capital to labor ratio and facilitated economic growth, in some cases, further aided by the remarkable human capital brought by the *olim*. Except for the *olim* who came during the major wave of *aliya* immediately after the birth of the State of Israel, the education level of the *olim* generally exceeded that of the established population and thus contributed remarkably to productivity. It is noteworthy that in general the massive investments in physical capital were financed by capital imports, as the *olim* themselves fled their former homes almost penniless.

Table 7.2 shows, for instance, that during the years 1922–32, when the number of *olim* each year was about 8.2% of the established population, output increased at a rate of about 16.4% per annum, so that

4. The Ottoman Empire occupied Palestine until 1917, when Palestine was conquered by Great Britain. A British Mandate was then in effect until 1948, when the State of Israel was established.
5. See Ben-Porath (1985).

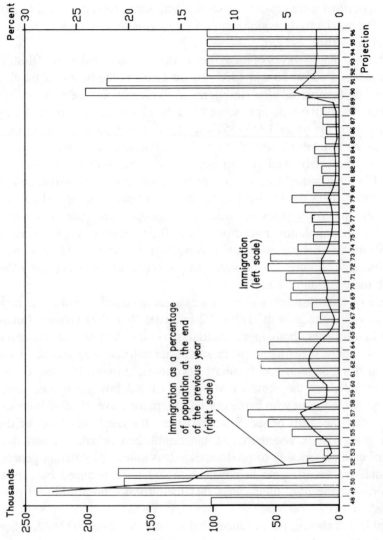

Figure 7.5: *Aliya.*

Table 7.2 *Aliya* and Growth, 1922–89
(annual percentage growth rates)

Period	*Olim* as a Percentage of Established Population	Population	Capital Stock (Excluding Housing)	Housing Stock	Per Capita Output
1922–32	8.2	8.0	—	—	7.8
1932–47	6.4	8.4	—	—	3.0
1947–50	19.8	21.9	—	—	—
1950–51	13.2	20.0	—	—	10.0
1951–64	2.2	4.0	12.8	11.6	4.9
1964–72	1.3	3.0	8.7	7.7	5.5
1972–82	0.9	2.1	6.1	7.7	0.8
1982–89	0.4	1.8	3.1	4.0	3.1

Sources: Ben-Porath (1985) for the years 1922–82, Central Bureau of Statistics (1992) and Bank of Israel (1991*b*) for the years 1982–89.

output per capita rose by a remarkable 7.8% per annum. Similarly, during the years 1950–51, when the number of *olim* each year amounted to about 13.2% of the absorbing population, output per capita increased by about 10% per annum. In contrast, during the years 1972–82, when *aliya* was virtually nonexistent, output per capita rose by the meager rate of 0.8% per annum. Obviously, one should not rely too heavily on *aliya* in explaining economic growth in Israel, as other factors such as political environment, internal economic policy, external shocks, and the like are also in play.

7.2.2. Main Characteristics of the Current *Aliya*

The collapse of communism in the Soviet Union, following the *glasnost* policy of Mikhail Gorbachev, opened the doors to *olim* from that huge, and by now loose, union of increasingly independent states. Excluding Israel and the United States, the former Soviet Union had the largest Jewish community in the world. Thus, the potential number of Soviet *olim* is huge and will likely dominate the number of *olim* from the rest of the world in this decade. So far, about 400,000 *olim* have arrived since the start of the new *aliya* in 1989. Many more are expected to come in the next few years. Originally, it was estimated that the total number of *olim* would reach about one million people, almost one-quarter of the 1989 Israeli population. However, after two years of high numbers of *olim*, the *aliya* has subsided considerably because of high unemployment among the *olim* and other obstacles to absorption. A

Table 7.3 The Occupational Distribution of *Olim* and Established
            Population

Occupation	*Olim*[a]	Established Israelis
Engineer or architect	24.9	1.9
Medical doctor	7.0	1.3
Paramedic	4.6	2.3
Technician	15.2	4.1
Executive	0.3	6.5
Clerical or administrative employee	3.9	17.6
Skilled worker	12.6	24.3
Unskilled worker	1.9	3.4
Salesperson	2.1	8.4
Farm worker	0.1	4.3
Service (financial, commercial, legal, etc.) employee	23.4	13.2
	100.0	100.0

Source: Bank of Israel (1991*b*).
[a] Based upon the occupational distribution of the Soviet *olim* who arrived in Israel between November 1989 and August 1990.

revised estimate puts the total expected number of *olim* at about 700,000. Still this will be by far the largest ''gathering-in of the exiled'' since the early years of the State of Israel.

A distinctive characteristic of the *olim* from the former Soviet Union is the high endowment of human capital that they possess. This contrasts sharply with their dearth of physical capital. This unique combination poses a great challenge to the economy: to invest in new physical capital sufficient to fully utilize such a blessed windfall of human capital.

As table 7.3 indicates, a very large proportion of the *olim* compared to the established Israeli population are college graduates with a strong bias toward technical skills and medical occupations. In a particular case of this group's remarkable composition, we note that there are currently about 30,000 engineers and 17,000 physicians and dentists employed in pre-*aliya* Israel with a population of about 4.5 million people. According to the occupational distribution of *olim* shown in table 7.3, there will be about 110,000 engineers and 30,000 physicians and dentists among the expected number of one million *olim*. On the other hand, we find only a few of the *olim* in Western, market economy–oriented occupations such as salesperson, executive, service employee (financial, legal, commercial, etc.), and the like. Furthermore, the relatively large number of engineers, technicians, and physicians among the *olim* poses a difficulty to the economy. Because their training and work experience come from the Soviet Union, it may take time to train and fit them into the relatively modern, Western-style techniques and rigors of the market economy in Israel.

Another distinguishing feature of the current *aliya* is its age composition which is significantly different from that of the established Israeli population. The fraction of people in the 19–49 age bracket is about the same in the two populations: 42% among the *olim* and 40% among the established Israelis. However, the 0–18 age bracket is much larger among the established Israelis (40%) than among the *olim* (24%). Consequently, the over-50 age group is much larger among the *olim* (35%) than among the established population (19%). The relatively aged population of *olim* will place a considerable burden on the national insurance system and other public services for the elderly (e.g., health care).

8

Future Macroeconomic Paths

In the past, *aliya* has been a trigger for an extended period of economic growth. In the short run, however, *aliya* has also been accompanied by unemployment, housing shortages, and strong pressures on the external balance. These are likely to be the effects of the current *aliya*.

In order to evaluate such effects of the new *aliya* quantitatively, we construct and calibrate a styled macroeconomic model of the Israeli economy. To focus on a small number of features pertaining to *aliya*—growth, capital formation, unemployment, and the external debt—we simplify the model as much as possible.

In the next eight sections we describe briefly the main features of the model and discuss and evaluate the plausibility of the model's assumptions concerning the future evolution of the population, the size of the labor force, and the supply of labor together with the rate of productivity. This description highlights key features of *aliya*. We also describe our conjectures about some fundamental policy variables which affect public sector employment, public expenditures (both civilian and military), public investment, private consumption, business sector investment, and investment in residential capital. Section 8.9 then describes the economic projections derived from this model about the path of the economy during the period of *aliya*. In particular, we analyze the behavior of private sector employment, the rate of unemployment, the rate of growth of the business sector product, and the rates of growth of GDP, capital formation, the current account deficit, and the size of the external debt. The reader who is not interested in the detailed features of the macromodel may skip sections 8.1–8.8 and turn to section 8.9 for the interpretation and discussion of the results.

Note that considerable uncertainty remains about the number of *olim* that will come to Israel in the next few years. In addition to the 400,000 that arrived in 1990–91, it was originally estimated that about 100,000 *olim* would come in each of the years 1992–97, bringing the total number of *olim* to about one million. However, this estimate looks less and less realistic with each passing month. Thus, a new estimate puts the number of *olim* at about 50,000 in each of the years 1992–97, bringing the total number to about 700,000. Therefore, the model is built to accommodate alternative scenarios. For brevity, we present only two cases, those of the original estimate of one million *olim* and the revised estimate of 700,000.

8.1. Population Growth and Labor Supply

The rate of population growth in this decade is likely to be dominated by the arrival of *olim* from the former Soviet Union. Thus far, about 200,000 arrived in 1990, 180,000 in 1991, and 75,000 in 1992. Recently, the arrival rate has slowed considerably. Originally, a semi-official estimate assumed that about 100,000 *olim* would come to Israel in each one of the years 1992–97. This would bring the total number of *olim* to about one million. For the established population, we estimate a fairly stable growth rate of 1.6% per annum, which has been the growth rate in the last decade. (The natural population growth rate of the *olim* is ignored during the first few years of their arrival.) An alternative estimate puts the number of *olim* that will arrive in Israel at about 50,000 in each one of the years 1992–97, bringing the total number of *olim* to about 700,000. Accordingly, table 8.1 shows the size of population at the beginning of each one of the years in the period 1991–98 for the two alternative scenarios for the number of *olim* designated as "high" and "low."

Given the age distribution of the existing population and of the *olim* and assuming a stable labor-force participation rate (equal for the two populations), table 8.2 shows the evolution of the size of the labor force (labor supply) until the end of 1997.

8.2. Production

There are two sectors in the stylized model, the business sector and the public sector. Gross product of the business sector (at factor prices) in

Table 8.1 Projected Population, 1991–98
(millions at beginning of year)

Year	Established Population	Olim		Total Population	
		High	Low	High	Low
1991	4.630	0.20	0.20	4.830	4.830
1992	4.707	0.38	0.38	5.087	5.087
1993	4.782	0.48	0.43	5.262	5.212
1994	4.859	0.58	0.48	5.439	5.339
1995	4.937	0.68	0.53	5.617	5.467
1996	5.016	0.78	0.58	5.796	5.596
1997	5.096	0.88	0.63	5.976	5.726
1998	5.178	0.98	0.68	6.158	5.858

year t ($\bar{Y}_{Bt}$) is given by a Cobb-Douglas production function:

$$\bar{Y}_{Bt} = A_t L_{Bt}^{\tilde{\beta}} K_{Bt}^{1-\tilde{\beta}}, \tag{8.1}$$

where L_{Bt} is labor employment in the business sector during year t and K_{Bt} is the net stock of capital in the business sector at the beginning of year t. $A_t > 0$ is a productivity parameter, and $\tilde{\beta}$ and $1 - \tilde{\beta}$ are the labor and capital shares in gross output, respectively.

Gross product of the public (government) sector in year t (Y_{Gt}) is

$$Y_{Gt} = w_{Gt} L_{Gt}, \tag{8.2}$$

where w_{Gt} is the real wage and L_{Gt} is employment, both in the public sector in year t.

Table 8.2 Projected Labor Force, 1991–97
(millions at beginning of year)

Year	High	Low
1991	1.771	1.771
1992	1.870	1.871
1993	1.957	1.911
1994	2.043	1.958
1995	2.132	2.005
1996	2.222	2.052
1997	2.314	2.100

Source: Economic Models Ltd. (1991*a*, table 5).

Gross product (at market prices) in year t (Y_t) is equal to gross business product plus public sector product in that year:

$$Y_t = Y_{Bt} + Y_{Gt}, \tag{8.3}$$

where Y_{Bt} is the gross product of the business sector at market prices.

8.3. Productivity, Wages, and Employment

As the chief mechanism which generates short-term unemployment we assume a downward real-wage rigidity in both the business sector and the public sector. Specifically, we assume that the real wage in the public sector remains constant at its 1990 level, despite the downward pressure associated with the influx of *olim*. Thus,

$$w_{Gt} = \$24.171 \text{ billion per one million employees.}^1 \tag{8.4}$$

(This figure corresponds to an annual wage income of $24,171 per employee.)

In general, conditions in the labor market affect real wages. Specifically, given the current high unemployment rate, we assume that the real wage in the business sector will rise at an annual rate of just 0.5% until 1992. As the unemployment rate stabilizes a little about that time in the high scenario, we assume that the wage rate starts to rise at a higher annual rate of 1% from 1993 on. As the low scenario generates a lower unemployment rate than the high scenario, we further assume that in the former the real wage in the business sector rises by 1.25% in 1996 and in 1997. In both scenarios, initially, productivity rises by 1.25% annually until 1993, and then, as the highly skilled *olim* are more integrated into the labor force, we assume that productivity rises by 1.5% annually. Note that the growth rate of the real wage in the business sector falls short of the productivity growth rate due to persistently high unemployment for most of the period. Given that the wage rate in the business sector in 1990 is $w_{B,1990} = \$24.427$ billion per one million employees,[2] we describe in table 8.3 the path of the real-wage rate in the business sector.

Employment in the business sector is determined to be that level

---

1. The number of employees in the public sector is 0.439 million (see table 8.4). Total wages in the public sector is $10.611 billion (Central Bureau of Statistics 1991a, table 3). The exchange rate is $1 = NIS 2.016. Notice that the product of the public sector is measured in constant prices (wages) in the national accounts. This means that the GDP is not affected by the assumption that real wages in the public sector remain constant.

2. See the calculations associated with table 10.4.

Table 8.3 Projected Real Annual Wage in the
Business Sector, 1990–97
(1990 $ per employee)

Year	High	Low
1990	24,427	24,427
1991	24,671	24,671
1992	24,918	24,918
1993	25,167	25,167
1994	25,419	25,419
1995	25,673	25,673
1996	25,930	25,994
1997	26,189	26,319

where the marginal product of labor is equal to the real wage (w_{Bt}):

$$L_{Bt} = K_{Bt} \left(\frac{\tilde{\beta} A_t}{w_{Bt}} \right)^{1/(1-\tilde{\beta})}, \tag{8.5}$$

or equivalently,

$$\beta = \frac{w_{Bt} L_{Bt}}{\bar{Y}_{Bt}}. \tag{8.5'}$$

We assume that the growth rate of employment in the public sector falls short of that of the population, because we suppose that certain subsectors within the public sector (such as defense) do not follow the trend of the general population. Specifically, we assume that employment in the public sector rises at a rate equaling 60% of the population growth rate (see table 8.4). Given the employment in the public sector, we can then use the public sector production function (eq. [8.2]) in order to calculate the product of the public sector (see table 8.4).

8.4. Calibration of the Production Function

We employ equations (8.1) and (8.5′) and the existing 1990 data on the capital stock K_B, labor L_B, the wage in the business sector w_B, and the product of the business sector at *factor prices*, $\bar{Y}_B$, in order to calculate $\tilde{\beta}$ and A_{1990}:[3]

---

3. $\bar{Y}_{B,1990} = \$28.871$, business sector's gross product at factor prices ($q_1 y_1$ in table 10.4, plus $\$3.571$ depreciation).
$K_{B,1990} = \$71.23$ billion (Bank of Israel 1991a, table B-A-8).
$L_{B,1990} = 1,053$ million (see table 10.4).

Table 8.4 Projected Public Sector Employment and Product, 1991–97

Year	Employment (millions)		Product (billion 1990 $)	
	High	Low	High	Low
1991	0.453	0.453	10.968	10.968
1992	0.468	0.465	11.306	11.236
1993	0.478	0.474	11.548	11.466
1994	0.488	0.481	11.789	11.633
1995	0.498	0.488	12.029	11.801
1996	0.508	0.495	12.270	11.968
1997	0.517	0.502	12.488	12.134

$$\tilde{\beta} = 0.845, \tag{8.6}$$

and

$$A_{1990} = 15.0884. \tag{8.7}$$

From now on, all macroquantities are expressed in *market prices*. (Note that the differences between market prices and factor prices are the *net excise taxes*.)

8.5. Private Consumption

Private consumption amounted to $32.094 billion in 1990. Excluding the actual rent paid on rented apartments and the imputed rent on owner-occupied housing ($6.753 million), we arrive at a figure of $25.341 million for private consumption in 1990.

It is estimated that per capita private consumption of the established population rose by 2% in 1991.[4] From 1992 on, this rate rises to the long-term trend of 3% per annum. Regarding the *olim,* it is postulated that their per capita consumption is initially (in 1991) only about 60% of that of the established population. Per capita consumption of the *olim* then rises each year seven percentage points closer to that of the established population, until the per capita consumption of the two kinds of population coincide in 1997. Accordingly, table 8.5 shows the projected path of total private consumption, excluding housing services, from 1991 through 1997.

4. Here and elsewhere in this chapter, the term "per capita" refers to the population at the beginning of the year.

Table 8.5 Projected Private Consumption,[a] 1991–97
              (billion 1990 $)

Year	By Established Population	By *Olim*		Total	
		High	Low	High	Low
1991	26.261	0.904	0.904	27.165	27.165
1992	27.482	2.016	1.716	29.498	29.198
1993	28.759	2.915	2.611	31.674	31.370
1994	30.096	3.627	3.002	33.723	33.098
1995	31.495	4.381	3.415	35.876	34.910
1996	32.959	5.176	3.849	38.135	36.808
1997	34.491	6.014	4.305	40.505	38.796

[a] Excluding housing services.

8.6. Public Consumption

Public consumption for 1990 totaled $13.632 billion, consisting of
$8.592 billion in civilian consumption and $5.04 billion in defense
spending (excluding direct military imports).[5] In general, the civilian
component of public consumption is closely related to the population
size: more people implies the need for more education, more health
services, and so on. Similarly, civilian consumption is associated with
the standard of living, so that its growth rate probably cannot persistently lag behind the growth rate of private consumption. Therefore,
we shall assume that civilian public consumption per-capita rises by 2%
annually from 1991 onward.

Military expenditures are a *pure* public good whose quantity need
not rise as the population grows larger. However, we assume that the
current mandatory army service of two years for women and three years
for men will not be significantly shortened. Thus, the larger population
will increase the size of the regular armed forces, necessitating an increase in military spending. Specifically, we assume that total military
spending will rise by 2% per annum from 1991 onward.

In addition to the above two items of public consumption, we assume
that the government will spend a one-time sum of $1,500 per *oleh*
during the first year of his arrival to Israel on relocation costs (teaching
Hebrew, providing for household start-up costs, etc.). Table 8.6 summarizes the path of public consumption.

5. See Bank of Israel (1991*a*, table B-1) or Central Bureau of Statistics (1991*a*, table 5).

Table 8.6 Projected Public Consumption,[a] 1991–97
(billion 1990 $)

Year	Civilian Consumption		Defense	Relocation Costs for *Olim*		Total	
	High	Low		High	Low	High	Low
1991	9.382	9.382	5.040	0.270	0.270	14.693	14.693
1992	9.971	9.871	5.244	0.150	0.075	15.365	15.190
1993	10.520	10.420	5.384	0.150	0.075	16.019	15.879
1994	11.092	10.888	5.455	0.150	0.075	16.697	16.418
1995	11.684	11.372	5.565	0.150	0.075	17.398	17.012
1996	12.297	11.873	5.676	0.150	0.075	18.123	17.624
1997	12.933	12.392	5.789	0.150	0.075	18.872	18.256

[a] Excluding direct military imports.

8.7. Investment and the Stock of Capital

We distinguish among three types of investment: (1) investment in the business sector, including public investments in public factors of production which are beneficial to the business sector such as roads, bridges, and so forth, (2) investment in residential structures, (3) investment in public services (school buildings, hospitals, etc.).

8.7.1. Investment in the Business Sector

We assume a very simple investment function that expresses gross investment in the business sector (I_{Bt}) as a constant fraction (γ) of gross business product (Y_{Bt}); that is,

$$I_{Bt} = \gamma Y_{Bt}. \tag{8.8}$$

To calibrate this equation, we note that in 1990 gross investment was equal to \$5.127 billion,[6] while gross domestic product was equal to \$35.230 billion (at market prices),[7] so that

$$\gamma = 0.1455. \tag{8.9}$$

The net stock of capital at the beginning of year $t + 1$, which serves in the production process in year $t + 1$, is equal to the net stock of capital at the beginning of the preceding year t, minus depreciation,

6. See Bank of Israel (1991a, table B-A-8, p. 96).
7. See Bank of Israel (1991a, table B-1, p. 12).

plus gross investment in year t; that is,

$$K_{B,t+1} = K_{Bt}(1 - \check{\delta}_B) + I_{Bt}, \qquad (8.10)$$

where $\check{\delta}_B = 0.05$ represents the depreciation rate.[8]

8.7.2. Residential Structures

We distinguish between investment in residential structures for *olim* and for the existing population.

We assume that an "average" *olim* family consists of 3 persons, so that the number of families (or households) of *olim* who need new housing is one-third of the number of *olim*. We also assume that the construction cost of a new dwelling unit of the size provided for *olim* is $70,000. Since the construction process is about one year long, we assume that about one-half of the dwelling units intended for the *olim* in a given year are built during that year; the other half are completed in the succeeding year.[9]

For the established population, we assume that the rise in the net stock of residential capital per capita lags behind the rise in per capita private consumption (due to an increase in the relative price of housing). Specifically, we assume that the net stock of residential capital per capita rises by only 1% per annum. The stock of residential capital at the beginning of 1990 was estimated to be $76.047 billion and the rate of depreciation 0.55%.[10] Accordingly, gross investment in residential capital is shown in table 8.7.

8.7.3. Investment in Public Services

The net stock of capital in the public service sector at the beginning of 1990 was estimated to be $23.413 billion and the depreciation rate 1.7%.[11] We assume that the government invests in this sector to maintain a constant net stock of capital per capita. Accordingly, table 8.8 shows the gross investment in the public service sector that is needed for this purpose.

8. See Bank of Israel (1991a, table B-A-8, p. 96). Depreciation in 1990 was $3.571 billion while the net stock of capital at the beginning of that year was $71.230 billion, so that $\check{\delta}_B = 3.571/71.230 = 0.05$.

9. Since these dwelling units are newly built, we ignore the small investment, if any, that is needed to replace the depreciation.

10. See Bank of Israel (1991a, table B-A-8).

11. See Bank of Israel (1991a, table B-A-8, p. 96).

Table 8.7 Projected Gross Investment in Residential Capital, 1991–97 (billion 1990 $)

| | By *Olim* | | By Established | Total | |
Year	High	Low	Population	High	Low
1991	4.434	4.434	2.520	6.954	6.954
1992	3.266	2.683	2.531	5.797	5.214
1993	2.334	1.167	2.611	4.945	3.778
1994	2.334	1.167	2.676	5.009	3.843
1995	2.334	1.167	2.741	5.075	3.908
1996	2.334	1.167	2.808	5.142	3.975
1997	2.334	1.167	2.895	5.228	4.062

Table 8.8 Projected Gross Investment in the Public Services Sector, 1991–97 (billion 1990 $)

Year	High	Low
1991	1.742	1.742
1992	1.343	1.073
1993	1.369	1.108
1994	1.389	1.123
1995	1.410	1.139
1996	1.431	1.156
1997	1.457	1.177

8.8. Solution of the Macromodel

We are now ready to employ our macromodel in order to solve for the expected path of the Israeli economy. The model is solved sequentially. First, given the stock of business capital at the beginning of 1990 ($71.230 billion),[12] investment in the business sector during 1990 ($5.127 billion),[13] and the rate of depreciation ($\check{\delta}_B = 5\%$), we calculate from equation (8.10) the net stock of business capital at the beginning of 1991: $K_{B,1991} = \$72.796$ billion. Second, as explained earlier, we assume downward rigidity of wages in the business sector (and in the public sector as well). Given the wage in the business sector, employment in this sector in 1991 is determined by the demand for labor in that sector (eq. [8.5]): $L_{B,1991} = 1.134$ million employees. Combining

12. See Bank of Israel (1991a, table B-1, p. 12).
13. See Bank of Israel (1991a, table B-A-8, p. 96).

business sector employment with public sector employment (table 8.4) yields total employment in 1991, and recalling total labor supply from table 8.2, we find the unemployment rate in 1991.

Third, combining the business sector stock of capital at the beginning of 1991 ($K_{B,1991}$) with the employment of labor in the business sector ($L_{B,1991}$) yields the gross product in the business sector ($\bar{Y}_{B,1991}$) according to the production function (8.1).

Fourth, given $\bar{Y}_{B,1991}$, we can calculate the investment in the business sector in 1991 ($I_{B,1991}$) according to the investment function (8.8).

Fifth, we can then use equation (8.10) again to calculate the net stock of capital in the business sector in 1992 ($K_{B,1992}$), and so on.

In this way the model solves for the gross business sector product, gross domestic product, and the unemployment rate. We then calculate the current account deficit (D_t) according to the following equation which states that the current account deficit is equal to the sum of domestic uses (absorption) minus the sum of national resources:

$$D_t = C_t + G_t + I_t - (Y_{Bt} + Y_{Gt} - r_t E_t) - B_t, \qquad (8.11)$$

where

C_t = private consumption in year t

G_t = public consumption in year t (excluding direct military imports)

I_t = total gross domestic investments in year t (in business capital, in residential capital, and in public services capital)

Y_{Bt} = gross product of the business sector in year t

Y_{Gt} = gross product of the public sector in year t

E_t = external debt at the beginning of year t

r_t = *real* rate of interest on the external debt at the beginning of year t

B_t = unilateral transfers from abroad to both the private and public sectors in year t (excluding direct military grant)

The interpretation of equation (8.11) is straightforward: the term $C + G + I$ denotes absorption, while the term $Y_B + Y_G - rE$ denotes gross national product which equals gross domestic product ($Y_B + Y_G$) minus payments to foreign capital (rE).

It is assumed that the real rate of interest (r) paid on the net external debt (E) is initially 4% per annum. But later, as the external debt increases, the interest rate rises to 6% per annum, reflecting a risk premium associated with a higher external debt. This increase in the interest rate takes place in 1992.

On the resource side, the unilateral transfer B must be added to the gross national product. This transfer is estimated to be about $4 billion in 1991. We assume that it stays constant in nominal dollars, which means that it falls in real terms at a rate of about 5% per annum (the expected future U.S. inflation rate).

The external debt at the beginning of year t (E_t) is equal to the external debt at the beginning of the preceding year (E_{t-1}) plus the current account deficit in the preceding year (D_{t-1}); that is,

$$E_t = E_{t-1} + D_{t-1}. \tag{8.12}$$

8.9. Output, Unemployment, Capital Formation, and External Imbalances

8.9.1. High Scenario

Table 8.9 describes the future path of the economy in the high scenario, in which about 100,000 *olim* arrive in Israel in each one of the years 1992–97.

The 400,000 *olim* (roughly) that had already arrived in Israel by the end of 1991 produce relatively high growth rates of total output: around 5%–6% per annum during the years 1992–97. However, given the initially large increase in population, the growth of GDP per capita is very moderate in the next few years—less than 1% per annum. Later, as the population growth rate subsides (down to 100,000 *olim* per annum), capital accumulates, and productivity continues to rise, then the growth rate of GDP per capita picks up to about 3% per annum toward the end of the six-year period. The growth is led by the business sector while public sector growth is kept under control. As a result, the share of the business sector in GDP rises from 79.2% in 1992 to 82.5% in 1997.

Unemployment is persistently high throughout the years 1992–97. The unemployment rate even rises initially and reaches almost 12% in 1993–94, but then gradually falls to just below 10%. This is due to the insufficient accumulation of capital in the business sector and the rigid real wage. The latter, though it lags behind the productivity growth rate, is still rising moderately in the presence of a relatively high unemployment rate.

As absorption (i.e., $C + I + G$) persistently exceeds output (plus unilateral transfers from abroad), by about $2 billion per annum, an

Table 8.9 Projected Output, Employment, and External Imbalances, 1992–97: One Million *Olim*

Year	GDP^a (billion 1990 $)	Gross^a Business Sector Product (billion 1990 $)	Gross Public Sector Product (billion 1990 $)	Gross Business Sector Product as a Percentage of GDP	Population at start of year (millions)	Per Capita GDP (1990 $)	Unemployment Rate	Investment in Business Sector (billion 1990 $)	Current Account Deficit (billion 1990 $)	External Debt at End of Year (billion 1990 $)	External Debt as a Percentage of GDP
1992	54.2 (6.1)	42.9 (7.0)	11.3 (3.1)	79.2	5.087 (5.3)	10,655 (0.7)	10.6	6.2 (7.0)	1.3	18.8	34.7
1993	56.4 (4.2)	44.9 (4.7)	11.5 (2.1)	79.5	5.262 (3.4)	10,737 (0.8)	11.9	6.5 (4.7)	1.6	20.4	36.1
1994	59.6 (5.5)	47.8 (6.5)	11.8 (2.1)	80.2	5.439 (3.4)	10,958 (2.1)	11.8	7.0 (6.5)	2.0	22.4	37.6
1995	63.1 (5.9)	51.1 (6.9)	12.0 (2.0)	81.0	5.617 (3.3)	11,234 (2.4)	11.5	7.4 (6.9)	2.2	24.5	38.8
1996	67.0 (6.2)	54.7 (7.0)	12.3 (2.0)	81.6	5.796 (3.2)	11,560 (2.9)	10.8	8.0 (7.0)	2.2	26.7	39.9
1997	71.3 (6.4)	58.8 (7.5)	12.5 (1.8)	82.5	5.976 (3.1)	11,931 (3.2)	9.9	8.6 (7.5)	2.0	28.8	40.4

Note: Numbers in parentheses are percentage rates of growth over preceding year.
^a Excluding imputed rent on owner-occupied housing.

Table 8.10 Projected Output, Employment, and External Imbalances, 1992–97: 700,000 *Olim*

Year	GDP[a] (billion 1990 $)	Gross[a] Business Sector Product (billion 1990 $)	Gross Public Sector Product (billion 1990 $)	Gross Business Sector Product as a Percentage of GDP	Population at start of year (millions)	Per Capita GDP (1990 $)	Unemployment Rate	Investment in Business Sector (billion 1990 $)	Current Account Deficit (billion 1990 $)	External Debt at End of Year (billion 1990 $)	External Debt as a Percentage of GDP
1992	54.1 (6.1)	42.9 (7.0)	11.2 (3.1)	79.3	5.087 (5.3)	10,641 (0.7)	10.4	6.2 (7.0)	1.0	18.5	34.2
1993	56.4 (4.2)	44.9 (4.6)	11.5 (2.7)	79.6	5.212 (2.5)	10,816 (1.6)	9.9	6.5 (4.6)	1.3	20.0	35.5
1994	59.4 (5.5)	47.8 (6.5)	11.6 (1.5)	80.5	5.339 (2.4)	11,134 (2.9)	8.3	7.0 (6.5)	1.6	21.4	36.0
1995	62.9 (5.7)	51.1 (6.8)	11.8 (1.4)	81.2	5.467 (2.4)	11,498 (3.3)	6.3	7.4 (6.8)	1.8	23.2	36.9
1996	66.0 (4.9)	54.0 (5.7)	12.0 (1.4)	81.8	5.596 (2.4)	11,780 (2.5)	5.2	7.9 (5.7)	2.4	25.6	38.8
1997	69.3 (5.1)	57.1 (5.9)	12.2 (1.4)	82.5	5.726 (2.3)	12,098 (2.7)	3.8	8.3 (5.9)	2.9	28.5	41.1

Note: Numbers in parentheses are percentage rates of growth over preceding year.
[a] Excluding imputed rent on owner-occupied housing.

annual deficit of this size is generated in the current account of the balance of payments. Consequently, the external debt rises by almost $12 billion at the end of the six-year period.

8.9.2. Low Scenario

The low scenario (a total number of 700,000 *olim*) is described in table 8.10. The lower number of *olim* in this scenario generates slightly smaller rates of growth of both the gross business sector product and GDP. However, as expected, the growth rate of GDP per capita is considerably higher in this scenario and the unemployment rate is markedly lower. The current account deficit and the external debt are also lower in the low scenario than in the high, but not by very much. Overall, the low scenario seems more realistic than the high scenario, because its relatively low rates of unemployment are consistent with a continuing influx of *olim*.

Both scenarios generate persistent current account deficits, and in the presence of country risk, they highlight the importance for Israel of loan guarantees from the U.S. government, which will enable Israel to finance these deficits through the international capital markets without an intolerable increase in the cost of borrowing. The importance of loan guarantees may be assessed through a comparison of the high and the low scenarios. The high unemployment rates in the high scenario make the assumption of one million *olim* quite implausible. The loan guarantees could enable the financing of more investments and thus the creation of more jobs. In this case the assumption of one million *olim* is not completely out of line.

A proper absorption policy requires job creation, mainly in the private tradable goods sector. Economists and policymakers more or less agree that jobs should be created in industries that are viable in the long run and can withstand the rigor of international competition. Therefore, there is absolutely no intent to return to protectionism but rather to promote international trade. The *aliya* generates needs for massive new investments in the business sector and elsewhere. There is a wide consensus in Israel that the capital market, both at home and abroad, should serve as the main channel for financing new investments. In this context, fiscal policy in general and tax policy in particular play a critical role in generating efficient savings and investments. Privatization of government-owned enterprises can further enhance economic efficiency. Accordingly, the next part deals with tax policy, international trade, capital market liberalization, and privatization.

V

Contemporary Issues

9

Tax Structure

This chapter treats tax policy in Israel. We first present some fundamental principles of efficient taxation. In particular, we elaborate on the concept of tax burden (section 9.1). We provide an overview of the main features of the Israeli tax system in sections 9.2 and 9.3, with special emphasis on the way Israel's tax system copes with inflation. Finally, in chapter 10, we succinctly analyze directions for tax restructuring. This analysis also provides an estimate for the effective cost of public funds when raised through taxes. Such an estimate is a key element of a proper cost-benefit analysis of public spending.

9.1. Tax Burden

To provide public goods and services, the government needs to purchase goods and services from the private sector and to employ labor. In the short run, the government may borrow, internally or externally, to finance these outlays. But, eventually, in the longer run, the government has to resort to taxes in order to pay for past, present, and future outlays. Taxes, however, are distortive. Thus, an important consideration in the design of the tax system is how to reduce the amount of distortions imposed by the system.

To illustrate, consider a one-consumer economy endowed with one unit of leisure or labor time. The labor is employed to produce goods. The consumption possibility set is bounded from above and from the right by the line TT in figure 9.1. Obviously, with no government, the tax burden issue does not arise, and in the absence of external effects, a competitive equilibrium must yield an efficient allocation of resources,

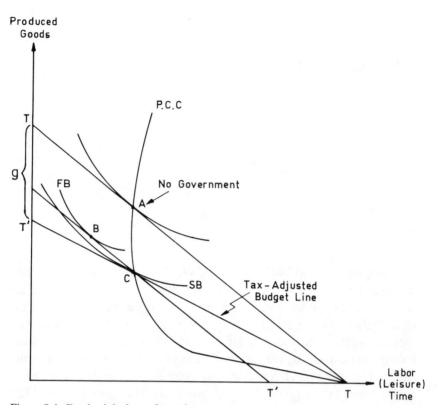

Figure 9.1: Deadweight loss of taxation.

say point A. At this point, as usual, the indifference curve of a representative household is tangent to the frontier of the consumption possibilities set, TT.

Now we introduce a government which needs labor services and other goods in order to provide public services. Suppose that these needs amount to the equivalent of g units of the produced good. In this case the relevant frontier for private uses of the produced goods and leisure becomes $T'T'$. If the government could obtain all the resources required for public uses by resorting to lump-sum taxes, which do not distort economic decisions, the ensuing equilibrium is the first-best allocation, represented by point B. If, however, only a flat-rate income tax is available to finance expenditures, the government must be restricted to a private consumption bundle which lies on the private sector's price-consumption curve (P.C.C.). The resulting (second-best) equilibrium is represented by point C. The difference between the indifference curve

FB (associated with the first-best equilibrium) and the indifference curve *SB* (associated with the second-best equilibrium) is called the *deadweight loss* (or the excess burden) of the tax system. At the heart of tax design is the attempt to reduce, as much as possible, the deadweight loss.

Entangled with, and affected by, the tax design problem is the issue of the cost of public funds. Since each sheqel of public expenditure has to be raised through distortionary taxes, the cost to the economy exceeds one sheqel. By how much? The cost depends on how distortive the tax system is: the more distortive the tax system, the higher the cost of public funds. Thus, the design of the least distortive tax system determines, at the same time, the cost of public funds and, consequently, the optimal overall size of the government. For, at the margin, the cost and benefit of public outlays have to be equated in order to determine the efficient size of government.

9.2. Facts and Figures

The two pillars of the Israeli tax system are the traditional income (and national insurance) tax and the relatively new value added tax (VAT). When it was first introduced in 1975, the VAT rate was only 8%. It was gradually increased and now stands at 17%. Before the introduction of VAT, the top individual marginal income tax rate was roughly 80%.[1] Now, it stands at 48% with a special, officially temporary surcharge of an extra 2.4 percentage points for the absorption of *aliya*.

More generally, one can detect a clear trend in tax revenues: heavier reliance on indirect taxation (mainly VAT) and, following tax reforms in many other industrialized countries (including, the United States and the United Kingdom), a smaller burden of direct taxation (income tax), with the total (both direct and indirect) tax burden falling noticeably. Tariffs and nontariff barriers have recently been gradually phased out following bilateral free-trade agreements with the European Community and the United States and a unilateral decision by the Israeli government to open up the Israeli economy to international competition from all countries (see chapter 11 below).

Table 9.1 demonstrates the fall in gross tax revenues, from over 42%

---

1. It is difficult to give an exact figure for the pre-1975 top marginal tax rate because a compulsory loan was imposed as a fraction of income and it is hard to assess the tax component of this nonvoluntary loan.

Table 9.1 Tax Revenues, 1985–91 (percentage of GDP)

| Year | Total Taxes | Direct Taxes | | | | Indirect Taxes | | |
		Total	Income[a]	National Insurance	Other	Total	On Domestic Production	On Civilian Imports
1985	42.0	22.5	15.3	6.3	0.9	19.5	12.5	7.1
1986	44.8	23.1	16.0	6.1	1.0	21.7	13.8	7.9
1987	44.1	21.8	15.6	5.6	1.6	22.3	14.0	8.3
1988	42.1	21.5	15.6	5.4	0.5	20.6	13.2	7.4
1989	38.3	19.5	13.6	5.3	0.6	18.8	13.4	5.4
1990	38.6	18.9	13.0	5.3	0.6	19.7	14.1	5.6
1991	38.7	17.7	12.1	4.9	0.6	21.0	14.9	6.1

Source: State Revenue Administration (1991).
[a] Includes VAT on wages in the public and financial sectors (see section 9.2.5).

Table 9.2 Individual Tax Rates on Earned Income, 1990 Tax Year

Annual Income Brackets ($)	Marginal Tax Rate (%)
0–9,226	20
9,227–15,208	30
15,209–21,647	35
21,648–33,581	45
Over 33,582	48

Source: State Revenue Administration (1991).
Note: A special, officially temporary, "absorption-of-*aliya* surcharge" of 5% of tax liability went into effect in 1990. Thus, the bottom marginal tax rate is effectively 21% and the top marginal tax rate is 50.4%.

of GDP in 1985 to a little less than 39% in 1990 and 1991. Similarly, direct tax revenues fell from about 22.5% of GDP in 1985 to 17.7% of GDP in 1991, while indirect tax revenues rose from about 19.5% of GDP in 1985 to 21% of GDP in 1991. Almost one half of all tax revenues are returned to the private sector as transfers to individuals and transfers or direct subsidies to the business sector.

9.2.1. Basic Features of the Individual Tax on Earned Income

The Israeli tax system does not allow personal deductions (for self, for spouse, or for dependent children), so that the lowest marginal tax rate (20%) applies from the first sheqel of income. The marginal (as well as the average) tax rate increases quite sharply with gross income, as shown in table 9.2. The income brackets are *fully* indexed to the consumer price index (CPI), and they are adjusted each time a cost-of-living adjustment (COLA) is paid to wage earners, even though the COLA itself is less than fully linked to the CPI. (Currently, the COLA is equal to 85% of the excess of the increase in CPI over 6% on an annual basis and is paid whenever the accumulated increase in the CPI exceeds 7%.)

Instead of personal tax deductions, an array of personal tax credits are granted. Ceteris paribus, credits (which are uniform across all income levels) are considered to be more progressive than deductions (which benefit individuals with higher incomes and higher marginal tax rates more than low-income individuals). Tax credits are described in table 9.3.

The tax schedule (table 9.2) does not distinguish between single and married people. Each member of a married couple is taxed separately (according to the above tax schedule) on his or her *earned* income and

Table 9.3 Personal Tax Credits, 1990 Tax Year

Type of Taxpayer	Annual Amount of Credit ($)
Married with nonworking wife	1,348
Married with working wife	933
Single	933
Married woman	415
Additional credit for each odd-numbered dependent child	415

Source: State Revenue Administration (1991).
Note: Since July 1990 an additional credit has been in effect. The credit is 4.8% of taxable income at low income levels and is gradually phased out as annual income reaches $46,567.

is entitled to a personal credit.[2] That is why a person with a nonworking wife receives a higher tax credit than a person with a working wife (she receives her own credit). Child-care costs are not deductible, but working mothers receive an extra credit for each dependent child. Overall, the Israeli tax system encourages married women to join the labor force.

Credits are limited to the amount of tax liability calculated according to the tax schedule. Thus, credits can reduce tax payments to zero, but not below. Combining the tax schedule (table 9.2) and the personal tax credits (table 9.3), we show in table 9.4 the amount of annual income that is exempted from taxes. Credits are fully linked to the CPI.

The tax system offers no credits for children except for those of working mothers (in lieu of deductions for child-care costs). However, dependent child allowances paid directly by the National Insurance Institute (the analogue of the Social Security Administration) should be viewed, for economic purposes, as part of the income tax system. In fact, they make Israel a negative income tax country. The amount of the child allowance is quite sizable and increases much more than in proportion to the number of children (see table 9.5). Child allowances, which because of the budget crunch had been suspended for families with up to two children and a relatively high income, were reinstated in April 1993.

9.2.2. Saving Incentives

An old controversy in the public finance literature is "the direct versus indirect tax" debate. It is beyond the scope of this book to attempt to

---

2. Unearned income is viewed as the husband's income for tax purposes. This is intended to subject all unearned income of a married couple to the presumably higher marginal tax rate of the husband.

Table 9.4 Zero-Tax Income, 1990 Tax Year

Type of Taxpayer	Annual Income ($)
Married with nonworking wife	7,550
Married with working wife	5,475
Single	5,475
Married woman	5,475
With one child	7,550
With two children	7,550
With three children	9,625

Source: State Revenue Administration (1991).

Table 9.5 Child Allowances, 1990 Tax Year

Number of Children	Total Annual Allowance ($)
1	415
2	830
3	1,660
4	3,320
5	4,565
6	6,018
7	7,470
8	8,923
9	10,375
10	11,828

Source: State Revenue Administration (1991).
Note: Until March 1993, child allowances for the first two children
were temporarily suspended for families with up to three children and income above 90% of the average wage.

even touch upon all aspects of this controversy. For our purposes in this section, it will suffice to mention that with a progressive income tax, income variations over the course of a given lifetime income increase tax liability. Economic theory suggests that, with perfect capital markets, individuals will attempt to smooth such income variations via borrowing and saving, so that the lifetime consumption path will not be affected (in the absence of taxation). In this respect, because of the progression of the income tax, a tax on consumption is fairer than a tax on income.[3]

3. One can say that a tax on consumption allows some kind of a substitute for income averaging which itself is not allowed.

This distinction between the income and consumption paths is particularly relevant to the proper taxation of the working versus the retired. In Israel, as in most other countries, the tax system allows individuals to put aside, tax-free, part of their income during their working years and to use it, after paying taxes, during their retirement. In principle, individuals deduct from their taxable income during their working years a certain amount of saving, invest it tax free, and then pay a relatively low marginal tax rate on this saving together with its accumulated return when it is actually withdrawn in order to finance consumption during retirement.

In practice, however, the word ''chaos'' perhaps best describes the many provisions regarding long-term savings. Incentives are given not only to retirement savings, but also to certain forms of long-term savings (e.g., provident funds) and life-insurance programs. Some medium-term (6 year) saving plans for employees (known as ''advanced training funds'') also qualify for tax benefits. Employees are subject to different provisions than are self-employed people: the ceilings on the contributions of employees and of their employers (on their behalf) toward pension or other retirement funds are generally more generous than those imposed on the contributions of the self-employed; but self-employed people are generally entitled to more favorable treatment than employees on withdrawals from these funds. Some saving plans qualify for tax deductions; others, for tax credits. Withdrawals from these saving plans are not treated uniformly: in certain cases, they are exempted from tax (even though the deposits were deducted from taxable income and the interest earned exempted from tax); in other cases, they are taxed at a reduced rate. And so on. . . .

What is urgently needed is a simple reform that will allow individuals to make pre-tax deductions from taxable income, up to some ceiling, to be deposited in certain, well-defined retirement funds; will exempt from tax all interest, dividends, capital gains, and the like that accumulate in these funds; and will tax any withdrawal from these funds as ordinary income. Of course, such a reform may require some complicated provisions for an extended transition period.

9.2.3. Housing

Tax treatment of houses and apartments, owned by individuals, is unique. Unlike many other countries, neither mortgage interest nor property taxes on owner-occupied housing may be deducted from taxable income. Also, unlike many other countries, capital gains on houses and apartments are *practically* exempt from tax. Originally, the idea was to exempt from tax only capital gains accruing on owner-occupied housing. So, originally, in order to be exempted from capital gains tax the owner had to reside in the house (or apartment) for at least the six months immediately prior to the sale of the house. As enforcement of such a provision proved difficult, it was later determined that exemption from tax on capital gains realized upon the sale of a certain house would be granted if no other house had been sold by the owner during the four years immediately preceding the sale of the said house. In 1992, the law was again changed to allow exemption from capital gains tax, if no more than two houses were sold during the same year, thus practically eliminating the tax on capital gains on houses sold by individuals.

Whenever capital gains *are* subject to tax, a distinction is drawn between inflationary and real gains. The real gains are taxed as ordinary income, while the inflationary gains are taxed at a flat rate of 10%. Also, there is a special, progressive sales tax (in Israel called ''a purchase tax'') on real estate transactions.

9.2.4. Capital Income

In 1992 the corporate tax rate in Israel is 40%, down from 61% only a few years ago. The rate is scheduled to go down to 36% gradually over the years 1993–96. There are also special reduced rates (all the way down to zero) for plants located in certain development towns and rural settlements and for direct foreign investment. Occasionally, accelerated depreciation allowances are granted, mostly in the manufacturing industry and for limited periods. For instance, an accelerated depreciation rate of 100% (immediate full expensing) was granted to the manufacturing industry in 1991 for investments made in 1991 and the first half of 1992. Accelerated depreciation schedules were introduced again for 1993.

Perhaps, the most unusual and intriguing feature of the taxation of business income (of both corporations and proprietorships) in Israel is the clever handling of inflation (which was well into the triple-digit range in the first half of the last decade and is still around 10%–20% annually at the present) in the computation of taxable income of businesses. We discuss this subject in detail in the next section.

There is no explicit integration between the corporate tax and the individual tax, but there is practically a reduced tax rate of 25% for dividend income to individuals. Thus, combining the corporate tax and the individual tax, when no special reduced rates apply, dividend income is taxed at a top rate of 40% + 25% × (100% − 40%) = 55%.

However, since capital gains on financial assets (stocks, bonds, etc.) traded on the Tel Aviv Stock Exchange are totally exempted from the individual income tax, payments of dividends in Israel are quite rare. Other capital gains are subject to a two-tier tax. A flat 10% tax is imposed on the inflationary component of capital gains, while the real component is taxed as ordinary income.

In principle, interest income is treated as ordinary income. However, in many cases, there are so many special benefits for interest income that one can safely assert that interest income is either tax-exempt or taxed at a reduced rate of 35%.

9.2.5. VAT and Other Excises

A general VAT of 17% is levied on sales of all goods and services; the only exempt item is fresh fruits and vegetables. The Israeli VAT is of the consumption, destination-based variety. Accordingly, imports are taxed and exports are exempt (or, more accurately, zero-rated). In addition, a credit is given against the VAT paid on investment goods. (In January 1993, the VAT rate was reduced from 18% to 17%.)

A reduced VAT rate applies directly to the value added of the public sector (namely, the wage bill), with no credits given against purchases of capital goods. An ordinary rate VAT applies also directly to the value added (wages and profits) of financial institutions.[4]

Excise taxes are imposed on tobacco, cigarettes, liquor, fuel, shoes, clothing, cosmetics, and many consumer durables, with highly varying rates. "Luxury" goods are subject to extremely high rates (e.g., private automobiles (100%), dishwashers (115%), etc.).[5] With such high rates, one may wonder whether the "wrong side" of the Laffer curve has already been reached, where tax rates must be *reduced* in order to raise tax revenues.

9.2.6. International Comparisons

The total tax burden in Israel, when measured by total tax revenue as a percentage of GDP, is significantly higher than in the United States,

---

4. In fact, the value added of the financial sector is doubly taxed because the value of the financial intermediation services it provides to the nonfinancial business sector is not excluded from the VAT base of the nonfinancial business sector.

5. Most of these durable goods are imported and the high excise taxes are, to a certain extent, substitutes for tariffs, since there is no domestic production.

Canada, and Japan, but about "average" or slightly higher than in the Western European countries (table 9.6). However, the direct tax burden is among the lowest in the world (table 9.6). Neither the top marginal tax rate nor the corporate tax rate in Israel are excessive, compared with other industrialized countries (table 9.7). But the indirect tax burden in Israel is very high, in fact, much higher than in any of the countries listed in table 9.7. This does not stem from extraordinarily high VAT

Table 9.6 Tax Revenue as a Percentage of GDP in Selected Countries, 1988

Country	Direct Taxes[a]	Indirect Taxes	Total Taxes
Israel	21.8	20.5	42.3
Belgium	34.0	12.2	46.2
Canada	21.3	12.9	34.2
France	28.2	14.6	42.8
Germany	28.3	12.2	40.4
Italy	25.9	10.1	36.0
Japan	22.2	8.5	30.6
Sweden	38.2	16.4	54.6
United States	20.8	8.2	29.0
United Kingdom[b]	21.3	16.2	37.5

Source: State Revenue Administration (1991).
[a] Includes national insurance or social security.
[b] Data for 1987.

Table 9.7 Tax Rates in Selected Countries, 1991

Country	Top Marginal Tax Rate[a]	Corporate	VAT[b]
Israel	50.4	40.0[d]	18.0
Belgium	65.0		19.0
Canada	49.9	42.5	0.0
France	57.0[c]	34.0	18.6
Germany	53.0	46.0	14.0
Italy		47.6	18.0
Japan	65.0	43.5	
Sweden	63.0	30.0	
United States	31.0	39.0	—
United Kingdom	40.0	35.0	16.0

Source: State Revenue Administration (1991).
[a] Excluding national insurance or social security.
[b] Standard rate.
[c] Rate in 1987.
[d] Rate in 1992.

rates. In fact, the VAT rate in Israel is no higher than in many EC countries. Therefore, the heavy indirect tax burden in Israel must result from the many excise taxes that are levied at extremely high rates.

9.3. Inflation and Taxation

The most interesting and genuinely innovative feature of the Israeli tax system is its treatment of inflation. The Israeli experience has shed new light on both the sign and the magnitude of the so-called inflation tax. The solution offered by the Israeli tax system for the effects of inflation is worthy of consideration by other high inflation countries.

Economists have long been interested in the inflation tax, defined as the real depreciation of money holdings. In a seminal paper, Bailey (1956) studied the welfare cost of inflationary finance; and Friedman (1969) investigated the optimal inflation tax and concluded that it should be negative. These early studies tended to ignore the fact that in the real world the alternatives to an inflation tax are not nondistortionary lump-sum taxes, but rather some other distortionary taxes. Therefore, the inflation tax should be considered in a second-best framework. Later, Phelps (1973) and Helpman and Sadka (1979) investigated the optimality of inflationary finance in such a "second-best" context, employing an optimal taxation approach similar to that adopted in the next chapter.

These studies considered only one aspect of inflationary finance: the real depreciation of money holdings or the revenues from printing money (seigniorage). These revenues tend to be relatively small as a percentage of GDP. In Israel, such revenues have averaged about 2% of GDP, with an inflation rate ranging widely between 40% and 500% annually (see, e.g., Eckstein and Leiderman 1989).[6] Furthermore, as the (perfectly foreseen) inflation rate rises, real money holdings decline; with a very high inflation rate a country may well find itself on the wrong side of the Laffer curve.

Tanzi (1977, 1978) identified another much more important and practical aspect of inflationary finance: the effect of inflation on the tax system.[7] According to Tanzi, real tax revenue is eroded by inflation owing to the *collection lag,* defined to be "the time that elapses between

---

6. See also Fischer (1982) for a study of other countries where the inflation tax revenues seem a bit higher.

7. Tanzi (1977) credits Olivera (1967) for first contemplating the possibility that inflation may lead to a decline in real tax revenues.

a taxable event (that is, earning of income, sales of a commodity) and the time when the tax payment related to that taxable event is received by the government" (Tanzi 1978, p. 419, n. 7). In fact, the overall revenue from inflationary finance may well be negative.

The collection lag can be shortened to lessen the effect of inflation on the tax system, but such measures are themselves not without costs. For example, when inflation reached triple digits, the filing period for the VAT in Israel was shortened from three months to one month. Accordingly, during the period 1979–85, businesses had to file a VAT return and pay the tax collected to the government every month, thereby increasing both their bookkeeping costs and the government's collection costs. Such private and public collection costs are another *real* cost of inflation that should be added to the lists compiled by Fischer and Modigliani (1978) and Fischer (1981).

The Israeli experience emphasizes yet another aspect of the effect of inflation on the tax system: the difficulty of properly defining income. The traditional approach followed in macroeconomic textbooks is that with a progressive individual income tax (i.e., one in which the *average* tax rate increases with income), nominal income, which rises in proportion to the rate of inflation, causes nominal tax liability to rise more than in proportion to nominal income and inflation. Hence, real tax revenues increase, and the progressive individual income tax serves as an automatic stabilizer. However, with full, and almost instantaneous, indexation of the income tax brackets, individual real tax liabilities no longer rise with inflation. Therefore, the effect of inflation rests primarily on the definition of business income. Since business income is defined according to nominal accounting standards, high inflation virtually destroys the income tax base in the business sector.

Many attempts have been made in the past to correct tax laws for the effects of inflation so as to reestablish a valid income tax base in the business sector during periods of inflation.[8] As the early (1975–82) Israeli experience suggests, these attempts were partial and not even-handed. Lawmakers were under pressure, first of all, to remove those effects of inflation that hurt taxpayers (e.g., the taxation of inflationary capital gains). Only much later did they deal with the effects of inflation that could be exploited by taxpayers (e.g., the tax deductibility of nominal interest payments). These "one-side-of-the-balance-sheet" adjust-

8. See Casanegra de Jantscher (1976) for a description of the early Latin American experience.

ments tended to worsen the already detrimental effect of inflation on the tax system (see also Kay 1977).

It took several years of high inflation before a law providing comprehensive adjustment to the effects of inflation on business income was enacted in 1982. Like any tax law, it contained several large loopholes, most of which were later closed or which became much less effective when inflation was brought down in mid-1985.

During the period of high inflation (1981–85), the tax on wage earners accounted for an unusually high fraction (about 65%) of all income tax revenue. Today, it accounts for only 40%. A key element in the mid-1985 stabilization program was the elimination of the fiscal deficit. A significant contribution to the elimination of the deficit came from the automatic increase in real tax revenues caused by the sharp decline in inflation. For this reason we make the conjecture that economists should abandon the traditional concept of the "inflation tax" in favor of the more realistic "inflation subsidy."

This section is organized as follows. Section 9.3.1 describes the main effects of inflation on business income; 9.3.2 summarizes early partial adjustments for inflation in the tax laws; 9.3.3 analyzes the main elements of the 1982 tax law, which was supposed to provide a comprehensive adjustment for inflation in the definition of business income; and 9.3.4 describes the major loopholes and exceptions to that law. Section 9.3.5 discusses the importance of withholding when income tax brackets are indexed and change *within the same* tax year. Section 9.3.6 discusses some alternatives to income taxation (e.g., consumption or cash flow taxation) during inflationary periods.

Throughout this discussion, inflation is assumed to take the form of an equiproportional increase in all prices, so that relative prices do not change. This assumption makes it possible to abstract from the question of which price index to employ in converting nominal values into real values.

9.3.1. Effects of Inflation on Taxable Business Income

Taxable income in the business sector is calculated according to standard accounting procedures, which are nominal in nature. In other words, one sheqel is treated as one sheqel regardless of the date on which it was paid or received. Nominal business income (or profit) so calculated, which is revenues (or sales) minus costs, is calculated by adding together sheqalim received at different dates (and having different real values) and subtracting from them sheqalim paid at different dates and having different real values. When inflation rates are 100%–500% per annum, a beginning-of-the-year sheqel may be worth, in real terms, as much as 2 to 6 end-of-the-year sheqalim. As a result, nominal income cannot serve as even an approximation of the real income of a business firm in periods of high inflation, such as those existing in Israel during the late 1970s and the first half of the 1980s.

Inflation creates several deviations of nominal income from real income. Some of these deviations or biases are negative and some are positive, but they do not offset each other. Furthermore, as we shall explain below, their incidence and magnitude are not independent of the behavior of the taxpayer. In other words, the taxpayer may take certain tax-avoidance actions that reduce his calculated nominal income even though his real income does not change. In such a case, a higher inflation rate reduces rather than increases real tax revenues; and the tax system fails to serve as an automatic stabilizer.

The deviations or biases of real income from nominal income that are caused by inflation may be classified into five main categories as follows:

(1) Nominal capital gains on an asset have two components: an artificial or inflationary component that merely reflects an increase in the general price level of all goods and services, and a true, real component that reflects the appreciation in the value of the asset that results from fundamentals such as increased demand for or scarcity of the asset. Thus, nominal income overstates real income by the sum of the inflationary component of capital gains. For later reference, it is worth pointing out that capital gains are normally taxed upon realization, rather than on an accrual basis, so that both the inflationary and real components of capital gains are taxed only when the asset is sold or otherwise disposed of.

(2) Analogous to the distinction between the inflationary and real components of nominal capital gains is the distinction between the inflationary and real components of the interest rate. Thus, allowing deductibility of nominal interest accumulations causes nominal income to understate real income by the sum of the inflationary component of the interest accumulations.

At first glance, one might argue that (1) and (2) above offset each other. On the one hand, inflationary capital gains on an asset are included in taxable income, but on the other hand, the inflationary interest charges incurred for the purpose of acquiring the asset are tax deductible. This argument is invalid on two grounds. First, the purchase of an asset may be financed by equity rather than by debt. Second, capital gains are taxed upon realization, whereas interest is deductible on an accrual basis. Suppose, for instance, that a firm takes out a fully indexed loan of 100 sheqalim to be repaid after five years in order to purchase a certain asset. If the annual inflation rate is 100%, then the firm will be allowed to deduct from taxable income an indexation differential (i.e., the inflationary component of the interest rate) of 100 sheqalim in the first year, 200 sheqalim in the second year, 400 sheqalim in the third year, and so on even though these differentials were not actually paid before the end of the fifth year.[9] The inflationary capital gains on the asset purchased, however, will not be taxed until the asset is sold.

(3) The depreciation allowance on a physical asset is calculated on the basis of the nominal (historic) cost of the asset. In this respect, nominal income overstates real income.

The above three sources of the deviation of real income from nominal income are well known and have received considerable attention. In fact, many economists have asserted that these are the only significant effects of inflation on real tax liabilities (see, e.g., Halperin and Steuerle 1988). Many believe that in order to eliminate the effect of inflation on real tax liability in practice, it would suffice to exempt inflationary capital gains from tax, disallow tax deductibility of inflationary interest charges, and allow replacement cost depreciation.

This simple prescription for dealing with the effect of inflation on taxable income might well be adequate for relatively low rates of inflation, say up to 10%–15% per annum. But when the annual rate of inflation reaches triple digits, other, less obvious, factors come into force. The solution suggested above fails to recognize these factors and is therefore inadequate for dealing with the effects of inflation on real tax liabilities in the business sector.

When the monthly inflation rate reaches double digits, two additional major factors cause nominal income to deviate significantly from real income. These factors, unlike the first three, pertain primarily to the determination of real *operating* income (i.e., income before capital gains and long-term financing costs are taken into account). They relate to the nature of the production process, which takes place over time.

---

9. These indexation differentials, which are tax deductible for the borrower, would, in principle, be taxable income for the lender. However, in Israel, where major segments of the capital market were effectively nationalized, the lender is very often the government itself, so that in many cases, there is no taxable lender to pay the tax that the borrower saved.

(4) Given that the production process takes place over time, output is usually sold at the end of this process, while the costs of labor and other inputs and raw materials are incurred earlier. Thus, output is sold at high (inflated) nominal prices, relative to the low nominal prices of the inputs. As a result, the nominal operating income overstates the real operating income. Naturally, the duration of the production process is short relative to the lifetime of fixed assets and long-term loans. Thus, the bias in the operating income, unlike the biases caused by capital gains and interest payments, is significant only when the inflation rate is high (e.g., when the annual rate climbs into the triple-digit range).

A special case of the preceding bias applies in particular to retail firms.

(5) A retail firm normally buys and pays for its merchandise before it can resell it. Thus, the sale price is inflated relative to the purchase price. As a result, the nominal profit from sales includes an inflationary appreciation in the value of the merchandise. The firm is thus taxed on the inflationary appreciation of the merchandise it sells.

9.3.2. Partial Adjustments for Inflation: 1975–81

One might conclude from the preceding subsection that, since the various deviations of nominal income from real income are not all of the same sign, the effect of inflation on nominal taxable income, vis-à-vis real income, is ambiguous. However, such a conclusion ignores the long-run response of the taxpaying firm to the effect of inflation on nominal income. In the short run, when inflation rises unexpectedly, firms are caught by surprise and may either lose or gain from inflation. For instance, those firms that have invested heavily in fixed assets, financed by debt, usually gain (because, as we recall, capital gains are taxed upon realization, whereas interest charges are deducted on an accrual basis); those firms that have used equity capital to finance their production usually lose. But in the longer run, firms will have taken various tax-avoidance measures in order to reduce nominal taxable income. For instance, they will use less and less equity capital and invest more and more in buildings and real estate. Such tax-avoidance activity is further fueled, as we will discuss below, by changes that are made in the tax laws in the wake of inflation—changes that are partial and unbalanced.

As inflation persists, lawmakers start to introduce provisions in the tax laws aimed at eliminating the effect of inflation on real tax liabilities. However, the Israeli experience suggests that these provisions are generally introduced piecemeal and tend to be unbalanced. Lawmakers first yield to the public outcry of those who are hurt by inflation and grant relief against taxation of inflation (artificial) income. Only much later do they close up the loopholes that enable taxpayers to deduct inflationary expenses.

One of the earliest provisions introduced in 1975 in the wake of the stubbornly persistent inflation was a reduction in the tax rate on the inflationary component of capital gains to 10%, compared to the 61% rate on ordinary corporate income.[10] Similarly, the holders of indexed government bonds and certain other bonds were exempted from paying tax on the inflationary component of the interest (the indexation differential) earned. Owners of bank saving deposits were also granted an exemption on the inflationary component of earned interest. Another ad hoc relief measure allowed firms to take a deduction based on the size of their (finished or unfinished) inventories. The rationale for this deduction was the need to offset artificial inflationary effects on the operating income of the firm that were related to the temporal nature of the production process.

All these provisions affected only one side of the balance sheet—that is, they all pertained to the asset side. The liability side was initially ignored. Only later on did it become evident that it made no sense, for instance, to exempt inflationary capital gains or to tax them at a low rate, while still allowing taxpayers to deduct from ordinary income the total inflationary component of any interest which they owed. As a result of these lopsided measures, firms increased their borrowing in order to invest in buildings, equipment, machinery, inventories, stocks, and indexed government bonds. Attempts to restrict the tax deductibility of inflationary interest charges were partial and clumsy, and they failed.[11]

9.3.3. The Comprehensive Approach: 1982–Present

The partial adjustment measures discussed in the previous section proved to be inadequate, and in 1982 after some seven years, with inflation reaching an annual rate of 140%, a new law was introduced.

10. It is worth noting that the Israeli tax laws are usually very generous with respect to capital gains accruing to individuals, even when they are real gains. E.g., securities traded on the stock exchange are exempted, as is residential housing (even if not owner-occupied) under some (not significantly restrictive) conditions (see section 9.2).

11. These restrictions applied to interest charges that could be attributed to the financing of tax-exempt government bonds and other securities.

The aim was to remove in a comprehensive manner all effects of inflation on real tax liabilities. In principle, the law should have been applied to all businesses. However, since the various provisions of the law were based on the balance sheet of the firm, it was effectively confined to "big" businesses, which are usually required to provide balance sheets: namely, to corporations and some other proprietary firms (usually above a certain size).

Theoretically, the most logical method for eliminating the effects of inflation on taxable income is to evaluate each transaction in units of some stable currency (say, the U.S. dollar) instead of nominal Israeli sheqalim. Thus, if income is calculated by subtracting the cost of labor and other inputs, finance costs, and depreciation from receipts of sales, all evaluated in dollars, the result will indeed more closely reflect the real income of the firm. However, implementing this method would be difficult and costly. As long as the Israeli sheqel remains the only legal medium of exchange and transactions are consequently made in sheqalim, this method would require a record to be maintained of the exact date of each transaction, so that the nominal sheqalim involved in each transaction could be translated into dollars at the current rate of exchange between the sheqel and the dollar, which varies daily in periods of high inflation. It was therefore felt that this method of dealing with the effects of inflation on taxable income would be too complicated to implement in practice. Hence, an alternative, much simpler, but indirect, method was adopted.

The main features of the new comprehensive law that was enacted in 1982 are quite simple: first, calculate income in nominal terms according to standard accounting procedures; then for each of the five effects of inflation enumerated in section 9.3.1, perform an adjustment that either directly removes that effect or ensures that it is offset by one or more of the other effects. Income, after these adjustments, will then reflect the real income of the firm, evaluated at end-of-year prices.

The following describes in more detail the adjustments that are needed. Consider first, effects (4) and (5) of 9.3.1, which relate to the fact that costs (of labor inputs, raw materials, and merchandise) are paid for some time before sales receipts are cashed in. These effects inflate nominal income because revenues are evaluated at prices that are inflated relative to the prices at which costs are evaluated. But there are now two possibilities: if the costs were financed by debt, then these two effects are offset by item (2) (i.e., the deductibility of inflationary interest charges), if the costs were financed by equity, then these two effects are corrected for by the following adjustment, which puts equity on a par with debt:

(i) Allow a deduction equal to an *imputed* inflationary interest on equity (i.e., a deduction that is equal to the amount of equity × the inflation rate).

Next, consider item (1) from section 9.3.1, the inclusion of inflationary capital gains in taxable income. When inflationary interest charges—both the genuine interest on debt and an imputed interest on equity as allowed by (i) above—are tax deductible on an accrual basis, it is correct to include inflationary capital gains in taxable income. Furthermore, these inflationary gains should be included on an accrual basis. Thus, the following adjustment has to be made:

(ii) Add inflationary capital gains accruing (even if not yet realized) on all fixed and other nonmonetary assets (i.e., on all assets that appreciate in nominal terms during inflation). This means adding to nominal taxable income an amount that is equal to the book value of these assets × the inflation rate; upon realization of the capital gains, only their real component is taxed.[12]

Notice that once inflationary interest charges on both debt and equity are deducted from taxable income, then adjustment (ii) above should be applied to business inventories as well. Specifically, recall that the cost of sales is defined as beginning-of-year inventory, plus new purchases during the year, minus end-of-year inventory. The latter should be evaluated at end-of-year prices, so as to include in taxable income the inflationary capital gains accruing to it.

Adjustments (i) and (ii) above fully correct for items (1), (2), (4), and (5) of subsection 9.3.1. The following adjustment must be made to correct for item (3), which is the historic cost depreciation:

(iii) Allow a depreciation that is evaluated at end-of-year prices.

These three adjustments to nominal income make it a true representation of real income, evaluated at end-of-year prices. In practice, (i) and (ii) were combined. Since (i) calls for a deduction equaling equity × the inflation rate, while (ii) calls for an addition to income, which is equal to fixed (and some other) assets × the inflation rate, then the net effect of (i) and (ii) is to allow a net deduction that is equal to

$$(\text{equity} - \text{fixed assets}) \times \text{inflation rate}.$$

12. Notice that in view of the adjustments to income discussed in this section, dividends represent *real* income.

Notice that this net deduction may well be negative. It is referred to as "the deduction for the preservation of equity," since it could be interpreted as a deduction aimed at protecting that part of equity not invested in "inflation-proof" assets.

An alternative way of deriving this formula is to employ the definition of real income of the firm as the difference between the firm's net worth at the end of the year and its net worth at the beginning of the year, when both are evaluated at the same prices, say, end-of-year prices (see appendix 9.1).

9.3.4. Loopholes and Exceptions

The preceding section described in a schematic way the basic features of the 1982 law. However, the actual implementation of these features was complicated by the serious practical considerations, which are described below.

Equity may vary within any single tax year, since new equity may be issued and some old equity may be retired by paying dividends. Thus, according to adjustment (i) described in section 9.3.3, the firm has to keep track of the movements of equity within the tax year to be able to calculate the tax deduction to which it is entitled. Beginning-of-year equity, for instance, will be entitled to a deduction based on the *annual* rate of inflation (i.e., that is, from the beginning to the end of the year), whereas a new issuance of equity will be entitled to a deduction that is based on the rate of inflation only from the date of actual payment for the new equity to the end of the year.

A similar caveat applies to fixed assets (as described in adjustment (ii) in section 9.3.3).[13] Since one usually encounters only a few changes in equity or in the stock of fixed assets within the relatively short period of one year, the calculation of the deductions from and additions to income is fairly manageable. However, this is not usually the case with business inventories.

Business inventories. Business inventories are normally fast moving and typically include an extremely large number of items. Hence, calculating the inflationary capital gains accruing to end-of-year inventories is not feasible and has therefore not been put into practice, even though it was one of the principles embodied in the 1982 law. The effect of

---

13. In practice, fixed assets were somewhat penalized by the 1982 law, since the 10% tax on inflationary capital gains was not abolished. Furthermore, only *nominal* capital losses are deductible from taxable income rather than their *real* equivalent.

this deviation from the rule has been to postpone the tax on inflationary capital gains on end-of-year inventories to the next year.[14] A public committee recommended in 1985 that some accounting formula could be used to calculate the *average* holding period of inventories and, accordingly, adjust the value of the end-of-year inventories, but this recommendation was never adopted.

Industrial equipment and machinery. A second exception was granted to industrial equipment and machinery. Industry in Israel has traditionally been accorded favorable treatment via the tax-subsidy system, in the belief that such assistance is essential for long-term, export-led growth.[15] Until 1986, for instance, the corporate income tax rate on industrial firms was substantially lower than on nonindustrial firms. Similarly, industrial firms are exempted from a general payroll tax.

Following this tradition, the 1982 law provided for the inflationary appreciation of industrial equipment and machinery to be exempted from tax until the date of realization, to encourage investments in these capital assets. As a partial offset for this tax relief, depreciation allowances for industrial equipment and machinery were not indexed.

The tax relief reduced the effective tax rates on income from industrial equipment and machinery and generated an overinvestment in them. The problem was that the magnitude of the decline in the effective tax rates depended on the rate of inflation: the higher the rate of inflation, the lower the effective tax rates. A method for determining the magnitude of the reduction in the effective tax was suggested by Sadka and Zigelman (1990), who adapted standard effective tax rate formulas (see, e.g., Auerbach 1983, 1987; King and Fullerton 1984) to the 1982 law and concluded that the effective tax rate (t_i) on the income generated by asset i is given by

$$t_i = \frac{MPK_i - D_i - r}{MPK_i - D_i},$$

where MPK_i is governed by the profit-maximization condition:

$$MPK_i(1 - t) = (D_i + r)[1 - t(Z_i + U_i)],$$

14. It should be pointed out that using the last-in-first-out (LIFO) method (rather than the first-in-first-out [FIFO] method) for evaluating end-of-year inventories would only increase the disparity, because the LIFO method deflates rather than inflates the monetary value of end-of-year inventories.

15. Of course, most academic economists in Israel do not approve of favorable treatment for only one sector of the economy.

and where

MPK_i = marginal product of asset i,

t = statutory corporate tax rate,

D_i = physical depreciation of asset i,

r = real rate of return required by equity holders,

Z_i = real present value of the depreciation allowances for asset i,

U_i = real present value of the "equity preservation deduction" (see section 9.3.3).

The interpretation of the above formulas is straightforward. The effective tax rate (t_i) is the rate by which the before-tax marginal return to capital ($MPK_i - D_i$) exceeds the real rate of return required by equity holders (r). The firm invests up to the point where the net-of-tax marginal product of capital equals the tax-adjusted cost of capital ($D_i + r$). The tax-adjustment parameters are related to the depreciation allowances (Z_i) and the equity preservation deduction (U_i).

Employing the above formulas, table 9.8 presents the effect of inflation on the effective tax rates on income from industrial equipment and machinery (for $t = 52\%$, which, until 1986, was the statutory tax rate for industrial firms, and $r = 4\%$). As the annual inflation rate rises from 0% to 400%, the effective tax rates fall by about 12–15 percentage points.

A reduction in effective tax rates as a response to a higher inflation rate introduces a built-in automatic *destabilizer* into the tax system, against the conventional wisdom of public finance textbooks, which advocate fiscal automatic stabilizers. Indeed, the tax relief that was granted in 1982 to industrial equipment and machinery was abolished in 1985, when inflation in Israel reached its peak. Inflationary capital

Table 9.8 Effect of Inflation on Effective Tax Rates on Industrial Equipment and Machinery

Asset	Inflation Rate	
	0%	400%
General industrial equipment	28.9	16.5
Tools	27.3	15.4
Special industrial equipment	26.4	14.8
Construction equipment	34.7	20.5

Source: Sadka and Zigelman (1990).

gains accruing to industrial equipment and machinery became taxable, and the depreciation allowances were indexed.

Proprietorships and self-employed individuals. The 1982 law covered all corporations, but largely ignored the incomes of most proprietorships and self-employed persons (e.g., small businesses, brokers, law firms, plumbers, accountants, and clinics), opening the third loophole. Proprietorships were only somewhat restricted with respect to the amount of interest deductions they could claim. As a result, the 1982 law essentially created two tax sectors within the business sector: one to which the law did apply, which we shall call the *indexed sector* (mostly corporations), and one that escaped the provisions of the law, which we shall call the *nonindexed sector* (mostly proprietorships and self-employed individuals).

The nonindexed sector can maneuver the timing of its cash receipts and payments in order to deflate its taxable income and reduce its real tax liability. By advancing the date of the cash receipt for a given real revenue, one can deflate nominal revenues. Similarly, by postponing the date of the cash payment for a given real expense, one can inflate real tax liability.

A simple example can serve to illustrate this argument. Consider an individual whose real revenues, expenses, and net income, when measured in terms of a stable currency (say, the U.S. dollar) are as follows:

revenues	$250,000
expenses	$150,000
net income	$100,000

Suppose that the annual inflation rate is 100%, so that prices double from the beginning to the end of the year. Thus, if the rate of exchange is NIS 1 = $1 at the beginning of the year, it will be NIS 2 = $1 at the end of the year. Suppose further that the individual is able to advance the receipt of revenues to the beginning of the year and postpone the payment of expenses until the end of the year. The statement of nominal income will then show the following entries:

revenues	NIS 250,000
expenses	NIS 300,000
net income	−NIS 50,000

Thus, through a few simple maneuvers, positive real income can be turned into a loss for tax purposes.

Notice that the validity of the above example rests on the ability of the individual to advance cash receipts or postpone cash payments or both. However, a receipt for one agent is also payment for another agent. Therefore, there should be other agents in the above example for whom payments of expenses were advanced and receipts of revenues were postponed. Would not the incomes of these agents be inflated and their real tax liabilities increased? The answer is not necessarily, since these agents could belong to the *indexed* sector and their real tax liabilities would not be affected by the manipulations described in the example. Alternatively, they could belong to the nontaxable, nonprofit sector, or the public sector, or they could be foreign residents, or final consumers—in any of these cases, their tax liabilities would not be affected.

9.3.5. Wage Taxation: The Role of Withholding

Unlike taxpayers in the business sector, wage earners cannot maneuver with the indexed sector in order to reduce their real tax burden because of the tax withholding system. This system ensures that any manipulation of the timing of cash receipts for wages earned will have little, if any, effect on *real* tax payment.

A simple example will serve to illustrate this point. Suppose, for the sake of simplifying the arithmetic, that the tax year consists of just two months. Suppose that in the first month the income tax schedule is

Month 1

Income Bracket (NIS)	Marginal Tax Rate
0–1,000	0%
over 1,000	30%

Suppose further that prices double between the first and the second month. With full indexation of the income tax brackets (as is the case in Israel), the income tax schedule in the second month would be

Month 2

Income Bracket (NIS)	Marginal Tax Rate
0–2,000	0%
over 2,000	30%

The income tax schedule is calculated for the annual tax returns by adding up the brackets for the various months. Thus, the annual tax schedule will be

Annual Schedule

Income Bracket (NIS)	Marginal Tax Rate
0–3,000	0%
over 3,000	30%

Consider an individual who earns a steady real wage income of $1,500 per month. Suppose also that the rate of exchange is NIS 1 = $1 in the first month, and consequently, NIS 2 = $1 in the second month. Thus, the individual earns NIS 1,500 in the first month and NIS 3,000 in the second month. In the first month, the individual will be subject to a withholding tax of (NIS 1,500 − NIS 1,000) × 30% = NIS 150, which is worth $150. In the second month, she will be subject to a withholding tax of (NIS 3,000 − NIS 2,000) × 30% = NIS 300, which is worth $150. Altogether, NIS 450, or $300, is withheld at source. When this individual files a tax return at the end of the year, she will report an annual income of NIS 4,500, on which the tax liability is (NIS 4,500 − NIS 3,000) × 30% = NIS 450. This is the amount that was withheld, and hence she will pay no further taxes. *Real* tax payment is therefore $300.

Now, suppose the individual advances the receipt of her wage for the second month to the first month; that is, she receives her total annual wage of $3,000, or NIS 3,000, in the first month. The amount of tax withheld will then be (NIS 3,000 − NIS 1,000) × 30% = NIS 600, which is worth $600. When she files a tax return at the end of the year, she reports an annual income of NIS 3,000, on which the tax liability is zero. Therefore, she receives a refund of NIS 600, which is now worth only $300. Hence, her *real* tax payment is $600 − $300 = $300. This is exactly what she paid when her income was spread evenly over the two months.

In the above example, the individual gained nothing by maneuvering the timing of her wage receipts. Although one may be able to devise an example in which something could be gained, nevertheless, this example serves to show how withholding substantially curtails the gains from advancing wage receipts. When a wage receipt is advanced, the tax is withheld, thereby limiting the real gain that can be realized from such a maneuver.

9.3.6. Consumption Tax versus Income Tax with Inflation

The income (or direct) versus consumption (or indirect) tax controversy has been discussed at length in the literature (see, e.g., Atkinson 1977). Although this controversy can be addressed from several angles, we shall confine the discussion here to the relative performance of these two taxes in the presence of inflation.[16]

As was seen above, the presence of inflation creates some serious complications in the definition of business income, but the consumption tax appears to be unaffected by these difficulties. This is why many economists and policymakers argue in favor of a consumption tax in a period of high inflation. Indeed, a consumption-type VAT performed remarkably well in Israel, even during the peak inflation period of 1984–85.

However, a consumption tax is usually levied at a flat rate. In a life-cycle model, or in a Ricardian world, the present value of consumption is equal to the present value of wages. Hence, a proportional consumption tax has the same equity implications as a proportional wage tax (i.e., it is not progressive). In order to make the consumption tax more progressive, one could exempt from tax some necessities (such as food products, e.g.) and impose a higher tax rate on luxuries.[17] This is indeed the practice followed in many countries with respect to the VAT. Yet, it is highly questionable how much progression one can achieve through a three-tier VAT system (i.e., with a zero rate, a standard rate, and a luxury rate).

In order to strengthen the progression capacity of the consumption tax, the tax rate has to be tied to the *total* consumption of the individual (in the same way that the income tax rate depends on the total income of the individual). In other words, there should be a consumption tax schedule that is applied to the total consumption of each individual or household. Each individual would have to report her total consumption, which could only be done accurately by subtracting *real* personal saving from *real* personal income. For a typical wage earner, it presumably would not be difficult to calculate real personal income—real interest income, dividends, and real capital gains would be added to wage income to yield real personal income. The corporate income tax would

---

16. Atkinson and Sandmo (1980), e.g., point out that income tax causes both intra- and intertemporal distortions, whereas a consumption tax causes only intertemporal distortions—the so-called double-taxation-of-savings argument.

17. For the theoretical foundation of this result see Deaton (1977) and Balcer and Sadka (1981).

no longer be needed and would be abolished. But a self-employed individual or an owner of a small business (unincorporated) would still need to calculate real business income. Thus with this group of taxpayers, we are back to square one: how to define real business income in a period of high inflation. In addition, the problem arises of how to calculate real personal savings (i.e., the real increase in net [of debt] wealth). A progressive consumption tax therefore is not necessarily an easy alternative to the progressive income tax in a period of high inflation.

Another alternative to the business income tax is a business cash flow tax (see King 1987). This is a tax on the net cash flow a company receives from its real economic activities.[18] It differs from the income tax, in that it grants immediate expensing (100% first-year depreciation allowances) to all forms of investment.[19] This feature gives the cash flow tax an administrative advantage, since its implementation does not require a calculation of "true" or "economic" depreciation upon which to base depreciation allowances. After analyzing the positive implications of the cash flow tax for the efficiency of resource allocation, King (1987, p. 379) concluded: "It is attractive for a further reason, namely that the base of the tax requires no adjustment for inflation, and hence that the complicated indexation provisions for depreciation, for example, required under alternative corporate tax systems are unnecessary with a cash flow tax. . . . The tax eliminates the necessity of calculating 'economic profit.' Hence, there is no need to construct a true measure of depreciation or to make any adjustment for the effects of inflation."

Obviously, with a cash flow tax that grants immediate expensing, the need for indexation provisions for depreciation vanishes. However, with a high inflation rate, other adjustments for inflation still need to be made in the tax base. When the inflation rate is sufficiently high (say, in the triple-digit range), the cumulative price increase within any single tax year, from the first month to the last month, is quite substantial. In such a case, one cannot simply subtract cash outflows from cash inflows in

18. In order for the cash flow tax to have the same effect as the consumption tax, interest payments should still qualify as a deduction if interest income is taxed at the individual level; otherwise, the firm and the individual will be using different rates of discount—the firm's rate of discount will be the pretax rate of interest, while the individual's discount rate will be the after-tax rate of interest. Such a divergence between the firm's rate and the individual's rate causes an intertemporal inefficiency of resource allocation.

19. It is noteworthy that a 100% depreciation was allowed for tax purposes in Israel, mostly in the manufacturing sector, for investments made during 1991 and the first half of 1992.

order to calculate the annual net cash flow of the firm. The cash inflows may have occurred at points in time different from those at which the cash outflows occurred, even though both flows occurred within the same tax year. Thus, cash flows have to be indexed when calculating the annual net cash flow of the firm. Alternatively, the tax period can be shortened from one year to one month. (In fact, the idea of a cash flow tax on a monthly basis was briefly considered in Israel in 1984, but the time was not yet ripe for such a tax "revolution.") A large advantage of the cash flow tax in this respect is that, unlike the income tax, it does not require the calculation of depreciation allowances or a complicated evaluation of business inventories (especially inventories of unfinished goods in the production process). Hence, a monthly cash flow tax would not be excessively costly to administer.

However, the monthly net cash flow of the firm varies considerably over time; often, it may be negative. (E.g., one would certainly expect a negative net cash flow in a month in which the firm makes a major investment.) Therefore, it is essential for the smooth functioning of the monthly cash flow tax either to grant a full tax rebate in case the net cash flow is negative or to allow net negative cash flows to be carried forward with full indexation and real interest.

The cash flow tax deserves serious consideration as an alternative to the business income tax. In addition to its "fiscal neutrality" advantage over the standard income tax, it may also perform more effectively in a period of high inflation.

APPENDIX 9.1 Alternative Derivation of Real Income

In section 9.3.3 the real income of the firm, evaluated at end-of-year prices, is shown to be equal to nominal income adjusted by "the deduction for the preservation of equity," and by an indexation differential on depreciation. This appendix provides an alternative, but equivalent, definition of real income via the balance sheet of the firm.

If no new equity is issued within the tax year and no dividends are distributed, then the real change in the firm's net worth is equal to its real income. Thus, real income, evaluated at end-of-year prices, is equal to end-of-year net worth, evaluated at end-of-year prices, minus beginning-of-year net worth, also evaluated at end-of-year prices.

If the firm neither purchases nor sells any fixed asset during the year, then its nominal balance sheets at the beginning and the end of the year will typically appear as follows (a "0" subscript stands for the beginning of the year and a "1" subscript stands for the end of the year.

Beginning of the Year

Assets	Equity and Liabilities
FA	E
NNA_0	L_0

End of the Year

Assets	Equity and Liabilities
$FA - D$	E
NNA_1	NI
	L_1

where

FA = fixed assets at historic (i.e., beginning-of-year) prices

NNA = net nominal (nonindexed) assets. These may include, for example, cash, checking accounts, and balances due from clients (minus balances due to suppliers)

E = equity at historic prices

L = long-term indexed liabilities at current prices

NI = nominal income during the year

D = depreciation at historic prices

Notice that

$$FA + NNA_0 = E + L_0 \qquad (A9.1)$$

and

$$FA - D + NNA_1 = E + NI + L_1. \qquad (A9.2)$$

Suppose that the price level rises from the beginning to the end of the year at the rate π. Then, the beginning-of-year net worth of the firm, evaluated at end-of-year prices, is

$$(FA + NNA_0 - L_0)(1 + \pi). \qquad (A9.3)$$

Similarly, the end-of-year net worth of the firm, evaluated at end-of-year prices, is

$$(FA - D)(1 + \pi) + NNA_1 - L_1. \qquad (A9.4)$$

Hence, the real income of the firm, evaluated at end-of-year prices, is obtained by subtracting (A9.3) from (A9.4):

$$\begin{aligned} \text{real income} &= (FA - D)(1 + \pi) + NNA_1 \\ &\quad - L_1 - (FA + NNA_0 - L_0)(1 + \pi) \\ &= (FA - D + NNA_1 - L_1) + (FA - D)\pi \\ &\quad - (FA + NNA_0 - L_0)(1 + \pi). \end{aligned} \tag{A9.5}$$

Employing (A9.1) and (A9.2), equation (A9.5) reduces to

$$\text{real income} = E + NI + (FA - D)\pi - E(1 + \pi). \tag{A9.6}$$

Rearranging terms, equation (A9.6) becomes

$$\text{real income} = NI - D\pi - (E - FA)\pi. \tag{A9.7}$$

Notice that $(E - FA)\pi$ is the deduction for the preservation of equity that is given by the formula in section 11.4.3. The term $D\pi$ is the indexation differential on depreciation. Thus, equation (A9.7) suggests that real income is indeed equal to nominal income, adjusted by the deduction for the preservation of equity and by an indexation differential on depreciation. A similar formula is proposed by Harberger (1988), but he understated the difficulties involved in the evaluation of business inventories, especially unfinished goods in the production process (see also Tanzi [1981, eq. 9]).

10

Tax Design: Static and Dynamic Efficiency

This section develops a framework for identifying and analyzing directions of efficient tax changes. The complex tax system is first calibrated into this framework and then efficiently restructured. The effective cost of public funds is obtained as a by-product of this analysis. Understanding this section requires a fair command of elementary public finance tools and techniques. Indeed, this section is intended mainly for the professional economist. The nontechnical reader can, however, gain some grasp of the relevance of this analysis by going directly to section 10.3 for the estimates of the effective cost of public funds in Israel.

10.1. A Stylized Tax-Transfer Model

In our stylized tax-transfer model, the economy is aggregated into three goods: a consumption good (good 1), labor (good 2), and capital (good 3). To analyze the magnitude of the deadweight loss of the tax system, it is convenient to disaggregate government expenditure according to transfer payments, wage payments, and purchases of goods. Similarly, tax revenue is classified according to taxes on labor income, taxes on capital income, and excise taxes. In line with this three-good disaggregation, transfers ($\mathbf{b}$) and goods purchases ($\mathbf{g}$) should be understood as (3-dimensional) vectors. For example, the first component of the $\mathbf{b}$-vector (b_1) denotes government transfers in terms of the consumption good, while the second and third components, b_2 and b_3, are transfers in terms of labor and capital, respectively. In the case of transfers, however, the last two components of $\mathbf{b}$ are typically zero. Similarly on the expenditure size, g_1 denotes purchases of the consumption good, g_2

denotes government hiring of labor services, and g_3 denotes government hiring of capital services from the private sector which is typically zero.

We denote the consumer after-tax price vector by $\mathbf{p}$ and the producer (pretax price) vector by $\mathbf{q}$. Accordingly, the tax-rate vector $\mathbf{t} = (t_1, t_2, t_3)$ is measured as the difference between consumer prices and producer prices, that is, $\mathbf{t} = \mathbf{p} - \mathbf{q}$. These are *specific* tax rates, that is, they are given per unit of the respective commodity. For example, t_1 is the tax per unit of the consumption good. Typically, t_1 is positive, implying that consumption is taxed rather than subsidized. On the other hand, t_2 is typically negative, because when labor income is taxed, then its consumer after-tax price (p_2) is below its producer pretax price (q_2). Similarly, t_3 is typically negative. The vector of *ad valorem* tax rates $\tau = (\tau_1, \tau_2, \tau_3)$ may be calculated from the vector of *specific* tax rates $\mathbf{t} = (t_1, t_2, t_3)$ by $\tau_i = t_i/q_i$, $i = 1, 2, 3$.

Following Lucas (1991), we reduce the multiperiod economy into a single period (static) economy. An immediate implication of this simplification is that in the single-period model saving (standing for future consumption) must be added to current consumption of the aggregate consumption good in order to obtain a meaningful indicator of the economy (lifetime) consumption. Similarly, government deficit (representing future taxes) must be lumped together with current taxes to get a meaningful measure of the overall tax revenue. Specifically, we assume that the *real* deficit of the public sector is equal to D_1 units of the consumption good, which means that in terms of consumer prices the private sector must pay an additional amount of tax of $p_1 D_1$. We assume that this is a lump-sum tax. Also, we assume in the single-period model that the current account deficit is financed through unilateral transfers from abroad. For convenience, we assume that the transfer is made to the government and is made in units of the consumption good. We denote the amount of this transfer (in units of good 1) by B_1.

The household (private sector) budget constraint is

$$\mathbf{p} \cdot (\mathbf{x} - \mathbf{e} - \mathbf{b}) = \mathbf{q} \cdot \mathbf{y} - p_1 D_1, \tag{10.1}$$

where the 3-dimensional vectors $\mathbf{x}$, $\mathbf{e}$, $\mathbf{b}$, and $\mathbf{y}$ denote *gross* consumption, endowment, government transfers, and *net* output, respectively. Notice that the net consumption (purchase) vector is $\mathbf{x} - \mathbf{e} - \mathbf{b}$, so that the specific tax rates apply to this vector. For example, $x_2 - e_2 - b_2 = x_2 - e_2$ is the household *net* purchase of labor which is typically negative, that is, $e_2 - x_2$ denotes the supply of labor. Note also that, by convention, the first component of the net output vector y_1, which denotes the private-sector output of the consumption good, is positive, while the second and third components, y_2 and y_3, denoting, respectively, labor and capital *inputs*, are typically negative.

The value of net output in producer prices ($\mathbf{q} \cdot \mathbf{y}$) is equal to profits of the private sector. It constitutes a part of the household income, the right-hand side of (10.1). Assuming, however, constant returns to scale in production, $\mathbf{q} \cdot \mathbf{y}$ must equal zero. As was already mentioned, $p_1 D_1$ is viewed as a lump-sum tax paid by the household. Table 10.1 presents the household sector income and spending for Israel in 1990.

The government budget constraint is

$$(\mathbf{p} - \mathbf{q}) \cdot (\mathbf{x} - \mathbf{e} - \mathbf{b}) + p_1 D_1 = q_1(g_1 - B_1) + q_2 g_2 + q_1 b_1.$$
(10.2)

The left-hand side of (10.2) consists of revenues from: (1) excise taxes on net purchases of the consumption good by the private sector, $(p_1 - q_1)(x_1 - e_1 - b_1)$, (2) tax on labor income $(p_2 - q_2)(x_2 - e_2)$, (3) taxes on capital income $(p_2 - q_2)(x_3 - e_3)$, (4) lump-sum taxes, $p_1 D_1$. On the expenditure side (the right-hand side of [10.2]), the government must pay for *net* purchases of the consumption good used as direct public consumption $q_1(g_1 - B_1)$, transfers to the private sector, $q_1 b_1$, and hiring of labor, $q_2 g_2$.

The economywide resource constraint is:

$$\mathbf{g} + \mathbf{x} = \mathbf{e} + \mathbf{y} + \mathbf{B},$$
(10.3)

where $\mathbf{B} = (B_1, 0, 0)$ is the vector of transfers from abroad. Notice that the government's budget constraint (10.2) is implied by the private sector budget constraint (10.1) and the economywide resource constraint (10.3). Thus, by Walras's Law, the government budget constraint (10.2) is redundant.

Table 10.2 presents the inputs to the public sector budget constraint for Israel in 1990. Because of constraints on data availability it is more convenient to employ the resource constraint (10.3) in order to rewrite the public sector budget constraint (10.2) as:

$$p_1 y_1 - (-p_2 y_2) - (-p_3 y_3) + p_1 B_1 + p_1 D_1$$
$$= p_1 g_1 + p_2 g_2 + p_1 b_1.$$
(10.2′)

Assuming that the household derives no direct utility from capital, the utility function is given by:

$$u(x_1, x_2, x_3) = \alpha \ln x_1 + (1 - \alpha) \ln x_2,$$
(10.4)

where $0 < \alpha < 1$.

Table 10.1 The Household Sector, 1990
(billion 1990 $)

Description	Budget Item	Israel 1990
Private consumption plus saving[a]	$p_1 x_1$	28.265
After-tax labor income[b]	$p_2(e_2 - x_2)$	26.593
After-tax capital income[c]	$p_3 e_3$	0.572
Government transfers[d]	$p_1 b_1$	8.902
Public sector deficit[e]	$p_1 D_1$	7.802

Note: We assume that the household possesses no initial endowment of the consumption good and it consumes no capital services, that is, $e_1 = x_3 = 0$. We also assume constant returns to scale, so that $\mathbf{q} \cdot \mathbf{y} = 0$.

[a] Central Bureau of Statistics (1991a, table 19). Excluding imputed housing services (5.443), consumption plus saving is equal to total disposable income (35.332), minus transfers from abroad which were assumed to accrue to the government (1.625).

[b] Central Bureau of Statistics (1991a, table 5). Computations are based on the identity which states that total labor income is equal to the sum of labor incomes in the public and private sectors: $p_2(e_2 - x_2) = p_2 g_2 - p_2 y_2$. Accordingly, after-tax labor income in the public sector $(p_2 g_2)$ is equal to $q_2 g_2$ minus direct taxes in the public sector. Also, $q_2 g_2 = 17.116$ (Central Bureau of Statistics 1991a, table 5). Direct taxes on labor income, including national insurance in both the private and the public sectors, are 12.748 (Central Bureau of Statistics 1991a, table 22). These figures are divided between the private and public sector according to the private and public sector employment ratio (1.053/0.439) and the private and public sector wage ratio (2,441/2,035). Figures for the latter ratio are obtained from Economic Models Ltd. (1991b, table 8). Accordingly, direct taxes on labor income in the public sector are 3.288 and in the private sector are 9.460. Hence $p_2 g_2 = 6.860$. After-tax labor income in the private sector $(-p_2 y_2)$ is equal to $p_2 g_2$ times the product of the ratio of private to public employment (1.053/0.439) and the ratio of private to public wage rates (2,441/2,035). The above calculations show that after-tax labor income in the private sector is $-p_2 y_2 = 19.734$.

[c] Household receipts from capital, rented to private-sector producers, are equal to net (after depreciation) national income at market prices (Central Bureau of Statistics 1991a, table 17), minus national insurance payments (Central Bureau of Statistics 1991a, table 22), minus total direct taxes (Central Bureau of Statistics 1991a, table 22), plus direct subsidies to the business sector (Central Bureau of Statistics 1991a, table 18), minus total indirect taxes on domestic production (Central Bureau of Statistics 1991a, table 18), minus after-tax labor income (line 2, this table). The calculations implicitly assume that all income of the self-employed constitutes capital income. We also note that $p_3 e_3 = -p_3 y_3$.

[d] Government transfers are equal to the government (domestic) interest bill plus transfers to the household sector (Central Bureau of Statistics 1991a, table 18).

[e] Residual, obtained from the household budget constraint, equation (10.1).

Maximizing the utility function (10.4) subject to the budget constraint (10.1) yields the familiar constant expenditure-share rule:

$$\alpha = \frac{p_1 x_1}{p_2 e_2 + p_3 e_3 + p_1 b_1 - p_1 D_1} = 0.491, \tag{10.5}$$

where use is made of table 10.1.[1]

1. Table 10.1 presents a figure of $26.593 billion for $p_2(e_2 - x_2)$. Assuming a value of 2.984 million for e_2 (the total *effective* labor force) and a value of 1.419 for $e_2 - x_2$ (the total *effective*

Table 10.2 The Public Sector, 1990
(consumer prices; billion 1990 $)

Description	Budget Item	Israel 1990
Sources (left-hand side of [11.2a])		
Product of private sector[a]	p_1y_1	30.942
After-tax labor income in private sector[b]	$-p_2y_2$	-19.734
After-tax capital income in private sector[c]	$-p_3y_3$	-0.572
National imports minus exports[d]	p_1B_1	4.331
Public sector deficit[e]	p_1D_1	7.802
Total		22.769
Uses (right-hand side of [11.2a])		
Public sector purchases[f]	p_1g_1	7.008
After-tax public sector wages[g]	p_2g_2	6.859
Public sector transfers[h]	p_1b_1	8.902
Total		22.769

[a] This budget item is equal to the net domestic product of the business sector at market prices (Central Bureau of Statistics 1991a, table 3).
[b] See table 10.1, note b.
[c] See table 10.1
[d] Computed from disposable income (table 10.1, note a), minus transfers from abroad, plus purchases by the public sector (Central Bureau of Statistics 1991a, table 5), minus the product of the private sector at market prices (this table).
[e] See table 10.1.
[f] Central Bureau of Statistics (1991a, table 5).
[g] See table 10.1, note b.
[h] See table 10.1.

The technology is specified by a Cobb-Douglas production function, describing gross (before-depreciation) output, $y_1 + \delta(-y_3)$, as a function of labor input $-y_2$ and capital input $-y_3$:

$$y_1 = A[(-y_2)^\beta(-y_3)^{1-\beta}] - \delta(-y_3). \tag{10.6}$$

Profit maximization implies that β is the share of labor in gross national income, that is,

$$\beta = \frac{-q_2y_2}{q_1[y_1 + \delta(-y_3)]} = 0.846, \tag{10.7}$$

where the estimate of β is based on calculations made in computing the data for table 10.2 ($-q_2y_2 = \$24.4$ billion and $q_1y_1 = \$25.3$ billion),

---

employment), we conclude that $p_2e_2 = \$56.235$ billion. The use of efficiency units to measure labor is necessitated by the wage rate differential between the public and private sectors.

Table 10.3 Average Ad valorem Tax Rates

Base	Rate (percentage; absolute value)
Consumption[a]	22.3
Labor income[b]	19.2
Capital income[c]	34.5

[a] The tax rate is equal to $[(p_1/q_1) - 1] = [(p_1y_1/q_1y_1) - 1]$. For p_1y_1 see table 10.2. To compute q_1y_1, we note that $q_1y_1 = p_1y_1$, plus direct subsidies to business sector (Central Bureau of Statistics 1991a, table 18), minus indirect taxes on domestic production (Central Bureau of Statistics 1991a, table 18).

[b] The average rate of the tax is equal to $[q_2(e_2 - x_2) - p_2(e_2 - x_2)]/q_2(e_2 - x_2)$. Note that $p_2(e_2 - x_2)$ is given in table 10.1. We add to it direct taxes (including national insurance payments) on employees in both the public and private sectors in order to get $q_2(e_2 - x_2)$.

[c] The average rate of the tax is equal to $[-q_3y_e - (-p_3y_3)]/[-q_3y_3]$. To calculate $-q_3y_3$, we use the zero-profit condition ($q \cdot y = 0$) which implies that $-q_3y_3 = q_1y_1 - (-q_2y_2)$, where q_1y_1 is calculated in note a and $-q_2y_2 = -p_2y_2$ (table 10.2), plus direct tax and national insurance in the business sector (Central Bureau of Statistics 1991a, table 22). The figure for $-p_3y_3$ is presented in table 10.1.

and on the Bank of Israel (1991a, table B-A-8) from which we conclude that $\delta(-y_3) q_1 = \$3.571$ billion.

In order to express the various accounts in physical quantities we have to adopt a consistent normalization rule. Our choice is to set the price of consumption, at factor costs, equal to 1.0, the price of capital equal to 0.08 (corresponding to an annual rate of return of 8%),[2] and the price of labor, at factor costs, equal to the average labor cost in the business sector.[3] Given the calculated tax rates in table 10.3, we therefore have:

$$q_1 = \$1$$
$$p_1 = \$1.223$$
$$q_2 = \$23.32 \text{ billion per one million employees,}$$
$$\text{per annum} \qquad (10.8)$$
$$p_2 = \$18.740 \text{ billion per one million employees,}$$
$$\text{per annum}[4]$$
$$q_3 = \$0.08$$
$$p_3 = \$0.0524$$

2. Notice that output (y_1) in the production function is net (after depreciation) output. Therefore, the producer price of capital (q_3) is equal to the domestic rate of interest.

3. Labor income at factor costs divided by business sector employment (1.053).

4. Notice that the calculated average tax on labor income in table 10.3 is lower than the implied tax on labor income in the business sector $1 - [p_2(-y_2)/q_2(-y_2)]$, due to the progression of the income tax schedule.

Table 10.4 A Stylized Tax-prone Economy: Israel, 1990
(billion 1990 $)

Consumption	Labor-Leisure	Capital
	Quantities	
$e_1 = 0$	$e_2 = 2.984$	$e_3 = 31.857^a$
$x_1 = 23.111$	$x_2 = 1.565$	$x_3 = 0$
$y_1 = 25.3$	$e_2 - x_2 = 1.419$	$-y_3 = -31.857^a$
$g_1 = 5.73$	$-y_2 = 1.053$	$g_3 = 0$
$b_1 = 7.279$	$g_2 = 0.366$	$b_3 = 0$
$B_1 = 3.541$	$b_2 = 0$	
$D_1 = 6.380$		
	Prices	
$p_1 = 1.223$	$p_2 = 18.740$	$p_3 = 0.0524$
$q_1 = 1.000$	$q_2 = 23.320$	$q_3 = 0.08$
	Ad Valorem Tax Rates (percentage: absolute value)	
22.3	19.6	34.5

[a] The capital stock $-y_3$ is calculated from the profit-maximization equation $(q_3 + \delta)(-y_3) = (1 - \beta)q_1[y_1 + \delta(-y_3)]$, where $q_3 = .08$ and $\delta = .05$ (Bank of Israel 1991*a*, table B-A-8). Note that the figure for the capital stock reported here is different (lower) than the figure reported in chapter 8. In a sense, capital is measured here in some efficiency unit. The reason is that here we attribute the same productivity (q_3) to all units of capital and hence have to use some common efficiency unit in order to lump together old and new capital.

With these normalizations, we have matched up the static three-good open economy model with the data. The stylized resource allocation for Israel in 1990 and associated prices are presented in table 10.4.

It remains only to calibrate the production function coefficient A. This is done by setting

$$A = \frac{y_1 + \delta(-y_3)}{(-y_2)^\beta (-y_3)^{1-\beta}} = \frac{25.300 + 3.571}{(1.053)^{0.846} (31.857)^{0.154}} = 16.218$$

(10.9)

10.2. Optimum Tax Structure: Static Efficiency

We view as given the endowments, the existing size of government spending and transfers, the existing size of the public deficit (D_1) which is financed by a lump-sum tax, and the existing current account deficit.

All of these are given in real terms (i.e., in units of the relevant commodity). The optimal tax problem is then to choose tax rates so as to maximize the utility level of the representative household, subject to two sets of constraints: the first is imposed on the government by the decentralized nature of the market economy, while the second is imposed by economic feasibility.

The first set of constraints in the tax optimization problem, the so-called implementability constraint, incorporates (1) the representative household's utility-maximization decisions on allocation of its time between labor and leisure when facing after-tax market prices and (2) the firm's profit-maximization decisions on employment of labor and capital.

The second set of constraints consists of the private and public budget constraints and the country's resource constraints. It is well known, however, that the household budget constraint, the government budget constraint, and the economywide resource constraint are linearly dependent (the so-called Walras Law). Thus, once two of these constraints hold, the third constraint necessarily holds as well. Walras's law, therefore, permits us to employ only the household budget constraint, which is already incorporated in the implementability constraint, and the country's resource constraint.

We continue to normalize the producer price of consumption at one, that is, $q_1 = 1$. However, as the technology is nonlinear, the other two producer prices (q_2 and q_3) will be endogenously determined in the solution to the optimal tax problem, together with the consumer prices and the implied tax rates.

10.2.1. Implementability Constraints

The household chooses the level of consumption x_1 and the amount of leisure x_2 (and in turn the quantity of labor services, $e_2 - x_2$), so as to maximize its utility function, subject to the budget constraint, where the latter is expressed in terms of after-tax prices. (Since the household derives no utility from capital, x_3 is set equal to zero.) The Lagrangian expression associated with the household problem is given by:

$$
\begin{aligned}
L = {} & 0.491 \ln(x_1) + 0.509 \ln(x_2) \\
& + \lambda[(2.984\, p_2 + 31.857\, p_3) \\
& - 6.380\, p_1 - p_1(x_1 - 7.279) - p_2 x_2],
\end{aligned}
\tag{10.10}
$$

where $\lambda \geq 0$ is the Lagrangian multiplier, representing the marginal utility of income. The necessary (first-order) conditions for a maximum are:

$$\frac{\partial L}{\partial x_1} = \frac{0.491}{x_1} - \lambda p_1 = 0, \tag{10.11}$$

$$\frac{\partial L}{\partial x_2} = \frac{0.509}{x_2} - \lambda p_2 = 0, \tag{10.12}$$

$$p_1(x_1 - 7.279) + p_2 x_2 = 2.984\, p_2 + 31.857\, p_3 - 6.380\, p_1. \tag{10.13}$$

In the one-period model, the return on capital should be viewed as a pure rent. Hence, an optimal tax policy calls for a 100% taxation of the return to capital. That is, the government would drive to zero the (after-tax) consumer price of capital: $p_3 = 0$.

Consequently, we can rewrite the condition in (10.11)–(10.13) as:

$$\frac{p_2}{p_1} = \frac{0.491\, x_1}{0.509\, x_2}. \tag{10.14}$$

$$(x_1 - 7.279) + \frac{p_2}{p_1} x_2 = 2.984 \frac{p_2}{p_1} - 6.380. \tag{10.15}$$

Substituting (10.14) into (10.15) yields the implementability constraint (derived from the household's maximization of utility):

$$\frac{0.458}{x_1} + \frac{1.465}{x_2} = 1. \tag{10.16}$$

Profit-maximization behavior on the part of the firm implies two more implementability constraints: marginal products of labor and capital should equal their respective costs. That is,

$$A\beta(-y_2)^{\beta-1}(-y_3)^{1-\beta} = q_2, \tag{10.17}$$

$$A(1-\beta)(-y_2)^{\beta}(-y_3)^{-\beta} - \delta = q_3. \tag{10.18}$$

The last two implementability constraints can, however, be ignored in solving the optimal tax problem. Once a solution is found, they can be used in order to define q_1 and q_2. Thus, we are left with only one implementability constraint, condition (10.16). Generally speaking, the implementability constraint states that the allocation supported by the

optimal tax system must lie on the household's price-consumption curve
(P.C.C.).

It is worth pointing out that the implementability constraint (10.16)
was established following a partial optimization step; that is, after driving the after tax consumer price of capital to zero ($p_3 = 0$). In this sense,
the set (a curve) defined by the implementability constraint (10.16) is
the welfare frontier for a larger set which satisfies an implementability
constraint but does not a priori set p_3 at zero. By comparing the original
household's budget constraint (10.13) with (10.15) which assumes p_3
$= 0$, it can be verified that the larger set of implementability is given
by replacing the equality sign in (10.16) with a weak inequality sign:

$$\frac{0.458}{x_1} + \frac{1.465}{x_2} \leq 1. \tag{10.16'}$$

Indeed the existing 1990 allocation for Israel described in table 10.4,
which is suboptimal, satisfies the implementability condition in (10.16')
with a strict inequality: $(0.458/x_1) + (1.465/x_2) = 0.956 < 1$. This
calculation suggests that the existing allocation deviates significantly
from the welfare frontier. Hence, there could be a marked *static* gain
from an optimal design of the tax system, as will indeed be confirmed
later.

10.2.2. The Optimal Allocation

The optimal allocation can be found by maximizing the household utility function in (10.4), subject to (1) the implementability constraint
(10.16), (2) the resource constraint on consumption and labor,

$$x_1 = y_1 + B_1 - g_1, \tag{10.19}$$

$$x_2 = e_2 + y_2 - g_2, \tag{10.20}$$

and (3) the production function (10.6). (Note that the resource constraint
on capital is superfluous, since in the one-period model it is obvious
that $x_3 = 0$ and $-y_3 = e_3$.)

The policy (control) variables are x_1, x_2, y_1, and y_2. We are thus
left with four constraints (10.6, 10.16, 10.19, 10.20) and four control
variables. In this case the constraints themselves are sufficient to define
the optimal solution. This should not be surprising since once it has
been determined that $x_3 = 0$ and $-y_3 = e_3$ we are essentially left with
a two-good model (consumption good and labor-leisure good). In such

a case it does not matter whether we tax labor or tax consumption, since the two taxes are equivalent. That is, there is essentially one tax rate to choose and this is fully determined by the government's revenue needs.

The four constraints can be consolidated into a single constraint, as follows:

$$\frac{0.458}{A(e_2 - x_2 - g_2)^\beta e_3^{1-\beta} - \delta(-y_3) + B_1 - g_1} + \frac{1.465}{x_2} = 1.$$
$$(10.21)$$

Upon substitution for the values of e_2, g_2, B_1, and g_1 from table 10.4 and for the values of the coefficients A and β from (10.9) and (10.7), respectively, we obtain:

$$\frac{0.458}{16.218\,(2.618 - x_2)^{0.846}31.857^{0.154} - 3.571 + 4.551}$$
$$+ \frac{1.465}{x_2} = 1. \quad (10.22)$$

We first solve this equation to find the optimal quantity of x_2. We then use the production function (10.6) and the resource constraints (10.19) and (10.20) in order to find the optimal quantities of x_1, y_1, and y_2. Next, we employ the implementability constraints (10.17) and (10.18) in order to calculate the (pretax) producer prices of labor (q_2) and capital (q_3). (Recall that q_1 is normalized at 1.0.) The household's first-order condition (10.14) defines the (after-tax) consumer price ratio p_2/p_1. As was already pointed out, in our model it makes no difference whether we tax labor or consumption. We therefore normalize the consumption tax rate at zero (i.e., we set $p_1 = q_1 = 1.0$), and proceed to find the consumer price of labor (p_2) and the tax rate on labor income from the consumer price ratio (p_2/p_1). This completes the derivation of the optimal tax allocation (recall that $p_3 = 0$). This allocation is presented in table 10.5.

Point A in figure 10.1, the intersection point of the implementability constraint with $p_3 = 0$ and the private consumption possibility frontier, represents the optimum allocation. Point B, which lies on the private consumption possibility frontier but at which the household receives a capital income of p_3e_3, represents the actual 1990 allocation in Israel. Observe that point B corresponds to relatively more leisure and relatively less consumption, compared to point A, because the tax on capital

Table 10.5 Optimal Allocation in the One-Period Model

Consumption Good	Labor-Leisure	Capital Services
	Quantities	
$e_1 = 0$	$e_2 = 2.984$	$e_3 = 31.857$
$x_1 = 31.662$	$x_2 = 1.486$	$x_3 = 0$
$y_1 = 33.850$	$e_2 - x_2 = 1.498$	$y_3 = -31.857$
$g_1 = 7.279$	$-y_2 = 1.132$	$g_3 = 0$
$b_1 = 5.730$	$g_2 = 0.366$	$b_3 = 0$
$B_1 = 3.541$	$b_2 = 0$	
$D_1 = 6.380$		
	Prices	
$p_1 = 1.000$	$p_2 = 22.080$	$p_3 = 0.000$
$q_1 = 1.000$	$q_2 = 22.988$	$q_3 = 0.098$
	Ad Valorem Tax Rates (percentage; absolute value)	
0	4	100.00
	Welfare Gain (percentage)[a]	
	$\Delta = 29.880$	

[a] The compensating variation in consumption (Δ) is defined implicitly by

$$\alpha \ln x_1^* + (1 - \alpha)\ln x_2^* = \alpha \ln\left[\bar{x}_1\left(1 + \frac{\Delta}{100}\right)\right] + (1 - \alpha)\ln\bar{x}_2$$

where an asterisk (*) refers to the optimal allocation and a bar (–) refers to the actual allocation.

is relatively light and the tax on labor income and consumption is relatively heavy in the actual equilibrium which encourages overconsumption of leisure. Accordingly, the corresponding household's indifference curve at point B must be flatter than the corresponding indifference curve at point A. Evidently, this is consistent with the welfare ranking implied from the position of these indifference curves.

Indeed, the optimal tax structure calls for lowering the tax rate on labor income from 19.6% to 4%. The employment of labor in the business sector rises by 5.6% and net output in the business sector by 34%. The increase in the employment of labor in the business sector raises the labor–capital ratio, thereby reducing the pretax wage rate by 1.7% and increasing the return to capital by 1.8 percentage points. Private consumption (x_1) rises by 37%.

Finally, we use the estimated utility function to evaluate the welfare

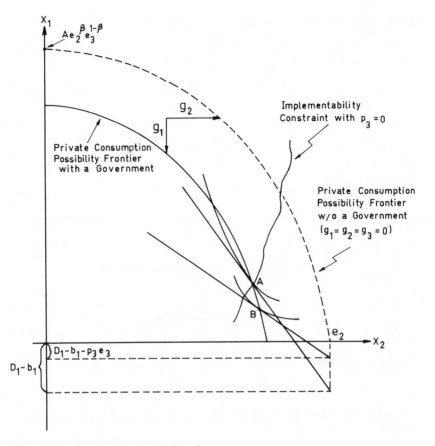

Figure 10.1: Actual and optimal allocations.

gain associated with the tax realignment. The gain is expressed in terms of compensating variation of consumption, that is, the percentage increase in 1990 consumption that could yield the same utility gain as the optimal allocation. The static welfare gain is large—about 30% of 1990 consumption.

10.3. The Economic Costs of Public Funds

When the government increases its expenditures by one dollar, and finances it, as it must, by distortionary taxes, it inflicts a cost on the private sector, exceeding the one dollar raised as taxes. That is, the economic cost of one dollar spent by the government is higher than one dollar. The difference is called the deadweight loss (or excess burden) of taxation. This loss or burden is due to the economic distortions caused by taxes.

Thus, when the government debates whether to spend one additional dollar on a certain public project (say, expanding the Jerusalem–Tel Aviv Highway) or to provide additional transfers, it must weigh the extra benefit derived from the additional outlays, not against the one dollar that the budget item nominally costs, but rather against the social cost of this one dollar, which is higher than one dollar. The economic costs of revenues financed by taxes are the cost of public funds.

In our economy, with variable prices of the produced good and inputs, the economic costs of government expenditures differ according to whether the expenditures fall on the produced good or on labor.

Employing our stylized model of the Israeli economy developed in sections 10.1 and 10.2, we estimate that the marginal (incremental) economic cost of one dollar spent on the produced good is $1.26. Similarly, the marginal economic cost of one dollar spent on hiring labor is $1.21. One can therefore state that the government must pay a marginal premium of about 26% when purchasing the produced good and a marginal premium of about 21% when hiring labor. Thus, for instance, a public project which costs one million dollars in terms of the produced good and one million dollars in direct wages is worthwhile only if it generates benefits in excess of $1.26 + $1.21 = $2.47 million.

We thus establish a key feature of our stylized model of the Israeli tax system. It provides a general-equilibrium-based estimate of the costs of public funds.

10.4. Optimal Tax Structure: Infinite Horizon

In the infinite-horizon model, capital income should not be viewed as a pure rent, calling for a tax rate of 100% as in the finite-horizon model. On the contrary, since heavy taxation of capital income discourages growth, the optimal tax rule typically calls for relatively light taxation. Indeed, in the steady state, capital income tax vanishes completely (see Lucas 1990; Razin and Sadka 1991).

A small open economy such as Israel's can take full advantage of its access to the world capital market in order to borrow (or lend) any amount needed to immediately close the gap between the desired and the actual capital stock, without adversely affecting its borrowing cost in the capital market. Thus, the optimal steady-state allocation can be reached within a relatively short time period.

Modifying the static tax rule structure from the previous section is quite straightforward. The resource constraint (10.19) must be adjusted to take account of the period-by-period debt service, incurred as the result of the increase in the capital stock.[5] Accordingly, the steady-state period-by-period resource constraint pertaining to good 1 is:

$$x_1 = y_1 + B_1 - g_1 - (k - e_3)(\rho^{-1} - 1), \tag{10.23}$$

where k denotes the steady state level of capital and ρ denotes the world's discount factor.

Substituting the labor-leisure resource constraint (10.20) and the production function (10.6) into (10.23) yields a single resource constraint:

$$x_1 = A(e_2 - x_2 - g_2)^\beta k^{1-\beta} - \delta k + B_1 - g_1 \\ - (k - e_3)(\rho^{-1} - 1). \tag{10.24}$$

A necessary condition for the existence of a steady-state optimal tax system in a small open economy is that the subjective discount factor of the representative household is equal to the world's discount factor. The optimal steady-state stock of capital is implicitly specified by equating the marginal product of capital (after depreciation) to the world's discount rate ($\rho^{-1} - 1$):

$$(1 - \beta)A(e_2 - g_2 - x_2)^\beta k^{-\beta} - \delta = \rho^{-1} - 1. \tag{10.25}$$

It therefore follows that the marginal product of capital (the pretax domestic interest rate) is equated to the household's subjective rate of discount (after-tax domestic interest rate) in the steady state. Thus, the optimal tax rule calls for zero tax on capital income.

With the subjective discount factor of the representative household being equal to the common world and domestic discount factor, the household does not save or dissave and maintains a constant stream of consumption bundles (x_1, x_2). The government essentially confiscates the household's *initial* stock of capital at the time the tax reform is put into place and from there on reduces the tax on *new* capital income to zero. Thus, the implementability constraint (10.16) now describes the steady-state, period-by-period, *intratemporal* implementability constraint. (Note that the *intertemporal* implementability constraint is embedded in the intratemporal implementability constraint which states

5. Note that it is implicitly assumed that in the steady state there is reinvestment of depreciation, since the production function describes output net of depreciation.

Table 10.6 Infinite-Horizon Optimal Allocation

Consumption Good	Labor-Leisure	Capital Services
	Quantities	
$e_1 = 0$	$e_2 = 2.984$	$e_3 = 31.857$
$x_1 = 30.968$	$x_2 = 1.487$	$x_3 = 0$
$y_1 = 31.153$	$e_2 - x_2 = 1.497$	$k = 66.060$
$g_1 = 7.279$	$-y_2 = 1.131$	$g_3 = 0$
$b_1 = 5.730$	$g_2 = 0.366$	$b_3 = 0$
$B_1 = 3.541$	$b_2 = 0$	
$D_1 = 6.380$		
	Prices	
$p_1 = 1.000$	$p_2 = 21.589$	$p_3 = 0.03$
$q_1 = 1.000$	$q_2 = 25.743$	$q_3 = 0.03$
	Tax Rates (percentage; absolute value)	
0	16.1	0
	Welfare Gain (percentage)[a]	
	$\Delta = 27$	

[a] The compensating variation in consumption (Δ) is defined implicitly by

$$\alpha \ln x_1^{**} + (1 - \alpha)\ln x_2^{**} = \alpha \ln\left[\bar{x}_1\left(1 + \frac{\Delta}{100}\right)\right] + (1 - \alpha)\ln \bar{x}_2$$

where a double asterisk (**) refers to the optimal allocation and a bar (–) refers to the actual allocation.

that the household spends his entire income and does not save at each point in time.)

The government finances its constant **g** via the interest on the confiscated initial stock of capital and the temporal labor and consumption taxes. We assume that the subjective discount rate and the world *real* rate of interest are both 3% per annum.

Table 10.6 reports the optimal allocation, obtained as a solution to the set of the steady-state equations: the implementability constraint (10.16), the resource constraint (10.24), and the marginal productivity condition (10.25). The corresponding prices and tax rates are reported as well.

Due to the world's low rate of interest, relative to the initial domestic rate of interest (= marginal product of capital), there is a large inflow of capital from abroad. The steady-state stock of capital is about double the initial stock of capital. However, due to the low level of the capital elasticity of output $(1 - \beta = 0.155)$, this influx raises output in the business sector by only 23%. The size of the welfare gain is large: 27% compensating-variations gain in consumption, compared to the 1990 allocation.

11

Israel and the World Market

Israel has never been an economic enclave, isolated by trade barriers from the rest of the world. Its volume of trade has always been remarkably high. The government's heavy involvement in Israel's external economic relations was not intended as much to constrain the volume of trade as to control its composition among different categories of goods and services (e.g., capital goods and raw materials vs. luxury goods) and between the trade account and the capital account. Over the forty-five years since its birth, Israel has gradually, although with many ups and downs, undergone a process of liberalization both on the trade side and on the capital side. The highlights of this process have been the two agreements with the European Community and the United States, allowing essentially free trade between Israel and each one of these two giant economies. Further, a unilateral process of liberalizing trade with the rest of the world is currently under way. Similarly, and this is discussed in the next chapter, significant deregulations of international capital movements have started.

Israel's high level of economic openness has contributed greatly to its rapid development. Protectionism in Israel nowadays is passé. Even in the wake of a massive *aliya,* and an extremely high unemployment rate, there has been no reversal of the liberalization process.

11.1. Volume of Trade

From its very inception, the Israeli economy relied on and benefited from international trade. Israel's volume of trade is described in table

Table 11.1 Volume of Trade, Selected Years

| | Civilian Imports | | Exports | |
| | Total (billion current $) | As a Percentage of GDP | Total (billion current $) | As a Percentage of GDP |
Year				
1980	12.6	62	10.4	51
1985	13.4	59	11.2	49
1990	22.6	44	19.0	37

Source: Central Bureau of Statistics (1991*b*).

11.1. Civilian imports in 1990 amount to about $22.6 billion or 44% of GDP. Exports in 1990 were about $19 billion, or 37% of GDP. The shares of imports and exports in GDP were even higher in 1980 (62% and 51%, respectively). The calculated shares of imports and exports in GDP are obviously highly sensitive to the real exchange rate, or over time to the gap between the change in the nominal exchange rate and the excess of the domestic inflation rate over the world's inflation rate. There is no doubt that a major portion of the decline in the calculated shares of imports and exports in GDP during the 1980s stems from the real appreciation of the sheqel. In fact, the cumulative real rates of growth of imports and exports over the last decade were 59% and 58%, respectively, while real GDP grew by only 39%. Thus, the volume of trade as a percentage of GDP, measured in constant relative prices, grew significantly over the last decade.

Israel's openness is remarkable compared to other countries. Table 11.2 shows that the share of imports in GDP, a standard measure of openness, is higher in Israel than in most other countries. The exceptions are small European countries (Belgium, Ireland, the Netherlands) whose openness to the other EC members, in particular, is facilitated by the low transport costs and the borderless feature of the EC market. The openness of the European Community vis-à-vis the rest of the world is significantly lower than that of Israel.

The European Community is the largest trade partner in terms of the origin of Israel's imports and the destination of its exports. Table 11.3 shows that almost 50% of Israel's imports of goods in 1990 originated from the European Community. Similarly, the destination of about 35% of Israel's exports in that year was the European Community. Israel's

Table 11.2 Imports of Goods and Services as a
Percentage of GDP in Selected
Countries, 1987

Country	
Belgium	75.6
Ireland	60.0
Netherlands	59.3
Denmark	36.7
Germany	28.5
United Kingdom	28.2
France	25.0
Italy	23.5
EC12[a]	12.3
United States	10.1
Japan	11.4
Israel	50.4

Source: European Commission (1987).
[a] Imports of the twelve EC countries from sources outside the European
  Community.

total volume of trade with Europe is significantly larger than the volume
of trade with the European Community only. Thus, trade between Israel
and European Free Trade Association (EFTA) countries accounts for
11.5% of Israel's imports and 4.1% of its exports.

The United States is Israel's second largest trade partner. As shown
in table 11.3 Israel's imports from and exports to the United States are
about 17.8% and 28.8% of GDP, respectively.

Table 11.3 Israeli Imports and Exports of Goods by Origin and
Destination, 1990

Country	Civilian Imports (percentage of total)	Exports (percentage of total)
European Community	49.3	35.3
European Free Trade Association (EFTA)	11.5	4.1
United States	17.8	28.8
Other	21.4	31.8
Total	100.0	100.0

Source: Central Bureau of Statistics (1991c).

11.2. Integration into the World Economy

Israel's large volume of trade with the European Community prompted and at the same time was facilitated by the trade agreement between Israel and the then European Common Market (see appendix 11.1 for a brief overview of the single market in Europe). Following partial trade agreements which dated back to the 1960s, in 1975 Israel became an associate member of the European Community. A mutual process of total tariff phase-out for all manufactured products was completed in 1989. Currently, there are reduced tariff rates on agricultural products but still no concession for government procurements. Services (including capital services) are not yet covered by the trade agreement.

Many countries around the world, particularly the United States and Japan, are worried that the European union of 1992 may lead to a "Fortress Europe."[1] That is, they fear that, by increasing trade within the European Community, the union will reduce its trade with the rest of the world at the same time. In a scenario such as this, a united Europe will impose customs barriers and nontariff restrictions against nonmember states subject to the GATT constraints.

Israel, however, already has trade agreements with the European Community. Therefore it should not fear such a scenario. On the contrary, it is possible to identify three factors which could actually be to Israel's advantage. First, the new European standardization arrangements specify that a product which fulfills the standards of any community member will be regarded as fulfilling the standards of every other member. The EC countries have effectively regularized domestic standards by converging to the standards of the country which has the least stringent requirements. This will therefore improve Israeli exporters' opportunities for penetrating the markets of those countries which currently have the strictest standards. Although Israeli manufacturers will be faced with more intense competition from other EC member nations, multinational Israeli companies in Europe will be able to expand their activities in order to increase their competitiveness. Second, increased competition within the European Community, together with the exploitation of economies of scale, will to some extent, lower prices and improve the quality of goods. As Israel's imports from Europe are greater than its exports there, it will benefit from any fall in prices and

---

1. The recent difficulties in trade negotiations in the Uruguay Round, which revolve around European agricultural subsidy policies, are a concrete reminder of the trade barriers between Europe and the rest of the world.

improvement in quality of European goods. Third, the new procurement arrangements for the public sectors of EC countries will provide companies inside the community with easier access to these sectors in other member countries. If Israel manages to reciprocate in this respect, the public sectors of the EC member states will be open to Israeli manufacturers.

In contrast with its favorable arrangements for trade in goods, Israel has no special agreements with the European Community regarding capital movements and financial services. The spectre of Fortress Europe is therefore more real in this area, unless Israel increases the pace and scope of liberalization in its capital market.

Two principles have been emphasized in the discussions held within the European Community on its relations with other countries in the field of capital transactions. The first principle is that of reciprocity, whereby a financial institution from a nonmember country will only be able to operate in the European Community if that country adopts regulatory and administrative procedures identical to those accepted in the community. That is, a country outside the European Community that wishes to act on the principle of reciprocity will have to accept the liberal policy that is to be implemented within the EC's capital market.[2] For example, an individual or corporation outside the community wishing to partially or fully purchase a bank within the European Community will be able to do so only if his home country abolishes all restrictions on the maximum controlling share of banks which Europeans can purchase in that country. In another example, banking institutions in a nonmember country will be allowed to provide banking services within the European Community only if the nonmember country in question adopts the same capital adequacy rules for foreign banks as those followed in the community.[3]

The second principle is that of nondiscrimination between community residents (or corporations) and residents (or corporations) from a nonmember country. This principle is less stringent in its implications than the first one, since it does not require parity of regulatory and administrative procedures in the European Community and nonmember states. For instance, with respect to the subject of capital adequacy, under the principle of nondiscrimination a nonmember state cannot require from

2. It is noteworthy that Israel has a very liberal policy regarding licensing of foreign banks.
3. As is known, every bank is required to maintain a minimum ratio between its net worth and its total liabilities—the "capital adequacy ratio."

European banks a capital adequacy ratio which is different from that maintained by local banks. The nondiscrimination principle does, however, allow the country in question to prescribe a capital adequacy ratio for its local banks which differs from that existing in the European Community.

There is currently uncertainty over which of the two principles will apply in practice, and the question may be resolved in future, separate negotiations between each state or bloc of states (EFTA nations, e.g.). Should the principle of reciprocity be adopted to cover financial dealings between Israel and EC countries, Israel will have to remove its restrictions on foreign currency transactions and on investments by Israelis in Europe.

A free trade agreement (FTA) was signed in 1985 between the United States and Israel. Import tariffs and nontariff barriers and export subsidies, direct or indirect (e.g., via concessionary loans), are to be eliminated by January 1, 1995. Again, services are left out. Some mutual concessions were granted on government procurements.

Initially, the trade agreements with the European Community and the United States prompted a protectionist policy toward third countries (Japan, the new industrialized countries in South-East Asia and Latin America). Consequently, a considerable amount of trade was diverted away from these countries. Rough estimates for 1992 (by the Finance Ministry) put the share of imports from third countries out of total Israeli imports at about one-third to one-fifth of the average import share of other countries from these third countries. This low level of trade between Israel and third countries is partly due to the Arab boycott and the relatively high transport costs. But there is no doubt that Israel's protectionist policy has contributed to such trade diversion against these countries.

In 1991, the government decided to pursue a policy of unilateral exposure toward third countries. Accordingly, nontariff barriers will first be converted into tariffs and then all tariffs will gradually be reduced. At the same time the Arab boycott is losing its effectiveness. As a result, Israel's volume of trade with third countries is likely to increase in the 1990s.[4]

---

4. For instance, Mitsubishi, Honda, Toyota, Mazda, and Nissan Motors are starting to sell cars in Israel. In the last decade, only Subaru, Daihatsu, and Suzuki were selling cars in Israel, capturing a sizable share of the market.

Table 11.4 Import Duties, 1990

Commodity Group	Taxes (percentage)			Percentage of Total Imports
	Tariffs	Excises	Total	
Consumer nondurables	7.6	14.7	22.3	5.6
Consumer durables	5.5	63.8	69.3	4.9
Inputs and raw materials	2.2	2.0	4.2	74.9
Investment goods	3.3	15.1	18.4	14.5
Weighted average	2.8	7.6	10.4	

Source: Central Bureau of Statistics (1991c).

Indeed, as table 11.4 indicates the average tariff rate was already quite low in 1990, only 2.8%. However, this rate is an average rate over imports from all countries, of which the tariff-free imports from the European Community and the United States compose almost 70% (table 11.3). It is also an average over imports of all commodities. On certain consumer goods (such as sport shoes) the tariff rate is as high as 65% when they are imported from third countries. Furthermore, there are quite stiff excise taxes on commodities that are not produced domestically, so that these excises are equivalent to tariffs. For instance, the average excise tax rate on imported consumer durables was 63.8% in 1990 (table 11.4). Indeed, excise tax revenues from imported commodities amount to about 50% of total excise tax revenues (excluding VAT).

In summation, the average rate of import duties (tariffs and excises) in 1990 was fairly high, about 10.4%. Of course, a reduction of the excises is not a part of the trade agreements with the United States and the European Community, nor is such a reduction included in the policy of unilateral removal of trade barriers against imports from the rest of the world. Thus, one should expect the high import-based excise taxes to persist, and to lessen the scope of trade with the rest of the world.

APPENDIX 11.1 The European Community, 1957–92

The European Common Market (now known as the Single Market of the European Community) was established in 1957 with the signing of the Treaty of Rome by its six founding member states: France, the Federal Republic of Germany, Italy, and the three Benelux countries—Belgium, the Netherlands, and Luxembourg. The Treaty of Rome states that the European Community aims at creating a united bloc of borderless states, with free movement of goods and services and of labor and capital. In practice, however, the common market, which began operating in 1964, was a free trade area only for goods. In other words, tariffs on goods moving between member states were removed, while customs barriers on other countries' products remained.

European Community economic policy centered on agriculture, a sector that was traditionally highly protected and heavily subsidized in all of the member states. One of the main goals of the economic policy of the European Community was to design a common structure of protection against foreign agricultural products and to create a unified and subsidized internal market for production. Table 11.5 shows the gap between the high prices current in the European Community's agricultural sector and those prevailing worldwide. The high prices were paid by the consumers, and the agricultural surpluses generated as a result were purchased by the European governments. Expenses of purchasing agricultural surpluses were shared out among member states by a prior agreement. Table 11.5 provides an indication of the size of these surpluses. For instance, the price of milk in common market countries was almost five times higher than in neighboring countries. As a result of this protectionism in favor of local agricultural production, a 16% surplus of supply over demand was generated and purchased by the member countries' government (which subsequently apportioned the cost among them).

Despite the removal of customs duties on goods moving between member states, the free movement of goods was hindered by the extensive use of nontariff barriers, such as licensing and domestic standards. In addition, severe

Table 11.5 Agricultural Prices and Surpluses in the European Community, 1976–80

Product	Ratio of Domestic Supply over Domestic Demand	Ratio of EC Price over World Price (before tariffs)
Milk	4.76	1.16
Butter	1.43	1.16
Wheat	1.07–1.40	1.11
Meat	1.61	1.00
Sugar	2.04	1.19

Sugar: Giavazzi and Giovannini (1988).

restrictions remained on foreign exchange, capital movements, and imports and exports of financial services.

Since the Treaty of Rome was signed, the number of the community's member states has doubled. Britain, Denmark, and Ireland joined in 1972 and were later followed by Greece, Portugal, and Spain. Currently, the applications for membership by Austria and Sweden are being reviewed by the European Community. As mentioned earlier, the Treaty of Rome contained the seeds of a more complete European union, embracing a coordinated, joint macroeconomic policy and including an exchange rate policy. Following the expiration of the Bretton Woods arrangement of 1944, which specified fixed exchange rates among the industrialized nations, the Snake arrangement was established in 1975 among the common market countries.[5] This arrangement maintained the exchange rates among the member states within a fairly narrow range, and allowed them to fluctuate together, like a snake, relative to other world currencies. In other words, exchange rates were stable among the market's member states but flexible with respect to other currencies. The Snake arrangement did not last long, due mainly to lack of coordination in monetary policy.

In 1979, a more stable arrangement known as the European Monetary System was established. The new arrangement is still effective and is based on the same principles as its predecessor, but provides increased monetary coordination between member countries. Under this arrangement, until the summer 1992 currency crisis, each member country's exchange rate was allowed to fluctuate within a range of their common exchange rate with other outside currencies (the range is of ±2.25% for the member states' currencies, except for Portugal, Spain, and the United Kingdom which enjoyed the greater flexibility of ±6%). The common exchange rate was flexible with respect to other currencies such as the U.S. dollar and the Japanese yen. From time to time, the exchange rates of the member states were realigned according to a joint agreement. Twelve such adjustments had been made, a recent one being on January 4, 1990, when the Italian lira was devalued against the European Currency Unit (ECU) by 3.75%. Realignments were usually due to the disparity in the rates of growth of different countries' monetary aggregates. In recent years it seemed that both the growth rates of monetary aggregates and the domestic inflation rates of the different member states had converged, thus strengthening somewhat the stability of the monetary arrangement. However, in the summer of 1992, following the German unification, the effects of the wide interest rate differentials between the deutsche mark and the other European currencies were too strong to sustain the currency arrangement then existing in the EMS. As a result, Italy and the United Kingdom dropped out of

5. The Bretton Woods agreement expired in 1973.

the system temporarily, and the Spanish and Irish currencies underwent a devaluation.

In June 1985, the leaders of the EC countries issued a White Paper on Completing the Internal Market, which had been prepared by the European Commission. The White Paper contained some 300 specific recommendations (directives) for policy changes, which were intended to lead to the full economic union of the community nations by 1992. The recommendations center on three main areas: (1) the abolition of restrictions on the movement of capital between member states (liberalization of the capital market), (2) the abolition of restrictions on the import and export of financial services (such as banking and insurance services) between member states, and (3) the removal of the last remaining obstacles (mainly nontariff barriers such as domestic standards) to the free trade of goods between member states.[6] The white paper led to the passing of the Single European Act in 1987 as an amendment to the Treaty of Rome of 1957. Most of the white paper's recommendations have been endorsed by the Council of Ministers of the European Community and have become law.

Three types of trade barriers are being either phased-out completely or drastically weakened. They are: (1) physical barriers, such as customs inspections at border posts and the large amount of paperwork involved when crossing them, (2) technical barriers, such as varying standards in different countries, different commercial practices (e.g., different banking laws, including different liquidity requirements), and discrimination in favor of local manufacturers in public sector procurement (particularly in the case of government defense procurement), and (3) fiscal barriers, such as different rates of VAT and other sales taxes, these disparities in rates were drastically reduced.

In December, 1991, a new treaty was signed in the Dutch town of Maastricht, further strengthening the Treaty of Rome. The Treaty of Maastricht covered mostly social and monetary issues. It was agreed on an irreversible passage to a European Monetary Union (EMU) no later than 1999, with only the United Kingdom preserving an opt-out privilege. The unification procedures will begin in 1996. At that time, a qualified majority of the member states will decide on the conversion criteria that will allow member states to join the single currency (ECU) union. These criteria refer to the inflation rate, the long-term interest on government bonds, the rate of budget deficit out of GDP and the rate of public debt out of GDP—all in reference to the lowest rate that will exist in the European Community. The criteria would be set such that at least seven countries will qualify to join the union.

---

6. Many countries use domestic standards as a nontariff barrier for protecting domestic production. E.g., a standard can be specified for a product which is different from that which is accepted worldwide, thereby effectively allowing only a local manufacturer to supply the product in question in the local market.

The future of the Maastricht treaty on closer European political and economic integration has not yet been assured. The first Danish referendum rejected the treaty, while the Irish and French referenda approved it, in France by a narrow margin. The United Kingdom has yet to confirm it, and British domestic opposition grows. The alternative of a two-speed track—whereby countries such as France, the Benelux nations, and Germany will form a single currency union, first, and the rest of the EC countries join later—seems a likely scenario.

12

Deregulation and Privatization

12.1. The Government as "Invisible Hand" and the Ongoing Liberalization Process

For years, the government's hand and foot were very much visible in the capital market. One can say, in a nutshell, that the government used to suck in private domestic savings. The funds so collected were used mainly to finance the deficit in the government's current budget and development budget. The remaining funds, together with other funds borrowed from abroad (either directly by the government or through heavily regulated private institutions), were allocated to the business sector for investment and to the household sector for owner-occupied residential investment. Since the stabilization program and its associated fiscal tightness, rapid liberalization has been taking place. Much freer financial markets have started to play their natural role as a meeting place between savers and investors.

12.1.1. The Government as "Invisible Hand"

The Israeli capital market was traditionally characterized by extremely heavy government involvement, both in the supply of and the demand for various types of credits, and in the comprehensive regulation of the market. This government involvement created a segmented market with numerous distortions. A succinct and accurate description of the market is provided by David Klein.[1] "In 1987, the cost of borrowing foreign currency by local residents in the domestic market was more than *twice*

---

1. David Klein is a senior executive, in charge of monetary policy, at the Bank of Israel.

the cost of borrowing abroad; the real cost of borrowing short-term domestic currency was more than *thrice* the cost of borrowing long-term domestic currency; and the rate paid by short-term domestic currency borrowers was almost *four* times the rate paid to domestic currency depositors." He then goes on to conclude that, "It is obvious that such a state of affairs is sustainable only through a massive administrative intervention by the authorities. No market would bear for long such huge interest rate differentials" (Klein 1991). Following these observations one may distinguish several main lines of segmentation created jointly by the Finance Ministry and the Bank of Israel:

(1) The government directly channeled long-term savings, and especially the institutional retirement savings (pension funds, provident funds, etc.), to its budget. Pension funds, provident and life-insurance funds, and advanced training funds, and the like were required to be invested in either higher-return nonnegotiable or lower-return negotiable government bonds. These bonds served to finance both the large deficit in the regular government budget and the entire government development budget. It should be noted that at the same time this policy also ensured safe returns to institutional savings. Similarly, medium- and long-term saving deposits at commercial banks were subject to very high reserve requirements, so that they were effectively channeled to the public sector (through the Bank of Israel).[2]

(2) The government was explicitly involved in directing investments of the business sector toward favored geographical locations (e.g., development areas) and types of industry (e.g., manufacturing and agriculture vs. other industries). The main mechanism employed was the commercial banks' reserve requirements. The Bank of Israel exempted from the reserve requirements certain fractions of long-term deposits in commercial banks if the funds were used by the commercial banks to extend credit to certain, preapproved (i.e., by the proper government ministries) investment projects of the business sector. These credits were called "loans from approved deposits."

(3) The world short-term capital market was open essentially only to exporters and importers and access to the world long-term capital market was severely restricted. First, the Bank of Israel directly extends short-term credit to exporters (the "directed credit"). Initially, it was a disguised subsidy to export, since part of the short-term credit was

2. In 1987 these reserve requirements were on average 63% on CPI-linked deposits and 84% on foreign-currency-linked deposits.

extended in nominal domestic currency terms at a nominal interest rate which was far below the inflation rate. Currently, this credit is foreign currency–linked and at the going world market rates, such as the Libor rate. It is noteworthy that this occurs while Israel still has exchange controls. Ordinary individuals and enterprises were not allowed to borrow directly from abroad, so that they were effectively taxed on their borrowing from abroad. Through the directed credit facility, exporters were thus allowed to borrow at rates comparable to those available to their competitors abroad. Similarly, exporters were allowed to invest their export proceeds for the short term in foreign capital markets (or in foreign currency–linked domestic accounts with commercial banks). Second, importers were effectively allowed to finance imports of business equipment via long-term credit abroad, provided that the interest rate did not exceed a set ceiling imposed by the Bank of Israel. Importers were also allowed to use short-term suppliers' credit. Third, long-term borrowing from abroad was allowed only for large corporations and required specific permits, which were sparsely allocated.

(4) The Bank of Israel completely barred short-term loans and deposits with commercial banks from being linked to the CPI, or to any other price index (such as real estate price indices) or to any foreign currency. The minimal term of deposit or loan required for such indexation was two-and-a-half years. This regulation essentially separated the unindexed (usually also the short-term) segment of the credit market from the indexed (exclusively long-term) segment of the credit market.

In addition, to fully grasp the scope of government involvement in the financial market, one has to understand the special circumstances caused by inflation. High inflation necessitates a clear and operational distinction between *nominal* returns and *real* returns for tax purposes (see also chap. 9). The Israeli tax system, like any other system, is in general nominal. Interest is taxed, in principle, on a nominal basis. There are specific ad hoc provisions exempting many financial instruments from tax on the inflationary return component. But these provisions are incomprehensive and asset-specific. For instance, suppose a firm considers issuing bonds to the public. As explained in chapter 9, the firm will be allowed to deduct only the *real* component of the interest rate from its taxes. However, the household—the ultimate bond buyer—is liable to pay tax on the *nominal* interest, unless there is a specific provision exempting that particular bond issue from tax on the inflationary component of the interest. Since there does exist a specific provision exempting the inflationary component of the interest paid on bank deposits, the household prefers to lend the money to the firm through commercial banks. Therefore, the firm will be unable to borrow directly from the household sector (namely, to issue bonds to the public) without first obtaining a specific tax relief provision (i.e., a tax exemption for the inflationary component of the interest and a reduced tax rate for the real component). Thus, in effect, every bond offer to the public by the nonfinancial sector requires prior approval by the Finance Ministry and the Finance Committee of the Knesset (the Israeli parliament).[3] (As a contrast, imagine IBM requiring the approval of the U.S. Congress before issuing new bonds!) Similarly, the main reason for the absence in Israel of a market for nonfinancial firms' commercial paper is that tax-exempt status (for inflationary returns) has not been granted. This, of course, is advantageous to the banking industry. Likewise, if the government wants to allow Israeli residents to invest abroad, it will also have to issue specific tax-exempt provisions for the inflationary return (in domestic currency) on foreign financial assets. Otherwise, foreign assets will be dominated by tax-exempt domestic assets. This is currently the case. Evidently, the interaction between inflation and taxation provides the government and the Knesset with additional power to play in the domestic financial market.

As a consequence of such "invisible" manipulations by the government, most financial savings were directed into the government's hands. One part of these funds was used to finance the budget deficit, while the rest was directed to specific types of investments and to exports. Thus, the capital needed by firms in order to invest and expand was raised, in practice, by the government. Moreover, the net worth of firms was mostly derived from financial profits that resulted from large subsidies embodied in the government-granted credit. The little capital, if any, that the nonfinancial business sector raised directly from the public through the security exchange was obtained by exploiting waves of speculation, and not through a mechanism that would accurately assess the value of a firm and its investments. The residual capital of firms that was not raised from the government (or to a very limited extent from the security market) came mostly from the banking system. The banks in turn raised the funds for these loans from tax-exempted (on the inflationary interest component) indexed deposits made by the public and from share capital raised by them in the stock market.

The mechanisms through which banks raised their share capital was

3. Obviously, such approvals were routinely granted.

by far the greatest scandal in Israel's financial history. The banks, enjoying significant market power, "regulated" the price of their own shares. They used various schemes in order to ensure persistent demand (e.g., bank subsidiaries posting demand for parent companies' shares) for their own shares, thus regulating their price in a persistently upward direction. It should be made clear that this process was by no means a covert operation of the bank executives. Rather, it was done with the full knowledge (though not always with the explicit consent) of the government, the Knesset, and the Bank of Israel. Occasionally, the authorities even approved of the process. For instance, when a sales tax was imposed on transactions in the security market in 1982, the finance ministry requested, and the Knesset Finance Committee granted, reduced tax rates for transactions associated with the banking share regulation process. The regulation resulted in an average appreciation of the value of the banks' shares at a rate of 30%–40% per annum in real terms. After a few years of such share regulation, banks' shares were grossly overvalued, much above the banks' economic value. As had to be eventually the case, at a crucial moment the prices of bank shares collapsed abruptly. This occurred in October 1983 when expectations for devaluation of the sheqel (after a long period of devaluation slowdowns that resulted in a real appreciation of the sheqel) abruptly shifted the public's demand from bank shares to foreign-currency-linked assets, and the banks lacked the funds needed to continue to support the prices of their own shares.

At this point the government caved in to the pressure of the banks' shareholders (including the banks themselves which indirectly held sizable amounts of their own shares) and bailed them out. The government set a floor on the prices of the bank shares by obliging itself to purchase all the outstanding shares at a predetermined schedule of appreciating dollar prices over a period of six years. Since the guaranteed prices were above what would otherwise have been unfettered market prices, the government indeed was forced to buy and hold the bank shares. However, the regulated shares that the government obtained had almost no voting rights, even though they constituted almost 100% of the banks' equity. In a later move, the government, by brute force sweetened with some nominal compensation, procured for itself the voting rights from the original holders of the voting shares. However, this transfer of voting rights was, in practice, deferred to October 1993. By that time, if the government does not sell the bank shares it holds, the banking industry will be effectively nationalized.

In the early 1980s, arrangements existing on the capital market began to collapse; the government's development budget was curtailed substantially; the so-called Hevrat Ha'ovdim Scheme, whereby it was permitted to invest about half of all pension-funds deposits in the manufacturing sector, was stopped completely.[4] The government budget deficit increased and the public's readiness to buy government bonds fell from lack of confidence in the government's ability to honor its escalating liabilities. The government ceased to be a net supplier of funds in the capital market (i.e., the total amount of new loans granted to the business sector was less than the total amount of repayments of old loans). The cessation of bank share regulation in October 1983 and the non-banking shares crash in January 1983 had the effect of closing the security exchange as a source of capital for the business sector. At the same time, the government would not permit capital to be freely raised from abroad as an alternative to raising capital from internal sources. At this point, the need for a major reform was self-evident!

12.1.2. Recent Developments: The Process of Deregulation

The private sector's sources of finance changed radically after the July 1985 stabilization program. Indeed, the implementation of this comprehensive economic program resulted in a balanced budget for the government, which stopped being a net borrower on the capital market.[5] At the same time, a process of capital market reform began. The reform's main goal was to reduce the level of government involvement in financial intermediation and to rid the market of excessive regulations. The government began to permit the transfer of funds from savings schemes to private-sector borrowers, either directly or indirectly through nongovernment intermediaries (such as commercial banks). See appendix 12.1 for recommendations by a team of experts for major structural changes following the current reform measures.

The reform's main components were the following: (1) greater freedom on the part of private-sector firms to issue securities on the security exchange without government authorization and greater freedom in the choice of investments by institutional investors. The potential inherent in this move has not yet been fully exploited, (2) a reduction in the government's direct or indirect financing of investments. Nevertheless, investment financing by issuing shares or debt is still modest compared

---

4. Hevrat Ha'ovdim is the holding company of the Histadrut-owned enterprises.
5. This position was reversed again with the new wave of *aliya*.

with other countries, though it has sharply increased during the last year, and (3) some relaxation of the supervision of international capital movements. Nevertheless, substantial controls over these capital movements, particularly in the area of short-term transactions and capital exports (investment abroad) still have to be removed.

More specifically, the reserve requirements on both time and demand deposits were sharply reduced. The reserve requirement on unindexed deposits was reduced from 31.4% in 1987 to 8.7% in 1990 (see Klein 1991). Similarly, the reserve requirement on long-term saving accounts was reduced from about 83%–100% on most indexed accounts in 1983 to 50% in 1990 (see table 12.1). Naturally, these changes act to reduce the debitory interest rate and to increase the creditory interest rate since the interest paid by the Bank of Israel on liquid reserves is typically very low. The policy objective of the Bank of Israel is to further reduce the reserve ratios to what are termed by the Bank of Israel as "business ratios." These are defined as roughly the ratios that would be called for by prudent banking practices; the Bank of Israel believes that these should be about 7%–10% on most deposits.

The mandatory minimum rate of investment in government (mostly

Table 12.1 Institutional and Other Long-Term Savings: Mandatory Investment in Government Securities and Reserve Requirements (percentage)

Minimum	Indexed Time Deposits	Dollar-linked Saving Accounts	CPI-linked Saving Accounts	Pension Funds	Provident Funds	Advanced Training Funds
1983						
Mandatory	15	100	83	92	92	92
1987						
Mandatory	15	85	55	92	78	78
Actual	15	85	57	92	85	88
1990						
Mandatory	5[a]	50[b]	50[b]	92	50	50
Actual	—	—	—	97	81	81
Share in total assets (December 1990)	4.6	8.3	17.8	23.9	39.8	6.3

Source: Bank of Israel (1991c).

[a] In 1991 the mandatory minimum was abolished.

[b] This rate is scheduled to fall gradually to zero, starting in 1993. The rate on unindexed deposits will be maintained at 4%.

nonnegotiable) securities imposed on institutional investors (pension and provident funds, advanced training funds) was reduced from 92% in 1983 to a range of 50%–92% in 1990, with further reductions in 1991 and 1992, and still more to be implemented later. Since the interest paid on the nonnegotiable government securities held by the pension funds was fairly high, the new minimum requirements were not constraining for them (see table 12.1).

Furthermore, the granting of authorization for the issue of bonds and other (short-term) commercial papers by nonfinancial firms became very liberal. (Recall that such authorization was needed mostly to achieve parity in the tax treatment of inflationary interest between government bonds, bank deposits, and corporate bonds.) The minimum term required for granting CPI-indexation on credits or deposits was reduced from two-and-a-half years to one year. The minimum term required for granting foreign currency–indexation on credits or deposits was recently abolished. The minimum term of two-and-a-half years for obtaining foreign loans and the ceiling of 2.5 percentage points above the Libor rate on the interest were gradually removed altogether.[6] Israeli residents (businesses or individuals) are now free to borrow from abroad.

As a result, the sources of funds and the investment opportunities available for the private sector changed drastically. Table 12.2 shows the sharp decline in the share of outstanding government securities (gross public debt) in the total stock of financial assets held by the public. This share fell from 83% in 1985 to 65% in 1990. (As a percentage of GNP, the shares fell from 136% in 1985 to 94% in 1990.) Similarly, table 12.3 shows a sharp decline of the government's role as a direct or indirect supplier of loans to the nonfinancial private sector. While 57.6% of the stock of all loans to the private sector were supplied either directly by the government or under its directives in 1987, only 29.7% of this stock was so supplied in 1990. Furthermore the sheqel is now perfectly convertible for foreigners, that is, foreigners and foreign residents can manage their financial portfolios both in foreign and local currency, and reconvert their capital and earnings to foreign currency (as long as the assets were originally bought with foreign currency). However, the major source of capital for the nonfinancial private sector is still loans from the banking sector. As indicated by table 12.4, the

---

6. Libor (the London Interbank Offered Rate) is the interest rate at which prime banks offer dollar-denominated deposits to other private banks in London. This rate is often used as a basis for pricing Eurocurrency loans (a loan provided outside the home country of the currency).

Table 12.2 Domestic Public Debt, 1985–90

Year	Percentage of Total Financial Assets of Private Sector	Percentage of GNP
1985	83	136
1986	75	125
1987	74	106
1988	73	98
1989	65	98
1990	65	94

Source: Bank of Israel (1991c).

Table 12.3 The Nonfinancial Private Sector:[a] Composition of Outstanding Loans

	Total	Directed[b]	From Approved Deposits[c]	Unregulated[d]
1987[e]				
Total (billion 1990 $)	22.4	4.4	8.5	9.5
Percentage	100	19.6	38.0	42.4
1990[e]				
Total (billion 1990 $)	32.3	1.0	8.6	22.7
Percentage	100	3.1	26.6	70.3

Source: Klein (1991).
[a] Including households.
[b] Export and equipment import financing.
[c] Loans for government preapproved project from deposits exempted from reserve requirements.
[d] Loans from funds raised from the public by commercial banks (e.g., demand and time deposits, savings accounts) without government involvement.
[e] End-of-year figures.

net issues of securities by the corporate nonfinancial sector in the Tel Aviv Stock Exchange is negligible and often negative. But the last year has witnessed a sharp increase in the issuance of new shares.

The deregulation of the financial markets has already started to show an effect. The differentials between borrowing and lending rates and between foreign and foreign-currency-linked domestic rates have narrowed remarkably. For instance, figure 12.1 shows that the differential between average borrowing and lending rates in the unindexed banking

Table 12.4 Issues of Securities on the Tel Aviv Stock Exchange, 1986–90 (million current $)

| Year | Private Bonds | | Net Shares | Total |
	Gross	Net		
1986	427	−192	88	−104
1987	655	−89	217	128
1988	638	−210	108	−102
1989	456	−401	362	−39
1990	542	−433	359	−74

Source: Bank of Israel (1991c).

segment has shrunk by about one-half in the last five years. Similarly, figure 12.2 shows that the gap between the domestic interest rate on dollar-linked credit and the Libor rate has shrunk by about two-thirds.

It is noteworthy that large and established Israeli corporations manage to issue securities (mostly shares) on foreign security markets. The gross market value of the Israeli corporations whose shares are traded on the New York Stock Exchange constitutes about 36% of the gross total market value of publicly held Israeli nonfinancial corporations.[7]

Capital export, though somewhat liberalized in recent years, is still heavily regulated. Direct foreign investment by Israeli corporations was, until recently, subject to strict licensing. Equity and portfolio investments by corporations and by households were not generally permitted until 1991. More recently, households were allowed to make such investment only if channeled through Israeli mutual funds and banks. Other investments abroad, such as real estate, bank deposits, and so forth are still not allowed. Firms, in addition to investing as do households through mutual funds and banks, are currently also allowed to make direct foreign investments of up to 40% of their equity.

It should be noted that the controls on both imports and exports of capital were a part of the broader policy of exchange rate management. Since its establishment Israel has adopted a policy of a more or less administered exchange rate. In the 1970s, with inflation starting to pick up, this policy took the form of crawling peg. It became a bit more flexible during the high inflation period. With the stabilization program

7. As of January 31, 1992, the market value of shares of Israeli corporations traded on the New York Stock Exchange was $5.5 billion, whereas the market value of nonfinancial corporations traded on the Tel Aviv Stock Exchange was $15.2 billion.

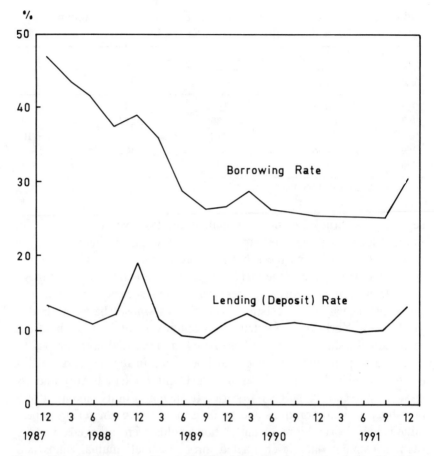

Figure 12.1: Average borrowing and lending (deposit) rates in the unindexed banking segment (percent per year).

of July 1985, the exchange rate was fixed with respect to the dollar and then in 1986 with respect to a basket of currencies with a few discrete realignments. In 1989, a 3% band was introduced, allowing the exchange rate to fluctuate by ±3% around the set mid-band rate, thus introducing some flexibility in the exchange rate. In 1990, the band was widened to 5%. Finally, in December 1991, the mid-band rate was no longer constant but rather adjusts daily at a 9% rate in annual terms (the so-called diagonal band). In principle this most recent refinement allows the exchange rate to be set by the market forces, but in practice the central bank intervenes daily in a determinant manner. Thus, the central bank still pegs the nominal exchange rate.

When the administered exchange rate is inconsistent with fundamentals underlying the financial markets, free mobility of capital undermines the government's control over domestic monetary aggregates and the domestic rate of interest (see also Part II). Thus, Israel employed, over the years, strict controls over exports and imports of capital. It follows that the deregulation of the capital market must be intertwined with restructuring the exchange rate regime.

With the prospect of freer movement of international capital, these intertwined problems of capital market liberalization and exchange rate management become central. If monetary policy is to concentrate its efforts on reducing the inflation rate, it cannot be involved in the day-to-day determination of the exchange rate because it loses control over the monetary aggregates. This is not to say that the central bank cannot

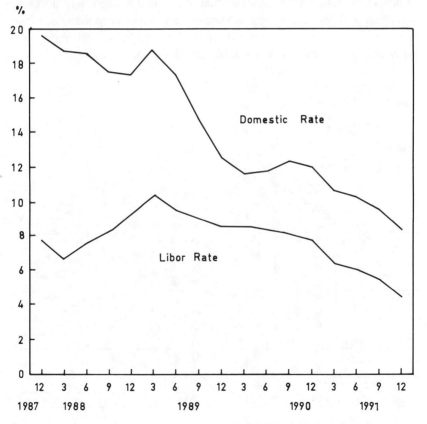

Figure 12.2: Average interest rate on domestic dollar-linked credit and Libor rate (percent per year).

intervene frequently in the foreign exchange market, but it should not do so daily and with the aim of determining the exchange rate as is the case even now with the present policy of the "diagonal band." The central bank now has appropriate instruments to conduct a monetary policy that can focus on reducing inflation through a preannounced path of the monetary aggregates. Monetary aggregates could be controlled either directly (e.g., through money auctions) or indirectly (e.g., through interest rate targeting).

12.2. Privatization

12.2.1. The Slow Pace of Privatization

State ownership of business-type corporations is pervasive in Israel. This is the case to a certain extent in many similar OECD countries as well. Indeed, figure 12.3 indicates that the United States is a remarkable exception with its extremely low state-ownership of corporations, while in many other countries (e.g., Austria, France, Italy, and West Germany) the government owns sizable chunks of major industries.

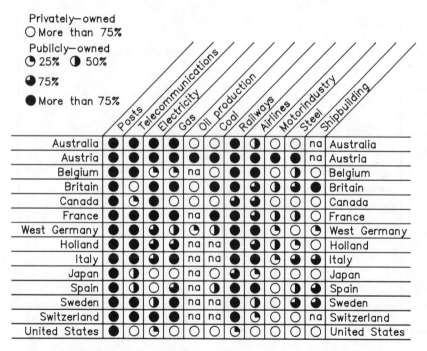

Figure 12.3: State ownership in OECD Countries.
Source: American Express (1986).

Because a government company does not have to operate according to criteria of profitability and can absorb losses by transferring them to the government, it is unlikely to operate efficiently. In addition, many government companies enjoy monopoly status, due either to the nature of their activity or to a government decision. Accordingly, the quantity and the quality of the goods or services which they provide are even more likely to be suboptimal. All these factors explain the recently heightened public interest in the privatization of the Israeli economy. Privatization is not unique to Israel and forms the basis of the economic policy of many countries in Western Europe, the Far East, and Latin America.

There certainly exist instances in which one can establish an economic case for government involvement in the provision and/or production of services, for instance, when there is a need for very large infrastructure investment, leading to economies of scale and the creation of a natural monopoly. In such a case, the government may acquire ownership of the monopoly in order to prevent a small group of interests from exploiting their monopolistic power at the expense of consumers. Examples are the supply of electricity and telephone services. But even in these cases, it might be preferable to regulate a private industry (e.g., by imposing rate ceilings which simultaneously ensure normal profits and provide incentives for efficiency) rather than to nationalize the industry.

Another area in which government involvement may be warranted is in the production and provision of health care. International comparisons do not unambiguously support private over public health care systems or vice versa. Existing private systems (such as in the United States) tend to provide excessive and overpriced services while public systems are more often characterized by overcrowded facilities.

Nevertheless, in Israel there are many government companies, or public companies which are partly owned by the government, whose activities and target markets, on the face of them, seem no different from those of any other privately owned firm (Israel Aircraft Industries or Israel Oil Refineries, e.g.). There are also cases in which the government has granted a monopoly to companies it owns, although these are not necessarily natural monopolies (El Al Israel Airlines, e.g.). Elsewhere, the government has established companies to exploit natural resources belonging to the state, even when there appears to be no reason why a private company should not be sold a license to exploit these resources (e.g., Israel Chemicals).

Table 12.5 State-owned Companies: Net Worth, Percentage of State
Ownership, and Employment, December 1990

Type of Company	Net Worth[a] (million 1990 $)	Percentage of State Ownership	Employment	
			Total	As Percentage of Total Business Sector Employment
Non-metallic minerals	642	100.0	4,276	0.4
Water and electricity	2,295	96.4	13,446	1.28
Research and servicing for manufacturing and commerce	480	48.2	667	
Transportation and communications	1,135	88.2	17,780	1.69
Oil and gas	568	82.8	1,981	0.19
Military industry	676	98.0	32,607	3.09
Agricultural R&D	17	91.4	1,117	
Housing and construction	86	95.5	1,235	
Servicing for the tourism industry	22	100.0	237	
Other	49	69.0	1,866	0.18
Total	5,970	90.2	75,212	7.14

Source: Israel Government Corporations Authority (1991).
[a] Adjusted for inflation for most companies; for a few exceptions, the net worth is adjusted by the dollar–sheqel exchange rate.

Table 12.5 describes the net worth (adjusted for inflation) and employment of state-owned companies by type (excluding municipal companies). There are about 75,000 people employed in these companies, over 7% of all employees in the business sector. Total net worth is about $6 billion which amounts to about 10% of the public debt.[8] We should point out that the purpose of privatization is not to alleviate the burden of the public debt (because the net public debt is not affected at all by privatization). Rather, the ultimate objective of privatization is to improve efficiency.

8. Incidentally, this figure suggests that the burden of the public debt is not exceptional by international standards, because it is backed, to a large extent, by the government's ownership of business firms and assets (such as land, water, etc.). The market value of the major state-owned companies is even higher than their book value (adjusted for inflation), for instance, Israel Chemicals Company is traded on the Tel Aviv Stock Exchange (as of February 1992) at a price that is about twice its book value.

Bearing in mind the efficiency criterion, it is imperative for a successful privatization process to start with a comprehensive restructuring of the would-be privatized firm and the industry in which it operates. The cost and investment structure of the government company in question and the market structure in which it operates must be analyzed in order to determine whether the company is a natural monopoly or whether competitive market conditions should prevail. This analysis will determine whether the company should be sold as a single package, or whether it should be split up into several companies, all or some of which will be sold in order to compete with each other. It is important to note that the overall benefit to the economy and the government's interest in obtaining the highest price from the sale of the companies are likely to imply very different sorts of packaging. Specifically, while granting monopoly power to a privatized firm would increase the government's financial gain, economic efficiency would suffer unless the company constitutes a natural monopoly.

When a natural monopoly supplying public utilities is concerned, it will first be necessary to define a pricing policy, the types and quantities of services to be provided, their supply availability and their regional distribution. In this context, the government should formulate a policy for subsidizing the services provided and for investment, and decide on the extent of the subsidy (if it is regarded as necessary for the natural monopoly) and its source of finance.

Table 12.6 demonstrates the slow pace of the privatization process. Out of the $5.4 billion of inflation-adjusted *book value* of state-owned companies (90% of $6 billion), only $150 million of *market value* was sold in 1991. (Recall that the market value is typically higher than the

Table 12.6 Sale of State-owned Companies to the Public, 1986–91

Year	Proceeds from Sale of Shares (million current $)
1986	125
1987	79
1988	498
1989	451
1990	246
1991[a]	149

Source: Israel Government Corporations Authority (1991).
[a] First eight months only.

inflation-adjusted book value.) In fact, up to now, one can single out only one major company (Paz Oil) which was fully privatized, and that was done before a restructuring of the oil industry was even conceived (a reform was implemented later). Thus, the price of the shares was necessarily determined in an arbitrary fashion. In 1990–91, the state telecommunication company (Bezek) was partly sold to the public, with the government still maintaining control. In February 1992, 19% of the equity of Israel Chemicals was sold to the Israeli public. Currently, a sizable portion of the remaining shares is being prepared for public issue on the NYSE, but still with the government maintaining over 50% of the equity. Israel Chemicals is a giant conglomerate estimated to be worth about $1.2–$1.5 billion. This offering of its shares may indicate some acceleration in the slow pace of the privatization process so far.

12.2.2. Nationalization of the Banking Industry?

The issue of government ownership of commercial firms became even more acute after the bank shares crisis of October 1983. As a result of its handling of this crisis and its aftermath (see section 12.1), the government is now the major shareholder of the four largest banking groups in Israel (Bank Hapoalim, Bank Leumi Le Israel, Israel Discount Bank, and United Mizrachi Bank). There is now only one major commercial bank (First International Bank) which remains in private hands. The assets of the four seminationalized banks account for about 95% of the total assets of commercial banks in Israel. Their total inflation-adjusted net worth was $3.5 billion at the end of 1990, over 90% of all net worth of commercial banks in Israel (see table 12.7). These banks are also major shareholders in nonbanking corporations (such as Clal

Table 12.7 Net Worth and Total Assets of the Banking Industry, December 1990 (million June 1991 $)

Banking Group	Net Worth[a]	Total Assets[a]
Bank Hapoalim	1,205	33,529
Bank Leumi Le Israel	1,340	28,393
Israel Discount Bank	709	15,576
United Mizrahi Bank	251	7,493
First International Bank	302	3,807
Total	3,807	88,798

Source: Financial statements of the above banks.
[a] Adjusted for inflation until 6/91.

Ltd.). So far, the government has committed itself to not exercising its voting rights until October 1993 (so that the previous holders of voting rights still control these banks). But, if the government does not sell its shares or otherwise extend the waiver of its voting rights, it will have full control over the four largest banks in Israel. In such an event the banking industry in Israel will be virtually nationalized.

The cost structure in the banking industry and its level of concentration complicate the process of its reprivatization. It can be safely assumed that the banking system exhibits economies of scale which could make a high level of concentration consistent with economic efficiency. For example, when a large business enterprise seeks a loan from a particular bank, the bank in question has to check its creditworthiness and keep track of its current business activities and long-term plans (investments). If the same loan request were to be divided between two different banks, both of them would have to follow the same procedures. In such a case, each bank would incur approximately the same operating expenses. Accordingly, subdividing the loan could double the intermediation costs, resulting in higher financial margins and commission fees. Other cited examples of economies of scale are in the area of computer services, international interbank relations, debt crisis management, and so forth. To the best of our knowledge, an in-depth study of economies of scale cum industrial structure of the banking industry in Israel has not been done.

A related question is the value of the would-be privatized banks. This value cannot be meaningfully determined without first resolving several critical policy questions: (1) the market structure of the banking system, that is, the number of banks which will be operating in the industry and their size; (2) the Bank of Israel's supervision and regulation policy on commission fees, financial margins, and required reserve ratios. These factors have been frequently revised (during the capital market reform) and final targets should be announced prior to any sale of the banks; and (3) the degree of government participation in support of various debt-ridden enterprises and organizations.

The qualifications required of a bank's controlling shareholders have not yet been defined in Israel. (Informally, however, some very restrictive criteria have been proposed by the Examiner of Banks.) Under U.S. Federal Reserve Bank regulations, for instance, a commercial firm may not have a controlling share in a commercial bank or share a roof with one in a holding company. It is feared that in such a case a bank might grant credit to a sister or parent commercial firm at conditions which do not reflect that firm's level of risk (creditworthiness). This commercial firm–commercial bank restriction does not exist in Europe. Under EC policy guidelines that are currently taking shape, large foreign investors (from outside the European Community) will be permitted to hold controlling shares in large banks only if the principle of reciprocity is maintained, that is, non-EC residents will be allowed to purchase bank shares in an EC-member country if and only if their own country allows EC residents to hold shares in its banks. The Israeli government's position and that of the Bank of Israel regarding foreign ownership of large Israeli banks is not clear. The Bank of Israel must approve any individual or company acquiring interest (over 10% of the equity) in a commercial bank. It seems that the Bank of Israel, as do the central banks in many other countries, will not approve a potential buyer of bank shares (over 10%), if it cannot show that the funds used for the purchase came from its own sources (i.e., not leveraged sources). Even more restrictive than this, at some point the Examiner of Banks informally suggested that to qualify as a buyer, the candidate must show evidence of having a net worth three times larger than its proposed investment in the bank. Given the large size of the three largest banks, it is doubtful that many Israeli residents (individuals or firms) could qualify as purchasers under this condition.[9]

Unfortunately, because of the great political power associated with holding strong the banks' controlling shares, alongside genuine difficulties in the process of privatization, we fear that government ownership of the banks is likely to continue for quite some time.

Appendices 12.1–12.4:

Recommendations by a Team of Experts

These appendices contain recommendations of the team consisting of Dan Bavly, David Klein, Nadine Trajtenberg, Efraim Sadka, Emanuel Sharon, and the late Eitan Berglas. The team was coordinated by Assaf Razin at the Israeli Democracy Institute, Jerusalem, November 1992.

We focus on four specific areas of reforms, for which we review the situation today and recommend steps for improvement. First, we examine the deregulation of the money market as embarked upon by the Bank of Israel and the Ministry of Finance, including the further opening of the Israeli market to international competition. We also touch on the conduct and goals of monetary

---

9. Institutional investors (e.g., pension funds) could raise adequate funds to purchase the banks. However, whether such a move is desirable, or what restructuring may be needed by the institutional investment sector for such a move, requires further serious and comprehensive study.

policy itself. Second, we suggest reforms of the tax structure pertaining to long-term savings instruments, which today is plagued by differential treatments and damaging distortions of economic incentives. Third, we focus on the actuarial imbalance of the pension system and the consequent need for reform, a problem faced by many Western countries in the past decade. Finally, we concentrate on the role to be played by the pension and provident funds in furthering the privatization program undertaken by the government, with an afterword on foreign investment in Israel.

APPENDIX 12.1 Reforms in the Money Market since 1985

In this appendix, we expand and elaborate on the discussion of money-market reforms in section 12.1.2. We discuss the impact of these reforms and make predictions and recommendations for the future.

A12.1.1 Deregulation

The implementation of deregulation has been gradual, following a preannounced path. This approach has thus been reassuring and credible at the same time. Deregulation was concentrated on the following five elements:

Cancellation of quantitative restrictions on credit. The ceilings on foreign-currency credit available through the banks has been abolished. This limit resulted in very high interest rates for the end-users who faced rates of up to Libor plus 13%. Directed credit arrangements (mostly for exporters) have also been cancelled. Similarly the quantitative restrictions on foreign-currency-denominated financial guarantees were also terminated.

Gradual reduction of the reserve requirement ratios. The reserve requirement ratios were extremely high (up to 100% for some long-term savings accounts in 1987), and the Bank of Israel embarked on a schedule of gradual reduction encompassing both unindexed (short-term) and indexed (medium- and long-term) deposits. The stated aim of the central bank is to reach "business level" reserve requirement ratios (i.e., levels that truly reflect the minimum required for sound business operations—approximately 5% to 8% depending on the type of deposits). The average reserve ratio on unindexed deposits has fallen from 31.4% in 1987 to 6.9% at the end of 1991. Similarly the average reserve ratio on deposits indexed to the CPI has dropped from 83% in 1987 to 60.6% at the end of 1991, and the corresponding ratio for deposits indexed to the exchange rate has decreased from 84% to 57.1% over the same period. The reserve ratio for long-term new savings schemes has fallen to 30% in 1992 and dropped to zero in January 1993. The 90% reserve requirement ratio on restitution deposits (in foreign currency) started falling by 1% per month, as of December 1991. The goal is to reach a normal level, from 4% to 8%, following this gradual process. This would stretch over a period of eight years.

Freeing institutional investors' portfolio. After the mandatory minimum rate of investment in government securities required of institutional investors was reduced to the 50%–92% range in 1990, it was dropped further to 50% during 1991. While the government stopped issuing high-interest-bearing securities for provident funds in 1985,[10] this practice continued for pension funds until now. After an agreement was reached with the Histadrut, the real interest rate on these securities was reduced from 6.2% to 5.5% in 1991.

In addition, the issuing of bonds by nonfinancial firms was greatly facilitated by the repealing of the required authorization from the Israeli parliament for tax parity with government bonds. Without this tax-parity, the interest income from corporate bonds were effectively taxed at a much higher rate than that from government bonds.

Liberalization of bank fees. Between 1981 and 1988 fees for different bank services had to be approved by the Bank of Israel. Moreover, their real value was significantly eroded during the hyperinflation period, and as a result bank fees did not reflect in any way the true cost involved in providing these services. Most bank fees have now been freed from supervision, and commercial banks are now left to determine the appropriate level for those fees according to economic and competitive considerations. There are still some fees under the supervision of the central bank, such as the service charges on demand deposits, checkbook orders, transfers of stocks from one account to another, and transfers of foreign currency from one bank to another. These fees are adjusted quarterly according to formulas incorporating both price and wage changes.

Elimination of time limits for indexed loans and deposits. In its effort to fight inflation, the central bank once imposed a minimum term for indexed loans and deposits. These minimum terms have been gradually lifted, and by the beginning of 1992 they were entirely removed for all loans and almost removed for deposits indexed to the CPI or to foreign currency. Hence the artificial segmentation between indexed and unindexed loans and deposits has almost vanished.

A12.1.2 Liberalization of Foreign Currency Restrictions

As of May 1992, almost all the remaining foreign-currency restrictions pertain to the movement of capital and not to flows related to trade of goods or services. In addition to making the sheqel convertible for foreigners, the most

---

10. Note that the interest borne by these special nonnegotiable securities was not always above market rates, which were particularly high after the 1985 stabilization program.

recent changes introduced in November 1991 allow banks to give sheqel loans to foreigners, against collateral in foreign currency.

These steps were important and may uncover an important source of future capital inflow. Indeed, a lot of large institutional investors, particularly in the United States, are seeking to diversify their portfolios by investing 1%–2% of their assets in different countries. (When Italy liberalized its capital market in 1990, it benefited from an important inflow of foreign capital and, by 1991, approximately 10% of all new issues of government bonds were held by foreigners.) In addition, foreign-currency deposits in Israel now held by foreigners are important, and with the fall in interest rates, these investors will be looking for higher-interest-bearing assets.

Israeli firms are now authorized to place 40% of their equity in direct investment abroad, up from 20%. Israeli citizens are now allowed to deposit in foreign-currency accounts funds or earnings earned or transferred from abroad. The implementation is now possible after the income tax commission's ruling on the taxing of capital income of individuals that makes appreciation due to exchange rate changes tax-exempt. Individuals are not allowed to convert domestic currency into these foreign-currency deposits. Israeli citizens are, however, now allowed to invest in securities and mutual funds abroad, through banks, brokerage houses, and domestic mutual funds.

A12.1.3 New Instruments

The Bank of Israel has introduced new financial instruments to further its monetary policy, such as money auctions to banks and the public and such risk-reducing instruments as futures and options on foreign currency and treasury bills.

Futures and options. Since 1989 the Bank of Israel has offered options to purchase dollars (three month and twelve month call options) and futures contracts to purchase treasury bills from the public. Starting in March 1991, the bank offered to the public futures contracts to sell treasury bills. In order for this market to develop, a number of tax changes were legislated. The lack of such legislation is one of the reasons the market did not develop on its own, aside from the fact that it is often too thin a market (i.e., there are not enough players on both sides). In fact, often in Israel, all the players were on one side only, but now the Bank of Israel is stepping in, filling the void.

Monetary auctions. The Bank of Israel has canceled "the basic interest rate" at which it used to offer a quota of discount window loans. Instead, it relies on monthly, weekly, and now daily monetary auctions to banks and to the public to determine the interest rate. In that sense the direct instrument of monetary policy is now similar to that used in the United States, Germany, France, and Italy, whereby the central bank's day-to-day operations center not on outright open market operations but on the selling and buying of money, taking government securities as collateral. This tool has proved to be a good one for controlling the money stock and, to a lesser extent, for setting interest rates. Thus the Bank of Israel no longer sets the interest rates administratively as it used to.

Exchange rate policy. The third instrument of monetary policy is the exchange rate, administered in the manner described in the latter part of section 12.1.2.

12.1.4 Impact of the Reforms

Looking at table 12.8, we can see that the amount of directed credit by the government has substantially been reduced, and the share of "free" credit has gone up from 45% in 1987 to 72.8% by the end of 1991. The earmarked deposits (*pamela* in Hebrew) include government mortgages, arrangements for the *kibbutzim,* and all government guaranteed loans.

Note: Table 12.8 is not an accurate picture of the reduction of government intervention, because there are some free loans for which the government is ultimately responsible and there are some *pamela* for which the government does not take responsibility. Though this complicates the picture, it is important to emphasize that it is when the government takes responsibility for a loan that it intervenes and not only when it officially channels the loan to sectors, individuals, or firms.

The average reserve requirement ratio has fallen significantly since 1987, as can be seen in table 12.9.

A12.1.5 Considerations for the Future and Recommendations

Macroeconomic stability. The most important consideration when envisaging future reforms is general macroeconomic stability in Israel. All of the

Table 12.8 Distribution of Commercial Bank Credit Available to Israeli Residents

Extent of Government Intervention	1987[a]		1991[a]	
	Total (billion NIS)	Percentage	Total (billion NIS)	Percentage
Free credit[b]	15.7	45	59.3	72.8
Directed credit	3.0	8.7	0.3	0.4
Earmarked deposits	16.1	46.3	21.9	26.8
Total	34.8	100	81.4	100

[a] End-of-year figures.
[b] Subject to no government intervention.

Table 12.9 Average Reserve Ratios on Bank Deposits Available to
Israeli Residents

Type of Indexation	1987[a]		1991[a]	
	Total (billion NIS)	Average Reserve Ratio	Total (billion NIS)	Average Reserve Ratio
Unindexed	9.6	31.4	22.6	6.9
Indexed to CPI	15.9	63.0	34.7	60.6
Indexed to exchange rate or foreign currency	14.3	84.0	25.9	57.1
Total	39.8	62.9	83.2	44.9

[a] End-of-year figures.

reforms achieved are in principle reversible, and few would have been possible without the relative economic stability seen since 1985. For instance, the 1977 liberalization program was entirely counteracted by the hyperinflation and recurrent balance of payment problems of the 1977–84 period. Similarly, the foreign-currency restrictions could be quickly reinstated if the country were to face balance of payment problems in the future.

Although such concern with stability is always appropriate, it is particularly so today because the challenge to integrate the large wave of immigration might not be met, and a lack of control of the government budget could seriously destabilize the economy. Thus, further progress in reforming the capital market might be hindered by the macroeconomic environment, and worse, changes in this environment might even endanger the reforms undertaken during these past few years. There are two, not unrelated, elements of the macroeconomic environment that are central in this context, the inflation rate and the size of the government debt (domestic and foreign).

The size of the government debt, and not only the size of the annual budget deficit, is an obstacle to further deregulation of the capital market. The credibility of deregulation policies requires a commitment to reduce the gross public debt, and not just to contain government deficits. To recall, the public debt now amounts to approximately 125% of GDP. In comparison, under the Maastricht treaty of December 1991, the European countries that will be allowed to participate in the single currency starting in 1996 will have to show a public debt no higher than 60% of GDP.

Hence our first recommendation should be to adopt a commitment to reduce the public debt burden (as a percentage of GDP) following a preannounced path and reaching eventually the Maastricht goal of 60% at the end of the decade.

Further deregulation and liberalization steps. Despite the caveat mentioned above, today, compulsory investment in government bonds by institutional investors can be reduced.

The mandatory minimum investment in government securities required of institutional investors should be gradually eliminated.

The Ministry of Finance may worry about such a move, despite the fact that for the moment many provident funds hold more government securities than their required minimum because of the attractive interest rate of such securities. Yet, if this is done gradually, those fears should be attenuated.

There are three areas for further liberalization of foreign-currency restrictions: advance payments for imports, firms' investment abroad, and limits on individual access to foreign currency and foreign assets.

Restrictions on advanced payment for imports before their arrival should be reduced.

Today such payments are limited to $50,000 which severely constrains importers. It is true that complete freedom will considerably increase the speed and potential of capital flight, but rules should not be set as if every day is a potential day of reckoning. In fact, the relative stability of the macroeconomic environment has diminished notably the number of "days of reckoning" during these past few years. Moreover, there are costs to advanced payments so that one should trust the importers to choose rationality not to systematically pay ahead of time if no large devaluations are expected. This again brings us back to exchange rate management and macroeconomic stability. Nevertheless, the present exchange rate policy of the diagonal band combined with the availability of options for foreign currency greatly reduces the potential for flight capital through the mechanism of advanced payment.

Restrictions on the proportion of its capital that a firm can invest abroad should be relaxed.

A firm's foreign direct investment is limited to 40% of its own capital. The tax revenue authorities fear that liberalizing this limit would encourage tax planning and thus shrink the tax base. At present the rules are that the tax liability of a firm depends on realization (i.e., profits from subsidiaries that are not directly controlled and managed from Israel are not liable to tax until they are repatriated, while profits from, say, a branch are directly tax-liable). Hence, if firms are allowed to purchase foreign firms or to establish subsidiaries, this could erode the tax base.

We recommend that the tax code be based on the residence (personal) principle and not on the source (territorial) principle.

We should point out that if Israel is to integrate into world markets, it might not be possible to keep more widely diverging tax rates than found abroad, because it will cause huge outflows of capital. This point has been an important obstacle to a more rapid monetary union in Europe and it is still a point of contention.

Restrictions on individual access to foreign-currency assets should be gradually reduced though not eliminated.

Individuals are still prohibited from investing in real estate abroad, from holding bank deposits in foreign currency here or abroad, and from directly purchasing foreign currency. Investing in foreign stock markets and mutual funds is now allowed through domestic banks, brokerage firms, and mutual funds. Gains (over and above the exchange rate changes) are taxed at the uniform 35%.

On this issue two diverging views are reasonable. The first view suggests that the near complete liberalization of the foreign-currency market is a goal that can be reached relatively rapidly. This view stresses that a credible promise of continued liberalization and of the cancellation of foreign-currency restrictions may itself repatriate funds now held abroad (as happened recently in Argentina and Mexico). Thus perhaps the most important point in this respect is that the liberalization process is contingent on the policy to be credible. As a first step, the approach to foreign-currency access must be changed from "everything is forbidden unless it is specifically permitted" to "everything is allowed unless it is specifically forbidden." Economic considerations dominate firms' behavior—this is perhaps less so for households—and these should be free to operate uninhibited. This implies that the last restrictions to be lifted should be those on the access of individuals to the purchase of foreign currency and foreign bank deposits, as has been the case in the recent European experience.

The diverging view states that the far reaching implications of a complete liberalization must be thoroughly investigated before taking any steps down this avenue. Indeed, there are reasons for not liberalizing entirely the access to foreign currency, or at least to justify a gradual process. First, the special security situation of Israel can cause panic outflows of capital in times of political or military tensions. Second, the general economic environment, particularly with respect to taxes, may not allow Israel to compete on an international basis for funds. This is particularly so as the security situation of Israel, combined with the challenge of integrating the wave of immigrants, will probably not allow Israel to reduce substantially its tax burden in the near future.

Conduct of monetary policy. With the prospect of more liberalized movement of international capital flows, the intertwined problems of higher inflation and exchange rate management become central. If monetary policy is to concentrate its efforts on reducing the inflation rate, it cannot be involved in the day-to-day determination of the exchange rate because it may lose control over the monetary aggregates.

The central bank should not be involved in the daily determination of the exchange rate.

This is not to say that the central bank should not intervene at all in the foreign exchange market, but it should not do so daily and with the aim of determining the exchange rate. This is so even with the present policy of the diagonal band.

The central bank should focus on reducing the inflation rate, through a preannounced path of monetary aggregates.

The central bank now has appropriate instruments to conduct such a monetary policy, although there is a debate as to the effectiveness of its policy with the present gap between debitory and creditory short-term interest rates.[11]

APPENDIX 12.2 Tax Reforms in the Capital Market

One possible objective of the tax reform could be to align the tax base with one of two benchmarks: the comprehensive income tax, according to which all sources of income (earned and unearned) are taxed equally, or the consumption tax, which completely exempts saving from tax. We recommend a middle road between a consumption tax and an income tax, mainly by deferring the tax on long-term savings.

All countries encourage long-term savings through various tax exemptions and deductions, and many solid arguments exist to justify such intervention in the capital market. First, such intervention corrects the bias against saving that is implied by the personal income tax (double taxation of savings). Second, a progressive income tax structure really wants to be progressive with respect to the standard of living, not so much with respect to income per se. Clearly,

---

11. There is considerable disagreement about the relevance of any comparison between very short term debitory and creditory interest rates. The Bank of Israel states that the large differential between creditory and debitory rates on short-term assets (such as the difference between the rate paid on time deposits and the rate charged on loans) does not allow it to conduct effective monetary policy. Commercial banks, however, claim that the Bank of Israel focuses unduly on this differential interest rate. They point to similar differentials abroad—between rates on credit cards and rates on demand deposits—and state that monetary authorities abroad are not concerned by these.

consumption is a better approximation to the standard of living than income, and thus it should be the appropriate object of taxation. In such a case, all savings ought to be entirely tax-deductible, and the proceeds and principal ought to be taxed only when withdrawn. Third, it is generally believed that many people do not save sufficient amounts for retirement purposes and that they should therefore be encouraged to save for the long term. Fourth, a progressive tax structure does not treat equally individuals with the same life-time income but with different patterns of income fluctuation. Since consumption expenditures are smoother than income, they allow for a fairer and smoother tax burden.

However, most countries impose a ceiling on tax relief for savings for reasons of social fairness. Indeed, the skewed distribution of sources of income combined with complete tax deductibility of all unearned income would make the tax structure a regressive one.

In Israel the existing practice is extremely complicated and "is the result of a patchwork of ad-hoc legislation passed over the years" (Swary and Yochman 1991). We basically endorse the recommendations for reforms of a committee of experts (1988), which are the following:

> **Unify the rules under which contributions to savings schemes may be made (level playing field), in order to encourage greater deregulation and innovation in financial markets and to reduce the segmentation of these markets.**

> **Exempt all contributions made toward retirement benefits (mostly pension and provident funds) at the point of creation and at the points of accumulation of interest, and to subject the entire sum (principal and interest) to ordinary income tax at the point of withdrawal. The exemption should apply to both the employee's and the employer's contributions.**

> **For earned incomes, an inclusive exemption (employees' and employers' payments) up to a certain fraction of income (about 20%) should apply. The exemption should be limited to an income of up to three or four times the average wage.**

> **Employees and the self-employed should be treated equally.**

To avoid compulsory individual filing for income tax purposes, which is costly to administer, a flat tax on unearned income, at the rate of 35%, is recommended.

> **Tax all sources of (real) income from capital at a flat rate of 35% at the individual level.**

APPENDIX 12.3 Retirement Savings: The Need for Reform

In Israel as elsewhere, saving for retirement takes different forms. An often used metaphor for describing a country's retirement income system is the three-legged stool. The first leg is the government provided pensions and welfare programs for the aged; the second is employer or labor union-provided pensions, and the third is direct individual savings. There is substantial variation, both across households and in different countries, in the mix of the three sources of retirement income (Bodie and Merton 1992). The Israeli National Insurance Institute constitutes the first leg of the stool, and it is a particularly short one. The second leg is made up of different pension systems, by far the largest being the government employee pension plan and the pension plan of the Histadrut. Finally, the most important private savings instruments include provident funds, executive endowment policies (in Hebrew, *bituah mena-halim*), life insurance policies, and severance pay schemes.

The areas that require reform concern (1) the lack of guarantees or insurance for pension plans, (2) the inappropriate supervision of the Histadrut pension schemes and their actuarial deficits, (3) the unfunded pension obligations of the public sector, and (4) the widely different tax treatment of the different savings instruments.

A12.3.1 Guarantees for Pension Plans

First let us stress the fact that the National Insurance Institute's role in providing retirement or disability benefits is relatively modest in proportion to total retirement benefits, and also when compared to other countries' social security programs. It is a system based on the principle of defined benefits, whereby the size of future payments is basically fixed (though indexed to the cost of living) and largely unrelated to past contributions. It is thus more an extension of the income tax's redistributive role than a pension scheme as such. Over the past few years, the government has repeatedly reduced the size of the contribution by employers without changing the stream of benefits, thus reinforcing the view that its role is one of redistribution and not of promoting long-term savings for retirement purposes. The redistributive role of the National Insurance Institute is emphasized by its providing, in addition to old-age benefits, a minimum guaranteed income for those who did not participate or did not accumulate sufficient benefits in any pension scheme. This is particularly important in Israel which has seen large waves of immigration, such as the recent one from the Commonwealth of Independent States.

Second, pension plans are very long term propositions, particularly given that the lives of individuals may be longer than that of the firm with which they placed their retirement savings. Because of the inherent risk involved in this enterprise, many countries provide government pension insurance of private sector defined-benefit pension plans, in addition to the implicit guarantee of benefits stemming from the social security schemes.[12] The United States has such insurance, even though in other respects it is notoriously frugal in the coverage of its social safety net.[13] To quote, "All private sector defined-benefit plan sponsors in the United States must participate in the federal program of pension insurance by paying premiums to the Pension Benefit Guaranty Corporation (PBCG). The PBCG was created . . . to guarantee only *basic retirement benefits*. There is therefore a ceiling on guaranteed benefits. . . . Germany and Japan also have government pension insurance schemes" (Bodie and Merton 1992).

Given the modest role of the National Insurance Institute and the intrinsic riskiness of pension plans, our first recommendation concerns the need for an explicit government guarantee.

The government must make explicit a pension insurance scheme for basic benefits (the amount of which have yet to be determined). For instance, it could be up to a ceiling equaling the maximum benefits to which an employee with thrice the average wage is entitled.

There is a controversy as to the actual implicit guarantee given by the government to holders of pension plans. In principle there is no legal guarantee signed by the government in any form. However the extensive government intervention in supervising the pension funds (it has changed the contributions of members, it has reduced the interest rate from 6.2% to 5.5% on earmarked government securities sold to the pension funds) signals that the government feels responsible for the promised stream of benefits. Moreover, the guarantee given to bank-share holders in 1983 makes it look improbable that the government would let pension funds go bankrupt and their members be left with little retirement savings.

In order to ensure that all individuals be covered by the guaranteed pension schemes, and in order to avoid moral hazard problems (i.e., individuals not contributing, and thus not paying a premium for the guarantee, but hoping that the government will bail them out if worse came to worse), our recommendation is:

Make compulsory participation in some government-insured pension scheme of the individual's choice.

12. For the same reason, some countries have their entire pension system in the government's hands, as is the case in Italy.

13. Major pension funds in the United States typically promise employees a fixed proportion of their salaries upon retirement. To meet this promise, they require employees to pay a fixed proportion of their wages into the scheme and employers to pay whatever more is needed. Thus, to a large extent, employees are shielded from poor investment earnings.

Let us recall that the government guarantee will be limited to a basic stream of benefits, thus insuring only a *minimum,* not all the benefits promised to individual members. This is particularly important given that the entire pension system in Israel has underfunded pension obligations (called an actuarial deficit, although some pension schemes are not funded at all, such as the public employees' pension which is a quasi-pay-as-you-go system since neither employees nor the public employer contribute on a regular basis). Quoting from the most recent National Comptroller Report: ''According to the data supplied by the pension funds on their actuarial balance, they stood in a state of actuarial deficit amounting to 21.3 billion NIS on 31.12.90'' (National Comptroller 1992, 3:80). (This figure does not include the unfunded obligations of the public sector.)

Making participation in government-insured pension schemes mandatory does not entail that the government will directly manage the funds or that it will simply extend its national insurance system. In fact, this ought to be avoided for two reasons: (1) as we have seen recently with national insurance, the government might arbitrarily change benefits from or contributions to the schemes for other than actuarial considerations, (2) in order to promote efficiency in the management of the funds, competition between funds must be encouraged.[14]

Choice in the pensions market should be greatly increased: a wider range of schemes, a wider range of pension providers, and a wider range of contribution rates. An increase in competition in the pension industry will discipline the relatively poor management of the existing funds and benefit their members.

> **Unify the income tax treatment of all retirement savings plans (pension and provident funds, executive insurance policies, severance pay schemes, etc.). See appendix 12.4.**

Provident funds, for instance, are basically used to supplement pension plans and are based on the defined-contribution principle. They should not be insured by the government, but they should be integrated with the pension schemes for tax purposes. Thus, contributions to pension and provident funds both should be exempt up to a ceiling (such as up to about 20% of wages, but then wages ought to be all-inclusive), but only the pension plan will have a guaranteed stream of basic benefits. At the time of retirement, individuals can choose to receive their benefits from the provident funds as a lifetime annuity (i.e., roll it over into their pension schemes) or to receive lump sum payments as is the case today.

---

14. Note that in order for competition to make sense, the members of pension schemes must participate in the profits made by such funds.

A12.3.2 Supervision of Pension Funds

In order to avoid excessive risk taking by managers of the pension funds covered by the government guarantee, their behavior must be closely monitored and the funds' actuarial balance maintained. This is important because the burden is on the government when the pension plans are in a state of actuarial deficit (i.e., when the expected present value of promised benefits is larger than the value of the assets in the funds).

The pension schemes must be self-correcting, in the sense that whenever the fund is in actuarial imbalance, it has rules by which it corrects the situation, for instance by adjusting contributions, benefits, age of retirement, and so forth. The pension plan of some commercial-bank employees in Israel has such a self-correcting mechanism, which takes into account the evolution of real wages, of the life expectancy of its members, and of the interest rate. Thus government supervision must be extensive, and the following recommendations are essential.

> **The government must supervise the actuarial balance of the guaranteed pension funds and regulate according to the promised benefits to set rules of appropriate investment management, rules for public disclosure on the situation of the funds, and rules to correct actuarial imbalance whenever necessary.**

The pension plan of the public sector employees is a defined-benefit system which suffers from imbalance. While we cannot speak of an actuarial deficit since the pension scheme is not funded, it suffers from a hangover due to the stream of liabilities it has incurred. The expected change in demographics will deepen the problem and require large future government deficits in order to fulfill its obligation to the pension plan members. Thus our first recommendation with respect to the public sector pension scheme is:

> **Switch from an unfunded pension system for public sector employees to a funded pension plan.**

This would require the accumulation of a fund, by instituting a compulsory contribution and providing benefits on the basis of past contributions. The United States did something analogous in 1983, when its social security system went to a funded system (note however that it covered the whole population while our recommendation applies to employees of the public sector only). Again actuarial balance must be maintained, and the respective ministries ought to be aware of the actuarial state of their own participation in the pension scheme.

> **Split the present public sector employee pension scheme into two portions: an insured pension plan and an uninsured provident**

**fund. This separation should also apply to the private pension
and provident fund systems.**

The insured pension plan portion and the provident fund do not both have
to be managed by the government, they can be left to the individuals to choose.
This, in effect, constitutes a privatization of the government pension scheme.
The experience of Chile is particularly relevant here, as this is exactly what
the Chilean government undertook in 1981 (Bodie and Merton 1992).

A12.3.3 Tax Treatment of Pension and Provident Funds

At present the tax treatment of different instruments for long-term savings
differs widely. Whenever there are lump sum withdrawals, as in the case
of most provident funds, the tax exemption is the most advantageous: the
contributions are tax-deductible, the yields are tax-exempt, and the benefits
are also exempt from tax. Pension benefits on the other hand are taxable,
although they benefit from a 35% tax deduction up to a certain ceiling.

All savings instruments that are basically for retirement purposes (i.e., paid
in annuity at retirement or after the death of the member) ought to be treated
uniformly for tax purposes. They include pension plans, provident funds, severance pay, executive insurance plans, and participating life insurance policies.
We suggest that the recommendations of a committee of experts (1988) be
adopted. (These recommendations were listed in appendix 12.2.) For convenience we briefly present again the basic principles:

> **Contribution to retirement saving schemes ought to be deductible
> up to a ceiling (say 20% of inclusive wages up to thrice the aver-
> age wage), independent of who is the contributor (employee, em-
> ployer, or self-employed).**

> **Accrued yields on these funds ought to be fully exempted, inde-
> pendent of where the funds have been invested.**

> **We recommend that benefits be taxed at a flat 35% income tax.**

In principle, benefits ought to be treated as ordinary income but this would
require compulsory individual income tax filing, which we do not recommend
at this stage. Thus, the basic tax rule for pension income should be the following: exempt contributions from tax, exempt the accumulated yields from tax,
and apply a flat 35% tax at withdrawal. Our recommendation is also to level
the playing field in the taxation of pensions, executive insurance, and participating life insurance policies.

APPENDIX 12.4 Role of Pension and Provident Funds in Privatization

The reformation of the pension system and of provident funds and privatization of state-owned enterprises are quite different matters, yet they can provide synergies and help solve each other's problems.

First, the focus is on the role of provident funds, and not so much on pension funds. Indeed, if pension funds are to be insured and thus regulated, the extent of their involvement in the stock market will be quite limited. Not so for the provident funds which can choose a much higher level of risk, and thus of expected returns, for its members.

Second, institutional investors are prudent investors who have a preference for well-established low-risk firms. Public utilities are obvious choices for them, whether in a competitive environment or in a state of regulated monopolies. A good many of the firms to be privatized are just those types of firms, such as Bezek (the telecommunication company), the electricity corporation, and so on. They would therefore make good candidates for privatization, attractive to institutional investors such as the provident funds. However, for this to be the case, the rules of the game by which they play must be made perfectly clear. That is, the extent of government involvement in the environment of these firms must be kept to a minimum (such as tariff regulation for monopolies or setting aside the part of the military industry that is deemed of national interest and leaving the rest to compete freely in the markets) and must be explicitly specified. No institutional investors, from here or from abroad, will participate in the privatization program before the economic, legal, and regulatory environment is made clear and clear of unnecessary government intervention. This is a necessary condition for the privatization program to continue and to truly take off.

If this condition is met, the role of provident funds can be important in two ways. First, institutional investors need assets with annual returns because they have payments to make and cannot afford to accumulate returns. Firms in Israel pay very little in annual returns, so that dividend payments are almost nonexistent. However, if our recommendation in appendix 12.2 is followed, the incentive to pay out dividends should be significantly strengthened. In order to make themselves attractive to institutional investors, firms will have to show more liquid assets and increase the distribution of their annual earnings. Newly privatized firms will probably show the way since their need to attract institutional investors is greater. Second, although institutional investors are prevented from taking control of firms (as elsewhere), they may be represented on the boards of directors of the companies to be privatized. Finally, the management of risk taking can be improved if the new financial instruments are used efficiently. For instance, to diversify risk, a domestic provident fund can make an equity swap arrangement with a foreign pension fund. If share prices in Israel perform better than abroad in a given year, then the Israeli fund will pay one-half of the differential to the foreign fund, and vice versa in a year in which foreign shares outperform the Israeli shares.

APPENDIX 12.5 Focus on Foreign Investment

The amount of foreign investment in Israel is quite limited when compared to the size of annual unilateral transfers (approximately $400 million compared to $5.8 billion in 1991). Most of the foreign investment is indirect investment (i.e., the purchase of financial assets), and very little direct investment has traditionally come from foreign sources. Most of the financial assets held by foreigners consists of foreign-currency deposits held in Israeli banks.

With the last stage of the money market reforms undertaken by the Bank of Israel and the Ministry of Finance, there are no restrictions left on foreign investment in Israel. It is believed that with the fall in interest rates, foreign investors will look for more attractive assets and will probably start diversifying their portfolios across liquid assets in sheqels, such as those offered by mutual funds.

A U.S. State Department study evaluated the reasons for the low level of foreign investment in Israel. It ranked the following reasons: (1) the security problem presented by the State of Israel was the principal obstacle to foreign investment, (2) a lack of credibility in government policies discouraged foreign investors, and (3) the extensive red tape involved when dealing with the Israeli government. Additional reasons may be that the size of the market in Israel does not warrant investment, which is why, for instance, there is a considerable amount of Japanese investment in Brazil but not in Israel (excluding for the moment the impact of the Arab boycott). The currency risk is not particularly large, particularly if one considers the developing hedging instruments such as futures and options.

The tax benefits given to direct foreign investors are very extensive, when one compares Israel to other countries. Foreign investment can get a grant for up to 40% of the investment, or alternatively enjoy tax exemption for 2–10 years depending on the geographical location of the investment and the extent of foreign control in the firm. Guarantees are also provided, and all the usual incentives provided by the "law for the encouragement of investment" are available to foreign investors. Clearly these benefits entail red tape, particularly as foreign firms have had the tendency to try to negotiate further benefits of all kinds. It is thus not surprising that they may have encountered more bureaucratic procedures than local Israeli firms or than they encounter elsewhere.

Such extensive benefits may paradoxically discourage some foreign investment as it may be taken as a signal that "there must be something wrong if so much benefits are available."

Epilogue

The *aliya* has already generated some growth of output. But so far, growth has been mainly confined to the housing industry and its associated manufacturing subindustries (e.g., steel, cement), and has not widely spread to other industries. This housing sector boom must soon subside.

At present, the most pressing problem for the Israeli economy and society is the record high level of unemployment. Several government measures taken to promote investment and create more jobs during the years 1990–92 have not proven adequate thus far. Among these measures are accelerated depreciation (up to 100% in the first year—full expensing), government loan guarantees and grants in substantial amounts for new investments, sizeable wage subsidies for new employees (not only *olim*), reduction of payroll taxes, and so forth. Perhaps, it is still too early to evaluate the full effectiveness of these measures as they have not yet run their course. Output did indeed rise, but unemployment is still very high and the stock of capital too low, relative to the size of the labor force. Furthermore, some of these measures, by generating low-yield investments, have adverse effects on productivity. Consequently, output per capita growth has been small. Thus, sustainable economic growth has not yet been achieved.

Growth can be sustained if it is led by the export industry. Growth pulled by expanded domestic demands must generate external imbalances and thus be short-lived, especially in a country which relies heavily on imports of raw materials and investment goods. When the Israeli sheqel appreciates in real terms, vis-à-vis the currencies of Israel's trade partners, the competitive strength of such an open economy is significantly eroded. In fact, the Israeli sheqel appreciated significantly over the years following the 1985 stabilization program. This proved to be extremely detrimental to the possibility of export-led growth. Indeed, prices of internationally tradable goods lagged behind wages, while prices of nontradable goods (e.g., most services, housing, etc.) surpassed wages quite significantly. As a result, output and employment in the nontradable sector have increased significantly over those in the tradable sector, tilting the balance of the Israeli economy against exports and import substitutes, and in favor of services and other sectors, which cannot be depended upon to lead growth.

In the long run, two forces drive economic growth: a high total-factor-productivity growth rate and a high saving rate. There are no shortcuts.

Productivity can be increased by investment in human capital and in infrastructure and by research and development (R&D). The infrastructure in Israel (excluding the West Bank and the Gaza Strip) has suffered severely from underinvestment in the last two decades. Recently, more public funds have been allocated to infrastructure investments, but they are vastly insufficient to compensate for the many years of neglect, and the stock of infrastructure capital is still low relative to the level of economic activity.

Research and development in Israel has been traditionally confined to the government-owned defense industry. With the end of the cold war, world demand for defense products is declining. Furthermore, spin-offs from R&D in the defense industry to the nondefense business sector have not been evident.

Investments in human capital in Israel are publicly funded. Despite the increase in population, the number of students in institutions of higher education has been more or less stable in the late 1970s and 1980s, and government funding of higher education was not increased. At the same time, the government does not allow private groups to open higher education institutes or public institutes to increase tuition. Consequently, there has been significant underinvestment in human capital. Furthermore, until the recent *aliya,* Israel has suffered from a net "brain drain."

These factors help explain the low productivity growth. Indeed, the total-factor-productivity growth rate in Israel was meager in the 1970s and 1980s, relative to the exceptionally high rates in the 1950s and 1960s. Evidently, a higher productivity growth rate during the years to come depends on renewed investment in human capital and infrastructure and on the ability of Israel to convert its R&D from defense to nondefense industries.

In the 1950s and 1960s, Israel managed to maintain very high national saving rates out of relatively low income levels. In the 1970s and 1980s, with much higher income levels, national saving rates have plummeted. Concurrently, economic growth rates also plunged. Somehow, saving rates will have to rise significantly in order to sustain economic growth.

At the same time, some structural changes are taking place. One such reform is in the area of international trade. Over the forty-five years since its birth, Israel has gradually deregulated the flow of both goods and services and capital. The highlights of this process have been the agreements with the European Community and the United States, allowing essentially free trade between Israel and each one of these two giant economies. Further, a unilateral process of liberalizing trade with the rest of the world is currently under way. Similarly, significant deregulations of international capital movements have started.

The capital market is also being reformed to gradually reduce the heavy role of government in financial intermediation (between savers and investors) and to rid the market of excessive regulation. Concurrently, the slow pace of privatization has recently been accelerated.

In addition to focusing economic policy in the years to come on the renewal of economic growth, we think that policymakers will not be able to avoid attending to several spots where crisis is imminent. One such spot is the health care system. Israel does not have national mandatory health insurance coverage. Neither does it have anything analogous to the U.S. government Medicare program for the aged. Instead, there are several nongovernmental sick funds (Kupot Holim); by far the largest sick fund belongs to the Histadrut. The sick funds provide health insurance, with some partial funding by the government, through the "parallel tax" (collected by the National Insurance Institute) which is earmarked for the sick funds. In general, any viable health system is based on the principle that the more healthy young subsidize the less healthy aged (as in the U.S. Medicare program). In a system of voluntary sick funds which are less than fully funded by the government, this principle cannot be enforced. As a result, in some of these sick funds a heavy concentration of elderly people could easily undermine their financial base. In addition, a major portion of health services are directly produced and provided by government-run hospitals which suffer from a badly distorted system of prices and incentives. The current *aliya* with its disproportionate number of elderly people exacerbates the health system crisis. There is no longer any doubt that a major reform of the health system is urgently required.

Another crisis spot is the pension system. In this context one can divide the population into three groups. First, employees in the public sector usually have an unfunded defined-benefit program, backed solely by the government (local and central) and other public sector employers (e.g., the universities). Given the size of the public sector in Israel (about one-third of the civilian labor force) and its generosity in granting concessionary and early retirement benefits, its pension liability is huge. The amount has not yet been calculated and is evidently not included in the public debt figure, which even so is quite large (about 125% of GNP).

Second, employees in large private enterprises (including those owned by the Histadrut) are members of Histadrut-run pension funds. The latter provide defined-benefit plans. They invest in nonnegotiable government bonds with yields which are currently (but have not always been) favorable. Nevertheless, over the past few years, these funds have accumulated significant actuarial deficits, mainly because they followed the lead of the public sector in providing generous benefits with the implicit expectation of government backing. For instance, these funds offered accelerated accumulation of benefits for new members (especially *olim* from the 1950s and 1960s) who joined the funds in mid-life, based benefits on wages in the near-retirement years, which are typically at the peak of the wage profile, and so forth. The deficits of these pension funds have been relatively stable in recent years, as the funds have changed their policies toward new members to match the expected benefits to the new members with their expected contributions. Nevertheless, the accumulated deficits are still enormous and require immediate attention from the government.

Third, a large fraction of the population (both employees and self-employed) do not participate in any defined-benefit pension plan. Many of them may still take advantage of various tax reliefs to accumulate their own private savings (especially in provident funds and participatory life insurance programs), but nevertheless they are not entitled to guaranteed pension benefits.

The pension system thus poses a severe fiscal and social problem. The new *aliya* will no doubt exacerbate this problem as many of the new *olim* from the former Soviet Union, who arrived in Israel in their middle age, lost their accumulated pension rights upon emigration. They will probably not be able to accumulate enough private savings and pension benefits in Israel to finance sufficient consumption after retirement. It is worth pointing out, in this context, that the old-age benefits provided by the National Insurance Institute (social security) are typically very low relative to the average wage.

Notwithstanding these two crisis spots, we look forward to the future with optimism. The Israeli economy faces great challenges in the years to come, but the various shadows of economic malaise are lightened by promise. After many years, Israel is again blessed with a massive wave of *aliya,* the gathering of the exiled, the very soul of existence of Israel. Renewed economic growth is within reach, especially since the new *olim* are richly endowed with human capital. The new world order, which emerged after the collapse of the Soviet Union, creates a new opportunity for peace and stability in the Middle East. We cannot overstate the contribution of peace to the investment environment in Israel: economic growth and peace are intertwined. Essentially, there cannot be a better companion to *aliya* in boosting long-lasting growth and economic prosperity than genuine peace in the Middle East.

Selected Data

Table 1 National Accounts: Sources and Uses, 1980–91
(million 1990 $)

Year	GNP	GDP	Private Consumption	Government Consumption	Gross Domestic Capital Formation	Exports	Imports
1980	37,118	36,950	18,810	14,911	7,154	11,307	15,232
	(3.5)	(−3.0)	(3.5)	(−8.2)	(6.2)	(−10.8)	
1981	39,857	38,600	21,252	15,880	6,373	11,895	16,785
	(7.4)	(4.5)	(13.0)	(6.5)	(−10.9)	(5.2)	(10.2)
1982	39,897	39,032	22,960	14,901	7,137	11,530	17,496
	(0.1)	(1.1)	(8.0)	(−6.2)	(11.9)	(−3.1)	(4.2)
1983	41,405	40,119	24,963	14,302	7,726	11,797	18,669
	(3.8)	(2.8)	(9.0)	(−4.0)	(8.2)	(2.3)	(6.7)
1984	41,298	41,039	23,208	15,144	7,735	13,434	18,482
	(−0.3)	(2.3)	(−7.0)	(5.9)	(0.1)	(13.9)	(−1.0)
1985	42,659	42,582	23,362	15,720	7,295	14,596	18,391
	(3.3)	(3.8)	(0.7)	(3.8)	(9.4)	(8.7)	(−0.5)
1986	43,632	44,151	26,820	14,228	7,809	15,428	20,134
	(2.3)	(3.7)	(14.8)	(−9.5)	(7.0)	(5.7)	(9.5)
1987	47,339	46,746	29,233	16,662	7,656	17,138	23,943
	(8.5)	(5.9)	(9.0)	(17.1)	(−1.9)	(11.1)	(18.9)
1988	48,486	47,989	30,471	16,380	7,717	16,856	23,435
	(2.4)	(2.7)	(4.2)	(−1.7)	(0.7)	(−1.6)	(−2.1)
1989	48,955	48,757	30,557	14,945	7,619	17,517	21,881
	(1.0)	(1.6)	(0.3)	(−8.8)	(−1.3)	(3.9)	(−6.6)
1990	50,889	51,225	32,094	15,498	9,492	17,903	23,762
	(4.0)	(5.1)	(5.0)	(3.7)	(24.6)	(2.2)	(8.6)
1991	53,173	53,837	34,732	16,495	13,450	17,547	28,313
	(4.5)	(5.9)	(8.2)	(6.4)	(34.0)	(−2.0)	(19.2)

Source: Central Bureau of Statistics (various years).
Note: Numbers in parentheses are percentage changes over previous year.

Table 2 National Accounts: Composition of GDP, 1980–91 (million 1990 $)

Year	GDP	Product of the Government and Nonprofit Institutions	Imputed Rent on Owner-occupied Housing	Gross Domestic Product of the Business Sector	Agriculture Sector Product	Manufacturing Sector Product	Electricity, Water, and Construction Sector Product	Trade and Services Sector Product	Transport, Storage, and Communication Sector Product
1980	36,950	9,306	4,435	23,209	2,012	5,549	3,538	9,967	2,141
	(3.5)	(−0.2)	(4.3)	(4.1)	(10.4)	(2.9)	(4.1)	(9.0)	(3.3)
1981	38,600	9,389	4,625	24,586	1,969	6,630	3,591	10,014	2,382
	(4.5)	(0.9)	(3.6)	(5.8)	(−2.2)	(19.5)	(1.5)	(0.5)	(11.2)
1982	39,032	9,690	4,797	24,545	1,470	7,096	3,496	7,587	4,895
	(1.1)	(3.2)	(3.7)	(−0.1)	(−25.3)	(7.0)	(−2.6)	(−24.2)	(105.5)
1983	40,119	9,777	4,936	25,406	1,232	7,192	3,073	9,488	4,422
	(2.8)	(0.9)	(2.9)	(3.3)	(−16.2)	(1.3)	(−11.1)	(25.1)	(−9.7)
1984	41,039	9,885	5,079	26,075	1,408	7,729	2,649	9,522	4,707
	(2.3)	(1.1)	(2.9)	(3.8)	(14.3)	(7.5)	(−12.8)	(0.7)	(6.5)

Year									
1985	42,582	9,835	5,226	27,521	1,619	7,674	2,071	10,783	5,374
	(3.8)	(−0.5)	(2.5)	(5.7)	(15.0)	(−0.7)	(−22.7)	(12.9)	(14.2)
1986	44,151	9,550	5,320	29,281	1,789	8,301	2,513	11,462	5,216
	(3.7)	(−2.9)	(1.8)	(5.9)	(10.5)	(8.2)	(21.3)	(6.3)	(−2.9)
1987	46,746	9,636	5,406	31,704	1,650	8,330	2,916	12,667	6,141
	(5.9)	(0.9)	(1.6)	(8.3)	(−7.8)	(0.3)	(16.1)	(10.5)	(17.7)
1988	47,989	0083	5,519	32,497	1,598	8,101	3,425	12,886	6,487
	(2.7)	(3.5)	(2.1)	(2.4)	(−3.2)	(−2.7)	(17.5)	(1.7)	(5.6)
1989	48,757	9,963	5,640	33,154	2,453	9,681	4,144	12,002	4,874
	(1.6)	(−0.1)	(2.2)	(2.0)	(53.6)	(19.5)	(21.0)	(−6.9)	(−24.9)
1990	51,225	10,152	5,770	35,303	2,824	10,238	4,554	12,497	5,190
	(5.1)	(1.9)	(2.1)	(6.6)	(15.1)	(5.8)	(9.9)	(4.1)	(6.5)
1991	53,837	10,528	5,923	37,386	2,617	10,805	5,421	13,085	5,458
	(6.5)	(3.7)	(2.6)	(6.0)	(−7.3)	(5.5)	(19.0)	(4.7)	(5.2)

Source: Central Bureau of Statistics (various years).
Note: Numbers in parentheses are percentage changes over previous year.

Table 3 Population and Employment, 1980–91
(thousands)

Year	Population Total	Population 15 Years Old and Older	Labor Force Total	Labor Force Participation Rate (%)	Unemployment Total	Unemployment Rate	Employment Total	Employment Public	Employment Private Total
1980	3,878	2,588	1,318	50.9	62	4.8	1,237	366	891
	(2.4)	(2.6)	(3.2)				(1.2)	(1.7)	(0.9)
1981	3,948	2,637	1,349	51.1	67	5.0	1,262	379	883
	(1.8)	(1.9)	(2.3)				(2.0)	(3.6)	(1.4)
1982	4,027	2,684	1,367	50.9	67	5.0	1,280	385	895
	(2.0)	(1.8)	(1.4)				(1.4)	(1.7)	(1.3)
1983	4,076	2,737	1,403	50.5	62	4.5	1,321	391	930
	(1.2)	(2.0)	(2.6)				(3.2)	(1.4)	(3.9)
1984	4,159	2,796	1,444	51.3	83	5.8	1,340	396	944
	(2.0)	(2.1)	(2.9)				(1.5)	(1.5)	(1.5)
1985	4,233	2,852	1,446	50.7	97	6.7	1,349	403	964
	(1.8)	(2.0)	(1.6)				(0.7)	(1.7)	(0.3)
1986	4,299	2,906	1,472	50.6	104	7.1	1,367	406	962
	(1.6)	(1.9)	(1.8)				(1.4)	(0.7)	(1.7)
1987	4,407	2,906	1,494	51.4	90	6.0	1,401	403	1,001
	(2.5)	(0.0)	(1.5)				(2.6)	(−0.7)	(4.1)
1988	4,477	3,021	1,553	51.4	100	6.4	1,453	422	1,031
	(1.6)	(4.0)	(3.9)				(3.5)	(4.7)	(3.0)
1989	4,559	3,082	1,603	52.0	139	8.7	1,460	423	1,037
	(1.8)	(2.0)	(3.2)				(0.5)	(0.2)	(0.6)
1990	4,821	3,201	1,649	51.5	158	9.6	1,491	439	1,052
	(5.7)	(3.8)	(2.9)				(2.2)	(3.7)	(1.4)
1991	5,059	3,427	1,770	51.7	187	10.6	1,583	468	1,115
	(4.9)	(7.1)	(7.3)				(6.2)	(6.6)	(6.0)

Source: Central Bureau of Statistics (various years).
Note: Numbers in parentheses are percentage changes over previous year.

			Employment			
			Private			
Agri-culture	Manu-facturing	Water and Electricity	Con-struction	Services and Commerce	Transport and Communication	Unclassified
73	290	13	78	321	86	10
(9.8)	(−1.3)	(12.3)	(−3.6)	(2.2)	(1.8)	(−19.7)
71	294	14	77	333	84	10
(−3.0)	(1.1)	(7.0)	(−0.9)	(3.7)	(−1.7)	(0.0)
67	291	14	79	348	88	8
(−4.9)	(−0.9)	(0.7)	(1.8)	(4.4)	(4.4)	
68	299	13	85	370	87	8
(1.0)	(2.8)	(−8.0)	(7.9)	(6.3)	(−1.4)	(0.0)
67	307	13	78	381	89	9
(−2.3)	(2.7)	(0.8)	(−8.2)	(3.1)	(3.0)	(12.5)
72	309	12	72	387	86	26
(8.3)	(0.6)	(−8.6)	(−7.3)	(1.6)	(−3.6)	(188)
70	322	12	62	400	87	9
(−2.9)	(4.2)	(5.1)	(−14.4)	(3.2)	(0.5)	(−65.4)
72	328	14	68	418	92	9
(2.9)	(1.9)	(16.7)	(9.7)	(4.5)	(5.7)	(0.0)
67	322	15	74	450	95	8
(−6.9)	(4.2)	(7.1)	(8.8)	(7.7)	(3.3)	(−11.1)
67	313	14	72	211	94	266
(0.9)	(−2.5)	(−0.4)	(−2.7)	(−53.1)	(−1.1)	(3225)
62	323	17	76	217	92	265
(−7.3)	(−3.0)	(13.0)	(5.7)	(3.2)	(−1.6)	(0.4)
55	340	17	96	224	97	286
(−11.3)	(5.2)	(1.2)	(26.3)	(3.2)	(5.4)	(7.9)

Table 4 Productivity, 1980–91 (percentage)

Year	Business Sector	Agriculture	Manufacturing	Water and Electricity	Construction	Commerce and Services	Transport, Storage, and Communications
1980	2.3	2.7	2.3	-4.7	7.4	0.5	-1.3
1981	4.0	13.8	2.3	-0.3	3.2	2.8	8.2
1982	-1.4	12.1	-2.0	-1.9	-3.1	-1.9	-5.8
1983	-0.3	1.2	-0.6	5.6	-5.6	-0.6	6.7
1984	0.3	1.5	3.7	2.9	-0.5	-4.9	6.0
1985	4.2	2.1	5.2	10.8	5.3	3.2	5.5
1986	3.8	1.7	2.1	4.5	10.8	5.7	6.4
1987	4.1	9.3	3.7	3.0	5.6	5.1	2.0
1988	-0.6	1.2	-1.0	-7.5	6.7	-3.5	-1.0
1989	0.1	6.6	-2.3	-0.7	-0.2	-0.2	4.0
1990	4.4	22.5	4.7	-4.3	1.5	1.8	3.6
1991	2.4	1.4	1.6	4.4	10.3	1.1	3.5

Source: Central Bureau of Statistics (various years).

Table 5 Real wage, 1980–91
(1990 $ per month)

Year	Total	Public Sector	Business Sector	Agriculture	Manufacturing	Electricity and Water	Construction	Commerce and Services	Transport, Storage, and Communications
1980	1,047	981	1,083	652	1,126	1,983	901	990	1,546
	(−3.2)	(−8.4)	(−0.4)	(−1.7)	(−0.4)	(2.0)	(−0.9)	(−0.6)	(1.4)
1981	1,157	1,083	1,194	700	1,260	2,410	980	1,087	1,685
	(10.4)	(10.3)	(10.3)	(7.4)	(11.9)	(21.5)	(8.8)	(9.8)	(9.0)
1982	1,151	1,032	1,214	716	1,287	2,301	1,028	1,111	1,675
	(−0.5)	(−4.7)	(1.7)	(2.2)	(2.1)	(−4.5)	(4.9)	(2.2)	(−0.6)
1983	1,221	1,130	1,270	737	1,357	2,478	1,025	1,177	1,709
	(6.1)	(9.5)	(4.6)	(3.0)	(5.5)	(7.7)	(−0.3)	(5.9)	(2.0)
1984	1,217	1,144	1,257	734	1,384	2,313	978	1,123	1,733
	(−0.4)	(1.3)	(−10.5)	(−0.5)	(2.0)	(−6.7)	(−4.6)	(−4.6)	(1.4)
1985	1,107	984	1,173	666	1,281	2,146	883	1,076	1,606
	(−9.0)	(−14.0)	(−6.7)	(−9.3)	(−7.4)	(−7.2)	(−9.7)	(−4.2)	(−7.3)
1986	1,194	1,024	1,281	733	1,372	2,150	997	1,198	1,755
	(7.9)	(4.1)	(9.2)	(10.1)	(7.1)	(0.2)	(12.9)	(11.3)	(9.3)
1987	1,286	1,096	1,385	802	1,469	2,436	1,159	1,291	1,933
	(7.7)	(7.1)	(8.1)	(9.4)	(7.1)	(13.3)	(16.3)	(7.8)	(10.1)
1988	1,351	1,203	1,450	835	1,522	2,573	1,199	1,363	1,999
	(5.0)	(9.7)	(4.7)	(4.2)	(3.6)	(5.6)	(3.5)	(5.6)	(3.5)
1989	1,344	1,208	1,427	829	1,536	2,614	1,173	1,328	1,934
	(−0.5)	(0.4)	(−1.6)	(−0.8)	(0.9)	(1.6)	(−2.2)	(−2.6)	(−3.3)
1990	1,360	1,212	1,406	789	1,539	2,564	1,121	1,294	1,935
	(1.2)	(0.4)	(−1.5)	(−4.8)	(0.2)	(−1.9)	(−4.4)	(−2.6)	(0.1)
1991	1,319	1,231	1,330	691	1,493	2,590	971	1,263	1,964
	(−3.0)	(1.6)	(−5.4)	(−12.4)	(−3.0)	(1.0)	(−13.4)	(−2.4)	(1.5)

Source: Central Bureau of Statistics (various years).
Note: Numbers in parentheses are percentage changes over previous years.

Table 6 Gross Investment, 1980–91
            (million 1990 $)

Year	Fixed Asset	Residential Buildings	Other Building	Transport Equipment	Machinery and Other Equipment
1980	7,358	3,053	1,514	659	2,132
1981	7,671	3,116	1,433	820	2,302
	(4.3)	(2.1)	(−5.3)	(24.4)	(8.0)
1982	8,094	3,017	1,410	1,086	2,581
	(5.5)	(−3.2)	(−1.6)	(32.5)	(12.1)
1983	9,150	2,855	1,494	1,636	3,165
	(13.0)	(−5.4)	(6.0)	(50.7)	(22.6)
1984	8,062	2,697	1,308	1,052	3,005
	(−11.9)	(−5.5)	(−12.4)	(−35.7)	(−5.1)
1985	7,378	2,373	1,260	623	3,122
	(−8.5)	(−12.0)	(−3.7)	(−40.8)	(3.9)
1986	7,387	2,232	1,294	789	3,072
	(0.1)	(−5.9)	(2.7)	(26.7)	(−1.6)
1987	8,308	2,417	1,492	1,087	3,312
	(12.4)	(8.3)	(15.3)	(37.7)	(7.8)
1988	8,301	2,470	1,542	1,184	3,105
	(−0.1)	(2.2)	(3.4)	(8.9)	(−6.3)
1989	8,048	2,653	1,560	706	3,129
	(−3.1)	(7.4)	(1.2)	(−40.4)	(0.8)
1990	9,563	3,047	1,583	1,033	3,900
	(18.8)	(14.8)	(1.5)	(46.4)	(24.6)
1991	10,528	5,363	1,595	706	2,864
	(10.1)	(76.0)	(0.8)	(−31.7)	(−26.5)

Source: Central Bureau of Statistics (various years).
Note: Numbers in parentheses are percentage changes over previous years.

Table 7 Net Capital Stock, 1980–91
(beginning of year, million 1990 $)

Year	Total	Residential Structures	Public Sector	Business Sector	Agriculture	Manufacturing	Construction	Commerce and Services	Transport and Storage	Other
1980	69,907	27,414	12,742	29,751	3,540	7,502	521	2,786	11,988	3,414
	(4.3)	(4.3)	(5.1)	(0.4)	(2.4)	(0.4)	(14.3)	(4.2)	(3.3)	
1981	71,906	28,634	13,206	30,066	3,527	7,584	520	2,338	11,926	4,171
	(2.9)	(4.5)	(3.6)	(1.1)	(−0.4)	(1.1)	(0.2)	(1.9)	(−0.5)	(22.2)
1982	73,992	29,844	13,643	30,505	3,516	7,659	484	2,989	11,955	3,902
	(2.9)	(4.2)	(3.3)	(1.5)	(−0.3)	(1.0)	(−6.9)	(5.3)	(0.2)	(−6.4)
1983	76,236	30,923	14,132	31,181	3,534	7,927	455	3,115	12,183	3,967
	(3.0)	(3.6)	(3.6)	(2.2)	(0.5)	(3.5)	(−6.0)	(4.2)	(1.9)	(1.7)
1984	79,287	31,846	14,750	32,691	3,603	8,371	467	3,368	12,805	4,077
	(4.0)	(3.0)	(4.4)	(4.8)	(2.0)	(5.6)	(2.7)	(8.1)	(5.1)	(2.8)
1985	81,216	32,581	15,261	33,374	3,599	8,755	433	3,495	12,920	4,172
	(2.4)	(2.3)	(3.5)	(2.1)	(−0.1)	(4.6)	(−7.4)	(3.8)	(0.9)	(2.3)
1986	82,334	33,001	15,735	33,598	3,587	9,127	379	3,563	12,761	4,181
	(1.4)	(1.3)	(3.1)	(0.8)	(−0.3)	(4.3)	(−12.4)	(2.0)	(−1.2)	(0.2)
1987–88	82,987	33,131	16,213	33,643	3,519	9,356	328	3,571	12,688	4,181
	(0.8)	(0.4)	(3.0)	(0.1)	(−1.9)	(2.5)	(−13.5)	(0.2)	(−0.6)	(0.0)
1989	84,592	33,595	16,748	32,249	3,459	9,505	322	3,585	13,183	4,195
	(1.9)	(1.4)	(3.3)	(1.8)	(−1.7)	(1.6)	(−1.9)	(0.4)	(3.9)	(0.3)
1990	85,530	34,133	17,217	34,180	3,327	9,458	308	3,564	13,657	3,866
	(1.1)	(1.6)	(2.8)	(−0.2)	(−3.8)	(−0.5)	(−4.3)	(−0.6)	(3.6)	(−7.8)
1991	87,481	34,952	17,631	34,898	3,211	9,590	361	3,607	14,176	3,953
	(2.3)	(2.4)	(2.4)	(2.1)	(−3.5)	(1.4)	(17.3)	(1.2)	(3.8)	(2.3)

Source: Central Bureau of Statistics (various years).
Note: Numbers in parentheses are percentage changes over previous year.

Table 8 National Income and Savings, 1980–91

Year	National Income as a Percentage of GNP	Disposable Income as a Percentage of National Income	Private Savings as a Percentage of Disposable Income	National Net Savings as a Percentage of National Net Income
1980	84.26	121.98	33.60	5.41
1981	84.50	119.27	35.80	4.23
1982	84.39	116.46	28.70	0.17
1983	84.72	117.96	25.60	2.79
1984	83.45	123.12	35.60	5.26
1985	82.60	131.16	29.20	7.91
1986	83.34	127.04	20.70	5.87
1987	83.83	122.72	20.20	2.56
1988	84.68	117.68	21.40	2.25
1989	84.29	116.54	24.50	2.59
1990	84.32	117.79	24.30	3.82
1991	85.09	117.86	26.10	6.72

Source: Central Bureau of Statistics (various years).

Table 9 Government Consumption, 1980–91
(million 1990 $)

Year	Total	Civilian Consumption	Domestic Defense Purchases	Domestic Defense Wages	Net Direct Military Imports
1980	14,991	7,384	2,539	2,373	2,695
1981	15,880	7,608	2,661	2,333	3,278
	(6.5)	(3.0)	(4.8)	(−1.7)	(21.6)
1982	14,901	7,489	2,729	2,598	2,085
	(−6.2)	(−1.5)	(2.6)	(11.4)	(−36.4)
1983	14,302	7,487	2,719	2,615	1,481
	(−4.0)	(−0.0)	(−0.4)	(0.6)	(−29.0)
1984	15,144	7,724	2,654	2,653	2,113
	(5.9)	(3.2)	(−2.4)	(1.5)	(42.7)
1985	15,720	7,816	2,597	2,571	2,736
	(3.8)	(1.2)	(−2.2)	(−3.1)	(29.5)
1986	14,228	7,632	2,458	2,409	1,729
	(−9.5)	(−2.3)	(−5.4)	(−6.3)	(−36.8)
1987	16,662	8,220	2,680	2,359	3,403
	(17.1)	(7.7)	(9.1)	(−2.1)	(96.8)
1988	16,380	8,561	2,533	2,509	2,800
	(−1.7)	(4.1)	(−5.5)	(6.4)	(−17.8)
1989	14,945	8,396	2,521	2,470	1,587
	(−8.8)	(−1.6)	(−0.5)	(−1.6)	(−43.3)
1990	15,498	8,618	2,542	2,492	1,846
	(3.7)	(2.6)	(0.8)	(0.9)	(16.3)
1991	16,495	9,559	2,335	2,492	2,109
	(6.4)	(10.0)	(−8.1)	(0.0)	(14.2)

Source: Central Bureau of Statistics (various years).
Note: Numbers in parentheses are percentage changes over previous year.

Table 10 Imports and Exports, 1980–91
(million 1990 $)

Year	Imports					Exports		
	Total	Direct Military Imports	Fuel, Ships, and Aircraft	Diamonds	Other	Total	Diamonds	Other
1980	15,232	2,827	1,248	1,811	9,346	11,306	2,018	9,288
1981	16,785 (10.2)	3,429 (21.3)	1,299 (−3.2)	1,031 (−43.1)	11,117 (18.9)	11,895 (5.2)	1,646 (−18.4)	10,249 (10.3)
1982	17,495 (4.2)	2,323 (−32.2)	1,299 (7.5)	1,188 (15.2)	12,685 (14.1)	11,529 (−3.1)	1,480 (−10.1)	10,049 (−2.0)
1983	18,668 (6.7)	1,606 (−30.8)	1,278 (−1.6)	1,566 (31.8)	14,218 (12.1)	11,797 (2.3)	1,570 (6.1)	10,227 (1.8)
1984	18,481 (−1.0)	2,161 (34.5)	1,237 (−3.2)	1,838 (17.4)	13,245 (−6.8)	13,433 (13.9)	1,829 (16.5)	11,604 (13.5)
1985	18,390 (−0.5)	2,755 (27.5)	1,144 (−7.5)	2,358 (28.3)	12,133 (−8.4)	14,595 (8.7)	2,294 (25.4)	12,301 (6.0)
1986	20,133 (9.5)	1,768 (−35.8)	1,379 (20.5)	2,936 (24.5)	14,050 (15.8)	15,427 (5.7)	2,892 (26.1)	12,535 (1.9)
1987	23,942 (18.9)	3,416 (93.2)	1,499 (8.7)	3,422 (16.6)	15,605 (11.1)	17,135 (11.1)	3,560 (23.1)	13,575 (8.3)
1988	23,434 (−2.1)	2,828 (−17.2)	1,699 (13.3)	3,796 (10.9)	15,111 (−3.2)	16,856 (−1.6)	3,809 (7.0)	13,047 (−3.9)
1989	21,880 (−6.6)	1,622 (−42.7)	1,598 (−5.9)	3,237 (−14.7)	15,423 (2.1)	17,516 (3.9)	3,463 (−9.1)	14,053 (7.7)
1990	23,762 (8.6)	1,866 (15.1)	1,711 (7.1)	2,891 (−10.7)	17,294 (12.1)	17,902 (2.2)	3,065 (−11.5)	14,837 (5.6)
1991	28,312 (19.1)	2,112 (14.0)	2,245 (31.2)	3,639 (25.9)	20,316 (17.5)	17,546 (−2.0)	2,610 (14.8)	14,936 (0.7)

Source: Central Bureau of Statistics (various years).
Note: Numbers in parentheses are percentage change over previous year.

Table 11 Current Account of the Balance of Payments and
External Debt, 1980–91
(million current $)

Year	Current Account Surplus (Deficit)	Imports	Exports	Unilateral Transfers from Abroad	Trade Deficit	Net External Debt
1980	(746)	13,523	9,795	2,982	2,554	11,972
1981	(1,335)	14,651	10,390	2,926	2,486	13,479
1982	(2,024)	14,748	10,108	2,616	2,925	14,848
1983	(2,004)	15,000	10,140	2,856	3,492	18,446
1984	(1,401)	15,257	10,490	3,366	2,450	19,780
1985	1,159	14,806	10,891	5,074	1,937	19,397
1986	1,477	15,610	11,706	5,381	2,352	17,832
1987	(969)	19,636	13,828	4,839	3,254	17,719
1988	(675)	20,489	15,163	4,651	2,846	17,945
1989	1,096	20,640	16,873	4,863	3,767	15,787
1990	704	23,577	18,491	5,790	5,086	15,200
1991	(822)	25,952	18,739	6,391	7,213	14,973

Source: Central Bureau of Statistics (various years).

Table 12 Interest Rates and Debt Service, 1980–91
(million current $)

Year	Interest Payments on External Debt		Average Interest Rate on Net External Debt	Interest Income from Abroad
	Net	Gross		
1980	954	1,797	8.6	843
1981	755	2,205	6.3	1,450
1982	1,087	2,746	8.1	1,659
1983	1,084	2,699	6.8	1,585
1984	1,774	2,966	9.6	1,192
1985	1,733	2,772	8.8	1,039
1986	1,712	2,564	8.9	851
1987	1,576	2,438	8.6	862
1988	1,633	2,633	9.0	1,000
1989	1,393	2,661	7.2	1,268
1990	1,243	2,739	7.0	1,496
1991	879	2,539	5.0	1,660

Source: Central Bureau of Statistics (various years).

Table 13 Annual Change in CPI, 1949–91

Year	Percentage Change
1949	2.3
1950	−6.6
1951	14.1
1952	57.7
1953	28.1
1954	12.2
1955	5.9
1956	6.4
1957	6.5
1958	3.4
1959	0.8
1960	2.9
1961	6.7
1962	9.5
1963	6.6
1964	5.2
1965	7.7
1966	8.0
1967	1.6
1968	2.1
1969	2.5
1970	6.1
1971	12.0
1972	12.9
1973	20.0
1974	39.7
1975	39.3
1976	31.3
1977	34.6
1978	50.6
1979	78.3
1980	131.0
1981	116.8
1982	120.3
1983	145.7
1984	373.8
1985	304.6
1986	48.1
1987	19.9
1988	16.3
1989	20.2
1990	17.2
1991	19.0

Source: Central Bureau of Statistics (various years).

Table 14 GDP, 1950–91
(million 1990 $)

Year	GDP
1950	3,453
1951	4,484
1952	4,677
1953	4,621
1954	5,504
1955	6,247
1956	6,803
1957	7,395
1958	7,927
1959	8,926
1960	9,515
1961	10,552
1962	11,597
1963	12,826
1964	13,915
1965	15,223
1966	15,390
1967	15,774
1968	18,189
1969	20,480
1970	22,139
1971	24,575
1972	27,621
1973	29,031
1974	30,569
1975	31,853
1976	32,363
1977	32,977
1978	34,296
1979	35,839
1980	36,950
1981	38,600
1982	39,032
1983	40,119
1984	41,039
1985	42,582
1986	44,151
1987	46,746
1988	47,989
1989	48,757
1990	51,225
1991	53,837

Source: Central Bureau of Statistics (various years).

Table 15 Civilian Labor Force and Unemployment,
1962–91

Year	Labor Force (thousands)	Unemployment Rate (percentage)
1962	818	3
1963	840	3
1964	884	3
1965	912	3
1966	943	7
1967	927	10
1968	970	6
1969	990	4
1970	1,001	3
1971	1,033	3
1972	1,077	2
1973	1,124	2
1974	1,131	3
1975	1,148	3
1976	1,169	3
1977	1,207	3
1978	1,255	3
1979	1,277	2
1980	1,318	5
1981	1,349	5
1982	1,367	5
1983	1,402	4
1984	1,444	6
1985	1,446	7
1986	1,472	7
1987	1,494	6
1988	1,553	6
1989	1,603	9
1990	1,650	10
1991	1,770	11

Source: Central Bureau of Statistics (various years).

Table 16 Imports and Exports, 1950–91
(million 1990 $)

Year	Exports	Imports
1950	191	1,616
1951	264	1,726
1952	346	1,588
1953	426	1,622
1954	605	1,785
1955	623	1,921
1956	708	2,236
1957	848	2,218
1958	943	2,489
1959	1,243	2,666
1960	1,570	3,081
1961	1,822	3,806
1962	2,140	4,376
1963	2,459	4,679
1964	2,554	5,325
1965	2,771	5,268
1966	3,065	5,237
1967	3,325	5,734
1968	4,243	7,449
1969	4,532	8,573
1970	4,966	10,091
1971	6,143	11,160
1972	6,979	11,294
1973	7,363	15,292
1974	7,775	15,368
1975	7,915	16,014
1976	9,071	15,533
1977	10,132	15,083
1978	10,599	16,682
1979	10,917	17,149
1980	11,306	15,232
1981	11,895	16,785
1982	11,529	17,495
1983	11,797	18,668
1984	13,433	18,481
1985	14,595	18,390
1986	15,427	20,133
1987	17,135	23,942
1988	16,856	23,434
1989	17,516	21,880
1990	17,902	23,762
1991	17,546	28,312

Source: Central Bureau of Statistics (various years).

Table 17 Government Consumption, 1950–91
(million 1990 $)

Year	Government Consumption
1950	1,710
1951	2,097
1952	2,254
1953	2,333
1954	2,683
1955	2,900
1956	3,164
1957	3,385
1958	3,731
1959	4,096
1960	4,379
1961	4,856
1962	5,366
1963	5,903
1964	6,534
1965	7,123
1966	7,258
1967	7,425
1968	8,420
1969	9,279
1970	9,557
1971	10,111
1972	11,112
1973	16,146
1974	16,598
1975	18,291
1976	16,517
1977	14,303
1978	15,505
1979	14,156
1980	14,911
1981	15,880
1982	14,901
1983	14,302
1984	15,144
1985	15,720
1986	14,228
1987	16,662
1988	16,380
1989	14,945
1990	15,498
1991	16,495

Source: Central Bureau of Statistics (various years).

References

American Express. 1986. *The Amex Bank Review*. New York.

Atkinson, Anthony B. 1977. "Optimal Taxation and the Direct versus Indirect Tax Controversy." *Canadian Journal of Economics* 10 (November): 590–606.

Atkinson, Anthony B., and Agnar Sandmo. 1980."Welfare Implications of the Taxation of Savings." *Economic Journal* 90 (September): 529–49.

Auerbach, Alan J. 1983. "Taxation, Corporate Financial Policy and the Cost of Capital." *Journal of Economic Literature* 21 (September): 905–40.

———. 1987. "Corporate Taxation in the United States." In *Economic Policy in Theory and Practice,* edited by Assaf Razin and Efraim Sadka. London: Macmillan.

Bailey, Martin J. 1956. "The Welfare Cost of Inflationary Finance." *Journal of Political Economy* 64 (April): 93–110.

Balcer, Yves, and Efraim Sadka. 1981. "Budget Shares and Optimal Commodity Taxes Without Computation." *Economics Letters* 7(3): 265–71.

Bank of Israel. 1987. *Economic Developments in Recent Months*. No. 42 (September).

———. 1988a. *Economic Developments in Recent Months*. No. 43 (March).

———. 1988b. *Annual Report 1987*. May (in Hebrew).

———. 1989. *Annual Report 1988*. May.

———. 1990. *Recent Economic Developments*. No. 51 (June).

———. 1991a. *Annual Report 1990*. May.

———. 1991b. *A Program for Absorbing One Million Olim*. April (in Hebrew).

———. 1991c. *Recent Developments in the Capital Markets—1990*. Monetary Division.

Ben-Porath, Yoram. 1985. "The Entwined Growth of Population and Product, 1922–1982." In *The Israeli Economy: Maturing Through Crisis,* edited by Yoram Ben-Porath. Cambridge, Mass.: Harvard University Press.

Bodie, Zvi, and Robert C. Merton. 1992. "Pension Reform and Privatization in International Perspective: The Case of Israel." Paper presented at Pinhas Sapir Center for Development, Tel Aviv University, March 22.

247

Bruno, Michael. 1989a. "Israel's Crisis and Economic Reform: A Historical Perspective." NBER Working Paper no. 3075.

———. 1989b. "Economic Recovery in Historical Perspective." *Economic Quarterly* 141(July): 113–89 (in Hebrew).

———. 1991. "From Sharp Stabilization to Growth: On the Political Economy of Israel's Transition." NBER Working Paper no. 3881.

Casanegra de Jantscher, Milka. 1976. "Taxing Business Profits during Inflation: The Latin American Experience." *International Tax Journal*, 128–46.

Central Bureau of Statistics. 1987. *Statistical Abstract of Israel 1987*. No. 38.

———. 1988a. *Statistical Abstract of Israel 1988*. No. 39.

———. 1988b. *The National Accounts of Judea, Samaria and the Gaza Strip, 1981–1987* (in Hebrew).

———. 1989a. *Israel's National Accounts 1988*.

———. 1989b. *Statistical Abstract of Israel 1989*. No. 40.

———. 1990. *Israel's National Accounts 1989*.

———. 1991a. *Israel's National Accounts*, May 13.

———. 1991b. *Israel's National Accounts, 1980–1990*.

———. 1991c. *Statistical Abstract of Israel 1991*. No. 42.

———. 1992. *Statistical Abstract of Israel 1992*. No. 43.

Deaton, Angus S. 1977. "Equity, Efficiency, and the Structure of Indirect Taxation." *Journal of Public Economics* 8 (December): 299–312.

Dixit, Avinash. 1988. "Hysteresis, Import Penetration, and the Exchange Rate Pass-Through." Princeton University. Mimeo.

Dornbusch, Rudiger. 1992. "Disinflation and Real Exchange Rates." MIT. Mimeo.

Eckstein, Zvi, and Leonardo Leiderman. 1989. "Estimating an Intertemporal Model of Consumption, Money Demand, and Seigniorage." The Foerder Institute for Economic Research, Tel Aviv University.

Economic Models Ltd. 1987a. *Macroeconomic and Sectorial Trends*, July (in Hebrew).

———. 1987b. *Macroeconomic and Sectorial Trends*, September (in Hebrew).

———. 1991a. *Macroeconomic Trends*, November, (in Hebrew).

———. 1991b. *Main Economic Indicators* (in Hebrew).

European Commission. 1987. *European Economy*. No. 34 (November).

Fischer, Stanley. 1981. "Towards an Understanding of the Costs of Inflation: II." *Carnegie-Rochester Series on Public Policy*. 15: 5–42.

———. 1982. "Seigniorage and the Case for a National Money." *Journal of Political Economy* 90 (April): 295–313.

Fischer, Stanley, and Franco Modigliani. 1978. "Towards an Understanding of the Real Effects and Costs of Inflation." *Weltwirtschaftliches Archiv* 114(4): 810–33.

Friedman, Milton. 1969. "The Optimal Quantity of Money." In his *The Optimum Quantity of Money and Other Essays*. Chicago: Aldine Publishing Co.

Giavazzi, Francesco, and Alberto Giovannini. 1988. *Limiting Exchange Rate Flexibility: The European Monetary System*. Cambridge, Mass.: MIT Press.

Halperin, Daniel, and Eugene Steuerle. 1988. "Indexing the Tax System for Inflation." In *Uneasy Compromise: Problems of a Hybrid Income-Consumption Tax*, edited by Henry J. Aaron, Harvey Galper, and Joseph A. Pechman. Washington, D.C.: The Brookings Institution.

Harberger, Arnold C. 1988. "Comments on Indexing the Tax System for Inflation." In *Uneasy Compromise: Problems of a Hybrid Income-Consumption Tax,* edited by Henry J. Aaron, Harvey Galper, and Joseph A. Pechman, 380–83. Washington, D.C.: The Brookings Institution.

Helpman, Elhanan, and Efraim Sadka. 1979. "Optimal Financing of the Government's Budget: Taxes, Bonds or Money." *American Economic Review* 69, no. 1 (March): 152–60.

Helpman, Elhanan, and Assaf Razin. 1987. "Exchange Rate Management: Intertemporal Tradeoffs." *American Economic Review* 77: 107–23.

Israel Government Corporations Authority. 1991. *Annual Report 1990,* September (in Hebrew).

Kay, J. A. 1977. "Inflation Accounting—A Review Article." *The Economic Journal.* 87 (June): 300–11.

Kiguel, Migel A., and Nissan Liviatan. 1991. "The Inflation-Stabilization Cycles in Argentina and Brazil." In *Lessons of Economic Stabilization and its Aftermath,* edited by Michael Bruno, Stanley Fischer, Elhanan Helpman and Nissan Liviatan. Cambridge, Mass.: MIT Press.

King, Mervyn A. 1987."The Cash Flow Corporate Income Tax." In *The Effects of Taxation on Capital Accumulation,* edited by Martin S. Feldstein. Chicago: University of Chicago Press.

King, Mervyn, and Don Fullerton. 1984. *The Taxation of Income from Capital.* Chicago: University of Chicago Press.

Klein, David. 1991. "Deregulating Financial Markets in Israel: Policy and Results." Paper presented at a seminar at Tel Aviv University, organized in cooperation with the Rothschild Bank AG (Zurich), 15 May.

Lucas, Robert E., Jr. 1990. "Supply side Economics: An Analytical Review." *Oxford Economic Papers* 42:293–316.

———. 1991. *Topics in Public Finance.* Unpublished lectures notes (Spring), University of Chicago.

Metzer, Jacob. 1985. "The Slowdown of Economic Growth: A Passing Phase or the End of Big Spurt?" In *The Israeli Economy: Maturing through Crises,* edited by Yoram Ben Porath. Cambridge, Mass.: Harvard University Press.

Metzer, Jacob, and Oded Kaplan. 1990. *The Jewish and Arab Economies in Mandatory Palestine: Product, Employment and Growth.* Jerusalem: Bialik Institute (in Hebrew).

Ministry of Finance. 1985. *Report of the Commission for the Taxation of the Business Sector Under Conditions of Inflation.* The Steinberg Commission (in Hebrew).

National Comptroller. 1992. *Annual Report No. 42.* March (in Hebrew).

Neubach, Amnon, Assaf Razin, and Efraim Sadka. 1988. *Economic Growth: Embarking on the 1990s.* Tel Aviv: Maariv Press (in Hebrew).

———. 1990. *Challenges to the Economy of Israel: Aliya, Growth and Integration into the World Economy.* Tel Aviv: Maariv Press (in Hebrew).

Olivera, Julio H. G. 1967. "Money, Prices and Fiscal Lags: A Note on the Dynamics of Inflation." *Quarterly Review,* Banca Nazionale del Lavoro, vol. 20 (September): 258–67.

Phelps, Edmund S. 1973. "Inflation in the Theory of Public Finance." *Swedish Journal of Economics* 75 (March): 67–82.

Razin, Assaf, and Efraim Sadka. 1991. "Vanishing Tax on Capital Income in the Open Economy." NBER Working Paper no. 3796.

Sadka, Efraim, and Avi Zigelman. 1990. "Inflation and Effective Tax Rates in the Industrial Sector." *Bank of Israel Economic Review* 64: 71–82.

Samuelson, Paul. 1939. "The Gains from International Trade." *Canadian Journal of Economics and Political Science* 5 (May): 195–205.

State Revenue Administration. 1991. *Annual Report No. 41.* Ministry of Finance, State of Israel, November (in Hebrew).

Swary, Itzhak, and Zvi Yochman. 1991. "Capital Market Reform-Myth or Reality." In *Capital Market Reform in Israel,* edited by Marshall Sarnat. Jerusalem: Floersheimer Institute.

Tanzi, Vito. 1977. "Inflation, Lags in Collection, and the Real Value of Tax Revenue." *International Monetary Fund Staff Papers* 24 (March): 154–67.

———. 1978. "Inflation, Real Tax Revenue, and the Case for Inflationary Finance: Theory with an Application to Argentina." *International Monetary Fund Staff Papers* 25 (September): 417–51.

———. 1981. "Inflation Accounting and the Taxation of Capital Gains of Business Enterprises." In *Reforms of Tax Systems: Proceedings of the 35th Congress of the International Institute of Public Finance,* edited by Karl W. Roskamp and Francesco Forte. Detroit: Wayne State University Press.

Zaka'i, Dan. 1989. *Economic Development in Judea and Samaria and the Gaza Strip, 1985–1988.* Bank of Israel (in Hebrew).

Index

251